Ambition

Ambition

An Essay on the Burning Desire to Rise

Eckart Goebel

Translated by James C. Wagner

BLOOMSBURY ACADEMIC
NEW YORK • LONDON • OXFORD • NEW DELHI • SYDNEY

BLOOMSBURY ACADEMIC
Bloomsbury Publishing Inc
1385 Broadway, New York, NY 10018, USA
50 Bedford Square, London, WC1B 3DP, UK
29 Earlsfort Terrace, Dublin 2, Ireland

BLOOMSBURY, BLOOMSBURY ACADEMIC and the Diana logo are trademarks
of Bloomsbury Publishing Plc

First published in the United States of America 2022

Copyright © Eckart Goebel, 2022

For legal purposes the Acknowledgments on p. 256 constitute
an extension of this copyright page.

Cover design is by Eleanor Rose.
Cover Image and Artwork © The Andy Warhol Foundation
for the Visual Arts, Inc./Licensed by ARS

Whilst every effort has been made to locate copyright holders the publishers
would be grateful to hear from any person(s) not here acknowledged.

All rights reserved. No part of this publication may be reproduced or transmitted
in any form or by any means, electronic or mechanical, including photocopying,
recording, or any information storage or retrieval system, without prior
permission in writing from the publishers.

Bloomsbury Publishing Inc does not have any control over, or responsibility for,
any third-party websites referred to or in this book. All internet addresses given
in this book were correct at the time of going to press. The author and publisher
regret any inconvenience caused if addresses have changed or sites have
ceased to exist, but can accept no responsibility for any such changes.

Library of Congress Cataloging-in-Publication Data
Names: Goebel, Eckart, author. | Wagner, James C., translator. | Goebel, Eckart. Ehrgeiz.
Title: Ambition : an essay on the burning desire to rise / Eckart Goebel ;
translated by James C. Wagner.
Other titles: Ehrgeiz. English
Description: New York : Bloomsbury Academic, 2022. | Includes bibliographical
references and index. |
Identifiers: LCCN 2021052336 (print) | LCCN 2021052337 (ebook) |
ISBN 9781501383847 (hardback) | ISBN 9781501383830 (paperback) |
ISBN 9781501383854 (epub) | ISBN 9781501383861 (pdf) | ISBN 9781501383823
Subjects: LCSH: Ambition.
Classification: LCC BJ1533.A4 G6413 2022 (print) | LCC BJ1533.A4 (ebook) |
DDC 302.5/4–dc23/eng/20211230
LC record available at https://lccn.loc.gov/2021052336
LC ebook record available at https://lccn.loc.gov/2021052337

ISBN:	HB:	978-1-5013-8384-7
	PB:	978-1-5013-8383-0
	ePDF:	978-1-5013-8386-1
	eBook:	978-1-5013-8385-4

Typeset by Integra Software Services Pvt. Ltd.
Printed and bound in the United States of America

To find out more about our authors and books visit www.bloomsbury.com
and sign up for our newsletters.

CONTENTS

Introduction	1
1 The Semantics of Ambition	25
2 Eris—Agon—Ambition	55
3 Ambition in Modernity	107
1 A New Era of Ambition *Jacob Burckhardt*	107
2 The Ambition of Equals *Alexis de Tocqueville*	132
3 Critique of Success *Gustav Ichheiser*	150
4 Critique of Contemplation *Karl Mannheim*	168
5 The Ambitious Spoilsport *Roger Caillois*	185
6 Hesiod's Return in the Achieving Society *David McClelland*	198
7 Burning Ambition *Sigmund Freud and Alfred Adler*	223
The Ambition to Reject Ambition: An Afterword with a View to Montaigne	245
Acknowledgments	256
Index	257

Introduction

*Always be the best [...] and hold your head up
high above the others.*

(THE ILIAD, VI.447F.)

Ambition. The word itself makes me want to run and hide.

(ELISA ALBERT)[1]

*L'ambition est en effet partout, et on en voit les
traces sur le visage des morts.*

(EMIL CIORAN)

Ambivalence

In the competitive, at times ambition-driven world of the academic humanities in which, in spite of everything, this book about ambition came to be, I encountered no shortage of mocking remarks while drafting and writing it. I was surprised by the ambivalent reactions, also reported by Robin Romm, the editor of a collection of illuminating essays titled *Double Bind: Women on Ambition*.[2]

---

[1]Elisa Albert, "The Snarling Girl: Notes on Ambition," in: Robin Romm, *Double Bind: Women on Ambition* (London: W. W. Norton, 2017), 193–212, 195.

[2]Romm strikingly describes the "passionate dialogues" that would ensue in all manner of different social contexts as soon as she brought up the topic of ambition, particularly "women and ambition." See Robin Romm, "Introduction," in: Romm, ed., *Double Bind: Women on Ambition* (London: W. W. Norton, 2017), 1–4 (2).

2 AMBITION: AN ESSAY ON THE BURNING DESIRE TO RISE

The subject evidently touches a sensitive nerve. But why does the question of ambition, understood here provisionally as the drive to accomplish a task as well as possible and thus achieve success,[3] elicit such "discomfort"?[4] The defensive joke among colleagues that I must be writing my autobiography was a running gag from beginning to end. There were reflexively ironic aperçus, such as the pronouncement that it is an ambitious undertaking to write on ambition, as well as expressions of dread. The topic, I was told multiple times, was "too close," somehow "objectionable," as though ambition were always about grandiose fantasies such as those of Thomas Mann, who confided to his diary that, with the publication of his *Doctor Faustus*, he ought to become the first author in history to receive a second Nobel Prize in Literature, and seemed actually to be upset when the 1948 prize was awarded to the "poet Elliot" (T.S. Eliot).[5]

But, one might ask, what other fantasy remains to inspire a successful author who already holds the highest honor and so has achieved everything? This is the essence of the logic of surpassing that defines insatiable ambition, which constantly requires a sensational "kick," like an addict needs another dose of his chosen drug. A writer who already has a Nobel Prize must, in order to remain "first," become the first to receive a second one; otherwise, it was "all nothing." The experience that having achieved "everything" is or at least can be accompanied by the bitter insight that "everything" is worth little or nothing at all follows the history of ambition as a shadow that threatens to fall over all ambitious people, whether opera divas, Nobel Prize recipients, competitive athletes, world conquerors, Oscar winners, or retired Germanists. Seneca, in his *Letters on Ethics*, writes of the ambitious:

> The pleasure of seeing many behind them is nothing to the pain of seeing even one still ahead. All forms of ambition have this defect: they never look back. Nor is it only ambition that finds

---

[3]On the complex relationship between accomplishment, success, and ambition, see the sections below on the sociology of success developed by Gustav Ichheiser and Karl Mannheim.

[4]Romm, "Introduction," 1.

[5]Thomas Mann, *Tagebücher 1946–1948*, edited by Inge Jens (Frankfurt am Main: Fischer, 2003), 329f.

INTRODUCTION 3

no rest, but every form of desire, for desire is always beginning afresh from its fulfillment.[6]

As even this brief look at Thomas Mann's diaries and Seneca's letters shows, to define burning ambition solely as the drive to accomplish a task well and thus achieve success is insufficient. Ambition is not quenched by success, but immediately flares up again, rushing from success to success, victory to victory. Montesquieu brilliantly says of the ambitious that "[t]heir ambition is like the horizon that always stands before them."[7]

Burning ambition—the young Nietzsche speaks of "the flame of ambition"[8]—leaves behind the objects it seizes upon as ashes, and so must always seek new objects or, if necessary, find some new field of activity: exiled to Elba, Napoleon optimized the cultivation of vegetables. Ambitious lives resemble each other. As early as the first century AD, Plutarch wrote of the comparisons that ambitious people themselves have long enviously drawn in order to establish themselves as incomparable. During his time in Spain, the no longer young Caesar broke down in tears reading about the life of Alexander the Great.[9] Alexander, meanwhile, studied the *Iliad*, calling it a "handbook of the military art."[10] He desired to be a new Achilles and even arranged a race with his friends around his gravestone.[11] Achilles for his part preferred an early death for the sake of immortal glory over a long life in obscurity. In the end, Marcus Aurelius, the stoic on the emperor's throne, exposed the meaninglessness of the ambitious thirst for glory given "how soon we're all forgotten."[12]

---

[6]Lucius Annaeus Seneca, *Letters on Ethics: To Lucilius*, translated by Margaret Graver and A.A. Long (Chicago: University of Chicago Press, 2017), 225.
[7]Fritz Schalk, ed., *Die französischen Moralisten*, vol. 1 (Munich: dtv, 1973), 242.
[8]Friedrich Nietzsche, "Homer's Contest," in: Nietzsche, *On the Genealogy of Morality and Other Writings*, translated by Carol Diethe, edited by Keith Ansell-Pearson (Cambridge: Cambridge University Press, 2017), 177–84 (180).
[9]Plutarch, *Lives*, vol. VII, translated by Bernadotte Perrin (Cambridge, MA: Harvard University Press, 1967), 469.
[10]Ibid., 243.
[11]Ibid., 263.
[12]Marcus Aurelius, *Meditations*, translated by Gregory Hays (New York: Random House, 2002), 38.

4 AMBITION: AN ESSAY ON THE BURNING DESIRE TO RISE

Ambitious people recognize each other in society and develop a rapport like the last nicotine addicts at a party of non-smokers. It can be concluded from this family resemblance that a phenomenology of ambition clearly must come down, on the one hand, to concrete aims and an analysis of the social contexts that establish the objects of ambitious desire. On the other hand, however, any analysis understanding ambition as a *need* for honor and glory must involve working out the overall relation to the world that so jealously dictates this need. Joubert exposed this intransigency: "Ambition is pitiless. In its eyes, any credit that does not serve it is contemptible."[13] Homer articulates the pitilessness of ambition in a famous line of the *Iliad* that Cicero—likewise driven by his ambition, according to Plutarch[14]—unashamedly adopted as his life's motto: "Always be the best [...] and hold your head up high above the others."[15] The career of the ambitious person is supposed to lead to the top, to the highest height, potentially even to the ends of the earth and beyond its borders: "As far as to the stars, no doubt!"[16]

Faust's mocking reply to Wagner's praise of human progress finds its echo in the violent, imperialistic colonial policies of the nineteenth century. Hannah Arendt quotes Cecil Rhodes' alarming assertion, "I would annex the planets if I could," and notes that this statement born of despair, this "moving principle of the new imperialist era" stands in "contradiction to the human condition."[17] The greater the success, the more painful the discrepancy between ambition's infinite demands and the finitude of human existence. Success does not protect against mortality, it rolls right off. "That nothing perfect's ever ours, oh but/I know it now," Faust realizes in the solitude of *Forest and Cavern*.[18] But this insight does not prevent Goethe's most ambitious character from rising, in the second part of the tragedy, to the position of an unscrupulous

---

[13]Schalk, ed., *Die französischen Moralisten*, 261.

[14]Cf. Plutarch, *Lives*, vol. VII, 141.

[15]Manfred Fuhrmann, *Cicero und die römische Republik* (Düsseldorf: Patmos, 2006), 23.

[16]Johann Wolfgang von Goethe, *Faust: A Tragedy, Parts One and Two, Fully Revised*, translated by Martin Greenberg (New Haven: Yale University Press, 2014), 23.

[17]Hannah Arendt, *Imperialism: Part Two of the Origins of Totalitarianism* (San Diego: Harcourt Brace & Co., 1968), 4.

[18]Goethe, *Faust*, 116.

INTRODUCTION 5

colonial magnate who is ultimately stricken with blindness, thus becoming a precisely imagined literary prefiguration of historical figures like Cecil Rhodes. Boundless ambition is, in its absurdity, a variant of the myth of Sisyphus or perhaps even its essence, as Robert N. Watson argues with respect to the ambivalent portrayal of ambition in Shakespeare's dramas:

> [A]mbition may be defined as the will to transcend the constricting self, provided by one's birth. The danger in moving from a received position toward some preconceived ideal is that the ideal new self may never attain the integrity and stability of the original self. [...] Upward motion can lead to a dangerous roll downhill; ambition is a Sisyphean task in Shakespearean drama, a perpetual quest for elevation that is baffled by some moral equivalent of the law of gravity.
>
> Shakespeare portrays a doomed but necessary struggle between human identity and its lineal constraints, a struggle toward which the plays express a powerful ambivalence.[19]

Plutarch's description of Alexander the Great's reaction to the rebellion of his Macedonian troops—who, having advanced into India, finally could not and would not go further—is emblematic of ambition's absurdly infinite demands:

> At first, then, Alexander shut himself up in his tent from displeasure and wrath and lay there, feeling no gratitude for what he had already achieved unless he should cross the Ganges, nay, counting a retreat a confession of defeat.[20]

As can easily be observed even in everyday life, ambition is widely seen as something shameful, even sinister, something to hide, and moreover a source of melancholy and resentment. Thus it seemed obvious to me also to consult psychoanalysis, particularly Alfred

---

[19]Robert N. Watson, *Shakespeare and the Hazards of Ambition* (Cambridge, MA: Harvard University Press, 1984), 3f. On the connection between ambition and the formation of an ego ideal, see the section on Sigmund Freud and Alfred Adler below.
[20]Plutarch, *Lives*, vol. VII, 401.

6 AMBITION: AN ESSAY ON THE BURNING DESIRE TO RISE

Adler's controversial theories about the "inferiority complex" and the resulting craving for recognition that, very much in Watson's sense, seeks to assert a "preconceived ideal." Ambition, as we shall see, is ridden with shame, notwithstanding that job applicants today are increasingly expected to brand themselves in interviews as ambitious, success-oriented, "highly motivated" achievers. "Motivation"—as I discuss below in the section on David McClelland's still influential motivation theory—is the current euphemism for ambition in a neoliberal society geared toward optimization.[21] And yet I cannot remember ever encountering a person, at least in a German context, who openly admitted to being ambitious—although there have been indirect, generalized confessions. A colleague from Vienna, defending the necessity of ambition for oppressed and marginalized groups and individuals, told me: "As a woman, one must be ambitious."

Nina Verheyen, in her excellent book *Die Erfindung der Leistung (The Invention of Achievement)*, shows how "ambition," though practically ubiquitous in the German Empire at the turn of the twentieth century, all the way up to Kaiser Wilhelm II, was at the same time vilified as a "social climber problem."[22] "Behind the critique of quantitative standards of assessment and a world that stoked ambition," Verheyen writes, were "massive social conflicts that pitted established elites against industrious, adaptable social climbers as well as career-oriented women."[23] Hence the title

---

[21]Cf. Dagmar Fenner's comprehensive book *Selbstoptimierung und Enhancement: Ein ethischer Grundriss* (Tübingen: utb, 2019), particularly pages 27–30, on the negative aspects of ideals of optimization.

[22]Nina Verheyen, *Die Erfindung der Leistung* (Berlin: Hanser Verlag, 2018), 46.

[23]Ibid., 204. Verheyen documents how the nineteenth century saw the spread of "increasingly universally acknowledged practices that allegedly objectively attributed achievements to people in order to compare them against each other, regulate their career opportunities, and direct their biographies" (ibid., 94). In contrast to this, she seeks to show that achievement is always the result of collective effort and in this respect is "*genuinely social*" (206f.). A comprehensive theory of ambition might use this approach to characterize excessive individual ambition as a self-interested project aimed at rendering the collective, social aspect of achievement and success as invisible as possible. Alfred Adler's 1927 book *Understanding Human Nature* offers some confirmation of Verheyen's arguments. Adler rejects as ideological the idea that social progress can be reduced to the ambition of "great individuals," writing that "accomplishments can occur only under the stimulus of a social feeling.

INTRODUCTION 7

of Robin Romm's edited volume of essays on women and ambition: *Double Bind.* The challenge for women from various professions writing about their own ambition in 2017 consisted not only in overcoming the shame of publicly sharing "deeply private impulses and actions that made them too vulnerable, that exposed things that felt less tidy than the façade they wanted to project."[24] They also had to break through and portray the specific double bind that feminine ambition finds itself subjected to in a modern society that views itself as committed to realizing the gender equality it has not yet achieved: being expected to be ambitious, but at the price of the loss of "femininity" and thus of identity. Ambition has been strictly male-coded since antiquity, as Aristotle confirms in his *Nicomachean Ethics*: "[W]e praise the ambitious person as manly."[25] Cristina Henríquez thus writes:

> A woman is denied her ambition on the grounds of gender. Ambition is active, not passive; it's forceful, not meek; it's stubborn, not yielding. It's everything that society tells women not to be. It's unfeminine, for goodness sake![26]

She adds that, as a woman of color, she finds herself subjected to a double denial:

> A woman of color who exhibits ambition and who makes good on that ambition to achieve something, no matter how big or small, is often told—subtly, overtly, it doesn't matter—that she didn't actually achieve much at all, and that what she did achieve, she didn't deserve. To be a woman of color is to be doubly denied.[27]

A work of genius becomes valuable only through its social connotation." Alfred Adler, *Understanding Human Nature*, translated by Walter Béran Wolfe (London/ New York: Routledge, 2013), 193f.
[24]Romm, "Introduction," 3.
[25]Aristotle, *Nicomachean Ethics*, translated by Robert C. Bartlett and Susan D. Collins (Chicago: University of Chicago Press, 2011), 81.
[26]Cristina Henríquez, "Doubly Denied," in: *Double Bind*, 253–64 (262).
[27]Ibid.

8 AMBITION: AN ESSAY ON THE BURNING DESIRE TO RISE

Given this double bind doubly bound by racism, the insatiable demand of ambition described above, the never-ending chase after ever new successes, turns out also to be a result of *being* chased. As the African American author Roxane Gay writes:

> I have achieved a modicum of success, but I never stop working. I never stop. I don't even feel the flush of pleasure I once did when I achieve a new milestone. I am having a moment, but I only want more. I need more. I cannot be merely good enough because I am chased by the pernicious whispers that I might only be "good enough for a black woman."[28]

The need to develop a comprehensive phenomenology of ambition in the light of gender theory has only recently been discussed in any detail. In the section on psychoanalysis below, however, I intend to show that this debate has an important precursor in Alfred Adler, who already in the early twentieth century was arguing for equality between men and women from the perspective of individual psychology. Adler's socialist critique of "masculine protest" is in keeping with Pierre Bourdieu's theory of "masculine domination." The expansion of our understanding of ambition in recent years to include women seems to have made it increasingly possible for men, too, to describe their own ambition and reflect on its consequences. Thus when I speak in this book of the ambitious person as a masculine figure, I do so in full awareness of the double bind that this implacable figure forces ambitious women (and men) into, namely having to become a "man."

As Roxane Gay's testimony makes clear, any substantive cultural theory of ambition must embrace diachronic cross-cultural analysis and will thereby, also serve as part of a critique of racism. William Casey King emphasizes this critical aspect with respect to the American concept of ambition, which he acknowledges as an idea of "white ambition" intended as a statement of racial superiority:[29]

> Ambition was purged of some of its ties to sin at a significant cost—the degradation of Native Americans and Africans. In this

---

[28]Roxane Gay, "The Price of Black Ambition," in: *Double Bind*, 129–38 (138).
[29]See also the section below on Tocqueville.

INTRODUCTION 9

case, as in other cases throughout history, superiority required inferiority to substantiate it—The *Übermensch* cannot proclaim itself *über* without the presence of an *Untermensch*. Ambition, while "American," has often been realized at the expense of a degraded other.[30]

If ambition rarely appeared in people's descriptions of themselves until quite recently, it has long been a frequent feature in assessments of others. In the academic humanities, for example, it is common to characterize a colleague as "terribly" or "horribly" ambitious. This is by no means a compliment, but it is illuminating, inasmuch as such standard phrases give expression to a certain fear, perhaps of one's own ambition and of the implications and consequences of ambitious striving, the tormentingly addictive and haunting character of which Roxane Gay so vividly describes. The person who is stigmatized as being ambitious is inevitably at risk of being disgraced or humiliated, which consequently is one reason for imputing malicious ambition to others. Vauvenargues remarks:

Above all, we disguise our ambition, which is a kind of humiliating recognition of the superiority of great men and an admission of the smallness of our own status and the arrogance of our own mind. Only those who desire little or have a good chance of realizing their aspirations may show it without violating decorum. The absurdities of the world rest on manifestly ill-founded or boundless aspirations. And because fame and fortune are so difficult to seize, those who fail at both are never spared mockery.[31]

It is particularly the pathological aspect of burning or "boundless" ambition that allows us to recognize family resemblances between the sufferings of Alexander in his tent and those of a contemporary African American author in the twenty-first century. As in the case

---

[30]William Casey King, *Ambition, a History: From Vice to Virtue* (New Haven: Yale University Press, 2013), 7.
[31]Schalk, ed., *Die französischen Moralisten*, 166.

10 AMBITION: AN ESSAY ON THE BURNING DESIRE TO RISE

of melancholy,[32] the strikingly similar symptoms point to a similar etiology that transcends the vicissitudes of time. In the excruciating pain they suffer at the hands of the insatiable ambition that drives them, Alexander the Great and Roxane Gay come as close to each other as do the aforementioned last smokers, from all different parts of society, huddled together in the narrow glass cubicles of an international airport. Politics has landed on "the will to create" (*Gestaltungswille*) as its preferred euphemism for a pursuit of power that expresses itself as the desire to take on more responsibility. In academic life, others are ambitious—in German, *ehrgeizig*: literally "greedy for honor"—but I myself simply have "aspirations," a word that admittedly suggests a certain panting or wheezing, but nevertheless sounds somehow spiritual, with a hint of *per aspera ad astra*.

Humanities professors are presumably not the only ones who think about ambition the way that Jean-Paul Sartre said we all think about death: as something that only afflicts other people. Ambition is a lonely concern that one is loath to admit to oneself or to others, even to one's spouse. Lady Macbeth receives a letter from her husband on the subject that infects her and leads to disastrous consequences. Typically, however, the ambitious person broods in solitude, in a way that suggests the sullen influence of Saturn. Goethe's Faust and Schiller's Wallenstein are the "classic" examples of this. As exemplified by the image of Alexander grumbling in his tent, ambition and melancholy are closely intertwined.[33] Ambition spills over into melancholy at the moment the process of continuous consumption of its object is cut off, when the ambitious protagonist of the drama—most often a tragedy—is deprived of satisfaction and stares into the void, delivering a monologue that can have a cathartic effect, should someone in the audience be ambitious himself.[34]

---

[32]Cf. Eckart Goebel, "Schwermut/Melancholie," in: Karlheinz Barck et al., eds., *Ästhetische Grundbegriffe: Historisches Wörterbuch*, vol. 5 (Stuttgart: J.B. Metzler, 2003), 446–86.

[33]On melancholy, see the section below on Jacob Burckhardt's *The Civilization of the Renaissance in Italy*.

[34]Cf. King, *Ambition, a History*, 71ff.: "In Elizabethan and Jacobean drama, ambition is firmly located, not surprisingly, in tragedy" (71).

INTRODUCTION   11

In his essay *Of Ambition*, the powerful Renaissance politician Francis Bacon, who has frequently been discussed as a possible author of Shakespeare's plays, emphasizes the connection between ambition and melancholy against the backdrop of the ancient tradition of humoral pathology. Stifled ambition, Bacon writes, burns down into a poisonous substance, unleashing the fumes of resentment:

> AMBITION is like choler; which is an humor that maketh men active, earnest, full of alacrity, and stirring, if it be not stopped. But if it be stopped, and cannot have his way, it becometh adust, and thereby malign and venomous. So ambitious men, if they find the way open for their rising, and still get forward, they are rather busy than dangerous; but if they be checked in their desires, they become secretly discontent, and look upon men and matters with an evil eye, and are best pleased, when things go backward.[35]

It is remarkable that there has been no other subject about which I have found so many helpful references, particularly from the gigantic archive of world literature (expertise in matters of ambition is evidently more extensive than it would seem). I did not conduct a statistical analysis, but alongside Plutarch and Shakespeare, Kleist and Hölderlin stood at the very top of the list, followed by Balzac and Stendhal. In the world of literature, at least, there is a clear difference between those authors who have produced exemplary portrayals of ambitious persons—Shakespeare and Balzac, for example—and those who can be said to have also been extremely ambitious themselves. Hölderlin's "Schiller problem" is as notorious as "Kleist's conflict with Goethe," which in turn raises the question: How ambitious was Goethe really?

Such an irreverent question suggests the next distinction, between those to whom ambition adheres as a stigma and those with whom one does not immediately associate it. In Goethe's case, it seems that everyone around him, Schiller included, is seen as distastefully ambitious, whereas he himself—was simply Goethe.

---

[35]Francis Bacon, "Of Ambition," in: Bacon, *The Major Works*, edited by Brian Vickers (Oxford: Oxford University Press, 2008), 414–16 (414f).

12 AMBITION: AN ESSAY ON THE BURNING DESIRE TO RISE

And yet this isn't quite right, either. Not only did Goethe bring ambitious characters to the stage, in *Torquato Tasso*, *Egmont*, and the aforementioned tragedy of *Faust*, he also translated into German the autobiography of perhaps the most ambitious of all Renaissance artists, Benvenuto Cellini, who also drew the particular attention of Jacob Burckhardt. Additionally, Goethe eloquently confesses to his own burning ambition in *Poetry and Truth*. Only he gives it a different, more striking name and describes it as an independent force and affliction. The ambition that chased Goethe from Frankfurt to Weimar, and from there into a complicated, decade-long political career, he calls "the daemonic": "It seemed only to accept the impossible and scornfully to reject the possible."[36]

The insight, exemplified in Goethe, that successful people ultimately must efface the burn marks left by the "pinch of purgatorial fire"[37] of their ambition is reflected upon by the sociology of success of the late 1920s, discussed in detail below. Success is only achieved when it can no longer be said to be the result of dogged ambition. Stars are never the product of all manner of strategies and machinations: a star is born. Oscar Wilde's aphorism, "Ambition is the last refuge of the failure,"[38] sharpens this insight into a paradox. A person who appears ambitious bears the odium of one who has secretly failed. From this perspective, ambition betrays a lack of self-assuredness, a gnawing self-doubt as to whether one attained one's success "by rights" and is potentially repulsive. In others, it nourishes skepticism of the legitimacy of one's claims to success, which are perceived as presumptuous. In a society of snobs such as the one in which Wilde pursued his objectives, success must come to the ambitious as a supposedly purely natural result of nonchalant, relaxed presence. La Bruyère thus appropriately remarks, without any illusions:

> We seek, we are busy, we intrigue, we torment ourselves, we petition, are refused, we petition again, and obtain; but say we,

---

[36] Johann Wolfgang von Goethe, "From My Life: Poetry and Truth (Part Four)," in: Goethe, *The Collected Works*, vol. 5, translated by Thomas P. Saine, edited by Thomas P. Saine and Jeffrey L. Sammons (Princeton: Princeton University Press, 1987), 597.
[37] Goethe, *Faust*, 80.
[38] Oscar Wilde, "Phrases and Philosophies for the Use of the Young (1894)," in: Wilde, *Complete Works of Oscar Wilde* (New York: HarperCollins, 1989), 598.

INTRODUCTION 13

without having ever asked for it, or so much as thought of it, and even when we had a quite different thing in view. This is the old style, an innocent lie, which nowadays deceives nobody.[39]

The "Dioscuri of Weimar," the sentimental, ambitious Schiller and the supposedly naturally self-possessed Goethe, find their counterparts in the realm of turn-of-the-nineteenth-century world politics in Thomas Jefferson and George Washington. Jefferson wrote clever memoranda, set the federal budget, and was a schemer. Washington, meanwhile, was a quiet man, a great man, who simply retired after two terms in office and through this clever act of renunciation attained the goal that fierce ambition so ardently courts: immortal glory. The capital of the United States is called Washington, not Jefferson. In contrast to Germany, where we still have difficulty unabashedly acknowledging our own ambition, in the United States—assuming the relevant studies adequately reflect social reality—ambition is the force that powers the "American dream." As William Casey King writes in his 2013 book on the evolution of ambition in America from vice to virtue: "America has historically been and continues to be a nation driven principally by ambition."[40]

Upon closer inspection—and this is the primary focus of this book—we can see that our relationship to ambition, ever since antiquity, has been characterized by *ambivalence*, which we encounter in everyday life in the form of the distinction between "healthy" ambition on the one hand and "pathological," "exceeding," "inordinate" ambition on the other. My use of a well-known search engine was illuminating in this respect. I wanted to search for "ambition in Balzac," but no sooner had I typed the first two words than I was immediately offered the autocompleted suggestion "arousing ambition in children." The search engine had given away the ambivalence with which we still approach ambition. The official reserve that the subject of ambition usually encounters

---

[39]Jean de la Bruyère, *Characters: Or, the Manners of the Age* (Dublin: J. Chambers, 1776), 117.
[40]King, *Ambition, a History*, 3. See also the section below on Alexis de Tocqueville, whom King strangely fails to mention, though Tocqueville urgently devotes much attention to American ambition in his still widely read book on democracy in America.

14 AMBITION: AN ESSAY ON THE BURNING DESIRE TO RISE

in conversation is countered by the clandestine belief that we cannot get by without it, that without ambition we presumably cannot succeed in our modern, neoliberal, "meritocratic" society. Ambition is a double-edged sword, to be handled with care: "*Ambition!* powerful source of Good and Ill!" exclaims Edward Young in his poem *Night Thoughts*, one of the great but now largely forgotten bestsellers of the mid-eighteenth century.[41] An awareness of ambition's double-edged character has shaped reflections on the subject ever since Hesiod in *Works and Days* distinguished between the good Eris and the bad, ever since Aristotle acknowledged in the *Nicomachean Ethics* that there is no name for the "middle" disposition between excessive ambition and a lack of ambition. In other words, it may well be necessary to arouse ambition in order to have any chance at all of achieving a goal like social advancement. But in return for this, we inevitably run into the problem of having to tame the "unbridled" ambition that tends to ensure our success. The question is whether it is even possible to tame what Jacob Burckhardt in *The Greeks and Greek Civilization* calls the "degeneration" of ambition once the genie has been let out of the bottle. Ambition can devolve into hunger for honor and glory, unleashing a (self-)destructive energy that the young Friedrich Nietzsche paradigmatically described in relation to Greek antiquity to modernity, and that prompted Roger Caillois to think of the ambitious person as a spoilsport who ruins the great social game.[42] The displacement of "ambition" by the euphemism "motivation" renders this ambivalence invisible. As can be seen from the example of McClelland, however, it has not disappeared but remains in effect.

The imperious, pathologically compulsive aspect of ambition that burns those who are afflicted by it, plunging them into the hell of an unfulfillable desire, appears again and again in history and literature. To quote Vauvenargues once again: "Fervent ambition banishes all joys in youth so as to rule alone."[43] The most striking mythological depiction of the hell of ambition is to be found, of

---

[41]Edward Young, *Night Thoughts* (1742), edited by Stephen Cornford (Cambridge: Cambridge University Press, 1989), 159.
[42]See the sections below on antiquity and on Caillois.
[43]Schalk, ed., *Die französischen Moralisten*, 109.

INTRODUCTION 15

course, in John Milton's ambitious epic *Paradise Lost*, in the fourth book of which Lucifer, the youthful, most beautiful, and most powerful angel, envious of Jesus Christ, falls prey to ambition and rebels in vain against the Lord. With deepest bitterness, the ambitious Lucifer is forced to realize that he has built his own hell, indeed that he *is* his own hell. Lucifer's fall confirms another aphorism of Vauvenargues, who notes that "fate has dealt the worst blow to ambitious men who are barred from the path to honor":[44]

Me miserable! Which way shall I fly
Infinite wrath, and infinite despair?
Which way I fly is hell; my self am hell;
And in the lowest deep a lower deep
Still threatening to devour me opens wide,
To which the hell I suffer seems a heaven.[45]

Faced with the overwhelming, largely untapped wealth of cultural-historical material about ambition that has been produced and passed down from antiquity to the present, I pestered colleagues from a variety of disciplines with endless questions, and I am grateful for all of the information they so willingly provided me, even as I was walking on thin ice. The best answer I received was from a Latinist in Tübingen, whom I asked what I should read from Cicero on the topic of "ambition." She looked me in the eye and said, "Everything."

The present book cannot and does not intend to analyze or even address "everything," not even everything by Cicero. With respect to antiquity in general, while Jacob Burckhardt and, after him, Nietzsche offer fascinating accounts of the passion of the ancient Greeks for competition in nearly every area of their lives, and spellbound readers of Sallust, Plutarch, Mommsen, Brecht, and others have encountered Roman history as a history of extremely ambitious men and women, strangely enough, a standard reference work on *Ambition in Antiquity* evidently has yet to be produced.

---

[44]Ibid., 166.
[45]John Milton, "Paradise Lost," in: Milton, *Complete Poems and Major Prose*, edited by Merritt Y. Hughes (Upper Saddle River, NJ: Prentice Hall, 1957), 279 (IV, 73–8).

16   AMBITION: AN ESSAY ON THE BURNING DESIRE TO RISE

There is also, as far as I can tell, no book on *Ambition in the Middle Ages* that coherently elucidates how Christian humility and the chivalrous thirst for glory come together against the backdrop of the Christian catalog of sin, particularly in light of the fact that in the Middle Ages, as in Sallust, *ambitio* was considered akin to *avaritia*—greed—and thus a mortal sin. Perhaps high *Minnesang*, the medieval literary genre of courtly love, with its paradoxical positing of an ever-unattainable object, provided a social playing field for medieval Christians to manage ambition. Future studies of ambition in the Middle Ages might also be inspired by Johan Huizinga, who in the course of his analysis of Burckhardt's book on the Renaissance cites personal ambition and the thirst for glory as characteristic aspects of the idea of chivalry:

> The thirst for honour and glory proper to the men of the Renaissance is essentially the same as the chivalrous ambition of earlier times, and of French origin. [...] The passionate desire to find himself praised by contemporaries or by posterity was the source of virtue with the courtly knight of the twelfth century and the rude captain of the fourteenth, no less than with the beaux-espirts of the *quattrocento*.[46]

As far as I know, there is also no *Psychoanalysis of Ambition*, even though, as I have already intimated, Alfred Adler's major writings could be collected under this title if one equates ambition with the "will to power," to which Adler ascribes "absolute primacy" over all human motivations.[47] It was these and other intriguing desiderata of literary and cultural research that inspired the project of this book, for which I chose the free form of the essay, as I offer nothing here but precisely that, a first attempt intended to show that there is simply a lack of comprehensive works on one

---

[46]Johan Huizinga, *The Waning of the Middle Ages: A Study of the Forms of Life, Thought and Art in France and the Netherlands in the XIVth and XVth Centuries* (London: Edward Arnold, 1924), 59. See also Chapter V of that book, on "The Dream and Heroism of Love," 66–73.
[47]Alfed Adler, *The Neurotic Character: Fundamentals of Individual Psychology and Psychotherapy*, translated by Cees Koen, edited by Henry T. Stein (Bellingham, WA: The Classical Adlerian Translation Project, 2002), 50.

INTRODUCTION 17

of the vital forces that defines political and cultural life.[48] What follows constitutes only an initial exploration of a vast terrain. I limit myself in Chapter 1 to a delineation of various aspects of the semantics of "ambition," followed in Chapter 2 by a series of sketches of historically influential examples from Greek and Roman antiquity. Finally, Chapter 3 presents a historical reconstruction of modern perspectives on ambition: Burckhardt's uncovering of the connection between the evolution of the individual and the emergence of modern ambition in his book *The Civilization of the Renaissance in Italy*, Tocqueville's theory of the bourgeois ambition of equals, Ichheiser's and Mannheim's studies of the sociology of success, Caillois' theory of play, McClelland's theory of motivation, and finally the psychoanalysis of Freud and Adler. The afterword offers a first attempt at grappling with Michel de Montaigne's powerful reflections on the inevitability of ambition, in which he concludes that what is necessary is to turn ambition against itself, to conceive of an ambition capable of forsaking ambition.

These initial explorations represent the extent of the ambition of this essay on ambition, which led me to the insight that, though the passion of ambition knows no end, though it stretches as far as to the stars, each arrival at the next station or plateau offers us another chance to stop, to get off the train. Reverence is one antonym of ambition. The other, less contaminated by religion— the actual antidote in the face of ambition's toxic potential—is disillusionment. It would be a misguided ambition simply to write a comprehensive book about ambition and its history. A historically, systematically relevant study requires collaboration and continuous interdisciplinary exchange with others. As early as antiquity, productive exchanges between equals were considered a cardinal

---

[48]William Casey King also confirms this with respect to American research through 2013. See King, *Ambition, a History*, 4f. The French philosopher and journalist Vincent Cespedes also published a book on ambition in 2013, *L'ambition ou l'épopée de soi* (Paris: Flammarion, 2013), that—as I note below in my own survey of the semantics of "ambition"—includes stimulating individual observations that maneuver brilliantly but very much associatively between the different conceptual registers "de Socràte à Madonna" (51). Nonetheless, Cespedes, who ultimately aims to describe a forward-looking, political concept of ambition that leads from liberty toward fraternity (cf. 291), confirms the approach of this book, which argues that ambition shows itself to be a relatively stable "syndrome" across history, indeed from Socrates to Madonna.

18   AMBITION: AN ESSAY ON THE BURNING DESIRE TO RISE

remedy against the always possible hypertrophy of ambition, and thus also against the ambition to write about ambition.

*

In the context of contemporary critiques of neoliberalism—which, contrary to the social democratic ideas of the welfare state, reduces "reform [...] to self-interest, or worse, competitive advantage" and demands "a return to markets in all spheres of social life,"[49] as Anson Rabinbach noted already in 1990—literary figures who can be read as allegories of resistance against a life defined by ambition or the "motivation to consistently optimize oneself" have drawn increasing attention in recent years. One notable example of this would be the numerous readings of Herman Melville's enigmatic novella *Bartleby, the Scrivener*, the eponymous hero of which, with a complex turn of phrase as meek as it is uncompromising, suddenly refuses to perform his duties as a copyist at a Wall Street law firm: "Bartleby, in a singularly mild, firm voice, replied: 'I would prefer not to.'"[50] Another figure of opposition to the world of merciless competition is Ivan Goncharov's listless antihero, the nobleman Oblomov, raised on a remote estate near the Volga whose inhabitants are "impervious to economic truths about the desirability of a quick turnover of capital, increased production, and exchange of goods."[51] At Oblomovka it is rather "a perpetual holiday"[52] (though one admittedly based on serfdom). Oblomov, who spends his life in St. Petersburg almost entirely in bed, famously dreams of his family estate as the antithesis of a harried world ruled by competition, avarice, and ambition, as a pre-capitalist idyll:

> They had never heard of the so-called hard life, of people who were constantly worried, who rushed about from place to place, or who devoted their lives to everlasting, never-ending work. They did not really believe in mental worries, either; they did

---

[49]Anson Rabinbach, *The Human Motor: Energy, Fatigue, and the Origins of Modernity* (Berkeley/Los Angeles: University of California Press, 1990), 294.

[50]Herman Melville, "Bartleby, the Scrivener: A Story of Wall Street," in: id., *Billy Budd, Bartleby, and Other Stories* (New York: Penguin, 2016), 17–54 (25).

[51]Ivan Goncharov, *Oblomov*, translated by David Magarshack (London: Penguin, 2005), 129.

[52]Ibid., 156.

INTRODUCTION   19

not think that life existed so that man should constantly strive
for some barely apprehended aims; they were terribly afraid of
strong passions, and just as with other people bodies might be
consumed by the volcanic action of inner, spiritual fire, so their
souls wallowed peacefully and undisturbed in their soft bodies.[53]

Goncharov employs the traditional imagery of fire and flames with
precision to characterize those people driven forward by ambition,
who file past Oblomov's bed at the beginning of the novel. In the
wake of Oblomov's dream, only his childhood friend Andrey, an
assertive and disciplined half-German with the telling surname
Stolz (German for "pride"), is able to drag him out of bed and
into society. Exhausted by these outings, Oblomov finds himself
confirmed in his refusal of the world:

Everything—this constant rushing about, this eternal interplay
of petty passions, greed especially, the eagerness with which they
try to get the better of one another, the scandalmongering, the
gossip [...]; listening to their talk makes your head swim and
you go silly.[54]

Bartleby and Oblomov are examples of figures who in contemporary
theory and media discourse are considered avant-garde modern
refuseniks, as they stubbornly defy the constant striving of the
ambitious from New York to St. Petersburg, which they recognize
as a meaningless rat race that is empty at its core: "Just see whether
you can find the centre round which all this revolves; there is no
such centre, there is nothing deep, nothing vital."[55]
    The ensuing pages are devoted primarily to the actors in that
society from which Oblomov has fled in his disgust to his bed,
and especially those scrambling simply to gain access to those
circles from which the wealthy Oblomov is able to withdraw. I
am particularly interested in the "parvenu[s]"[56] of low parentage
like Oblomov's childhood friend Stolz, in what goes on beyond the

---

[53]Ibid., 123f.
[54]Ibid., 172.
[55]Ibid., 173.
[56]Ibid., 156.

20 AMBITION: AN ESSAY ON THE BURNING DESIRE TO RISE

confines of Oblomov's room. From the perspective of the pariah and the ambitious social climber, the cozy bed of the "parasite" fed by his servants is something that one "must first be able to afford," and thus also a symbol of resentment toward those so privileged. As Goncharov's great double portrait of the contrast between these two friends makes clear, the ambivalence in ambition's assessment can never be entirely extinguished. It is in fact Oblomov, archetype of procrastination, who confirms that ambition is "the salt of life."[57] Stolz, for his part knows that Oblomov's trenchant social critique is merely a rehashing of age-old patterns and points to the texts passed down from antiquity to which a study of ambition must therefore look back: "[Y]ou talk like the ancients: they all used to write like that in old books."[58]

Carrion

Where do the origins of ambition lie? Probably in the history of the species, somewhere in the depths of our evolutionary development. The evolutionary biologist Josef H. Reichholf, in his book *Warum wir siegen wollen* (*Why We Want to Win*), considers the question of whether and to what extent athletic ambition can be seen as a "driving force in human evolution." It seems evident to him that "the desire to win by no means must first be learned, but rather is somehow innate in human beings." Nevertheless, this will to win, which manifests itself not only in sports, but also permeates and largely defines human economic, political, social, and cultural life, remains an "evolutionary-biological mystery"[59] that he hopes in his study to explain. Why do we even have this intense desire to be "first"?

Reichholf traces the breathless race run all around the world—from childhood on, with the goal of finding out who will jubilantly arrive "first" and "win" – to our biological ancestors' persistent need for haste, for which he identifies two fundamental reasons: "Either

---

[57]Ibid., 184.
[58]Ibid., 174.
[59]Josef H. Reichholf, *Warum wir siegen wollen: Der sportliche Ehrgeiz als Triebkraft in der Evolution des Menschen* (Frankfurt am Main: Fischer, 2009), 41.

INTRODUCTION 21

one was being chased by something dangerous or one wanted to be the first to reach something attractive."[60] The latter was particularly important for the gibbons, swinging from branch to branch through the jungles of the Tertiary period, from whom we inherited the design and suspension of our long arms as well as our front-facing eyes.[61] Being the first to find fruit was critical:

> Harvesting fruits meant coming across them at the right time. The decisive factor was not the date or the place, but only their ripeness. It was not enough to be at the right place at the right time in order to be able to reap the fruits' benefits. Competitors for food might have arrived earlier and already fetched the best fruits—or the entire harvest! It all came down to who got there first.[62]

The first hominids, having come down from the trees and mastered walking upright, evolved into endurance runners with long legs. They became runners because they had to follow enormous herds of large animals across the savanna in order to obtain fresh meat, which later turned out to be critical for the growth of the human brain. Before human beings became hunters, they were "exploiters of carrion"[63] who had to make haste to arrive at a freshly dead animal before any other competitors. The origins of not just racing, but throwing as humanity's earliest forms of play and sport likely lie in this primordial competition. Throwing, according to Reichholf, presumably goes back to the rocks that our ancestors on the savanna hurled at their competitors in order to defend the found carcass.[64] An upright gait did not change the need for haste: in the savanna, too, everything came down to being the "winner," meaning the first to find the carrion. Reichholf offers a spectacular explanation for a well-known gesture:

> What is more obvious than the conjecture that the victorious gesture of the runner who is the first to arrive at the goal and

---

[60]Ibid., 61.
[61]Ibid., 66.
[62]Ibid., 72.
[63]Ibid., 96.
[64]Cf. ibid., 100.

22 AMBITION: AN ESSAY ON THE BURNING DESIRE TO RISE

gives expression to his success by throwing his arms in the air represents the age-old signal deployed on the African savanna during the quest to find the desired cadaver of a large animal?[65]

Human evolution as a whole has been shaped from the beginning by competition, from the study of which the dubious theory of social Darwinism has drawn its controversial conclusions:

> "Wanting to win" has mutated into "needing to win." Now there are real losers. [...] Winning has had to become a permanent objective, the central leitmotif of "wanting to win." Giving up means being defeated by "others" and going extinct.[66]

From the perspective of evolutionary biology, ambition as the will to win is a function of self-preservation. In the history of the species, it constitutes our first "success." Ambition fades away once self-preservation has been achieved and only flames up again when self-preservation must be ensured anew. Evolutionarily speaking, ambition is originally nothing other than the successful will to survive under conditions of chronic deprivation. But as even a fleeting glance at the world of human beings makes clear, over the course of documented history, ambition has emancipated itself from this original function. A biological riddle has given way to a cultural conundrum, one that Reichholf—who goes on to consider the origins of war—does not further discuss. What is the function, if any, of an ambition that does not fade even after self-preservation, and thus a rationally comprehensible success, has been assured? Seneca, for one, recognizes just *one* form of "crazed [...] ambition."[67] From an evolutionary-biological perspective, this burning ambition—only occasionally discussed in philosophy, but frequently and powerfully described in world literature, sociology

---

[65]Ibid., 133. Verheyen, however, suggests that the trope of throwing one's arms in the air might also be a product of early sports photography, "which gradually came to settle on a pose that effectively conveyed 'victory.'" Verheyen, *Die Erfindung der Leistung*, 52.

[66]Reichholf, *Warum wir siegen wollen*, 138f.

[67]Seneca, "On the Tranquility of the Mind," in: id., *Dialogues and Essays*, translated by John Davie (Oxford: Oxford University Press, 2007), 118.

INTRODUCTION 23

(of success), psychology (of motivation), and psychoanalysis—is excessive, latently hostile, and self-destructive. Its self-destructive aspect is even registered in everyday language in our distinction, mentioned above, between healthy and pathological ambition, or when we say, in a frighteningly dramatic turn of phrase, that someone is "eaten up by ambition," as though devoured by a predatory animal, corroded by acid, or consumed by an uncontrollable fire. This burning, potentially corrosive ambition, which seems to be a purely human phenomenon, is the primary interest of this book.

1

The Semantics
of Ambition

"The world is a quagmire, let's try to remain above it."

(THE DUCHESSE DE LANGEAIS, 1819, IN BALZAC'S *PÈRE GORIOT*)[1]

Ambition as Desire

In an excellent 2007 essay titled "Ambitions," the moral philosopher Glen Pettigrove, having examined all of the available philosophical literature, comes to the conclusion that ambition is a largely neglected topic in both ethics and political philosophy. Although authors from Plato to Machiavelli to Rousseau to Santayana have repeatedly cited personal ambition—unquestionably a driving force in political life—as one of the greatest threats to political security, philosophical literature since antiquity, Pettigrove finds, contains scarcely more than a few scattered passages on the subject.[2] A look at the brief entry for "Ehrgeiz" in the *Historisches Wörterbuch der Philosophie* (*Historical Dictionary of Philosophy*) confirms a lack of philosophical interest in the German-speaking world, as well: there

---

[1] Honoré de Balzac, *Père Goriot*, translated by A.J. Krailsheimer (Oxford: Oxford University Press, 1991), 71.

[2] Cf. Glen Pettigrove, "Ambitions," in: *Ethical Theory and Moral Practice* 10.1 (2007), 53–68 (53f.).

26 AMBITION: AN ESSAY ON THE BURNING DESIRE TO RISE

is nothing there but a desultory florilegium spanning the millennia, with no effort toward any argumentative integration.[3] Cicero—who addresses ambition in *De officiis*, among other texts, and defines it there, in keeping with Plato's *Politeia*, as "an altogether wretched practice"[4]—is not mentioned, nor is Francis Bacon, who penned the short but insightful essay on ambition quoted above.

Faced with this situation, Pettigrove aims to provide "a long overdue analysis of ambition."[5] The following pages of this chapter are intended as a reconstruction of and critical commentary on his short essay, which provides a clarifying outline of the semantics of ambition and offers numerous prompts for further reflection and thus presents an eminently useful approach to the topic. The overarching question that Pettigrove poses as a moral philosopher is the same one that has been posed again and again since antiquity: should ambition be considered a virtue or a vice?[6] And he, too, ultimately comes to the conclusion that "[a]mbition is double-edged."[7]

Pettigrove's look at the philosophical tradition first shows him that ambition has repeatedly been construed as "a kind of desire" that can be directed at various objects. While David Hume defines ambition as a desire for power, other philosophers identify respect, admiration, glory, honor, victory, and success as objects of ambition, as well as wealth, knowledge, and perfection. It goes without saying that this desire can also be directed at a combination of the objects just named (in addition to many others), inasmuch as victory, for example, may bring with it honor, power, and maybe wealth as well. Alexis de Tocqueville, in the course of his reflections on democracy, convincingly deduces the reason why, in an ideally imagined *society of equals*, money ultimately and inevitably rises to become the primary object of ambitious desire:

> When fellow citizens are all independent and indifferent [in the sense of being equal, EG], it is only by paying that you can obtain

---

[3] Joachim Ritter, ed., *Historisches Wörterbuch der Philosophie*, vol. 2 (Basel: Schwabe Verlag, 1971–2007), 324–5.
[4] Cicero, *On Duties*, edited by M.T. Griffin and E.M. Atkins (Cambridge: Cambridge University Press, 1991), 34.
[5] Pettigrove, "Ambitions," 53.
[6] Cf. ibid., 54.
[7] Ibid., 67.

THE SEMANTICS OF AMBITION 27

the cooperation of each one of them; this infinitely multiplies the use of wealth and increases its value.

Since the prestige that was attached to ancient things has disappeared, birth, state, profession no longer distinguish men, or scarcely distinguish them; there remains hardly anything except money that creates very visible differences between them and that can put a few of them beyond comparison. The distinction that arises from wealth is increased by the disappearance and lessening of all the other distinctions.[8]

Pettigrove's preliminary definition of ambition—as desire for an open set of objects that, following Hume (and later Nietzsche), are all potentially subject to the "will to power" and can cumulate in wealth—immediately prompts further questions: What exactly does "desire" mean here? How does this desire emerge, and what is it rooted in? Ambition is at least somewhat distinct from the two basic drives named by Freud, the ego and sex drives. Does ambition consist in their intensification or hypertrophy? Acquiring power and wealth can be necessary for self-preservation, but at what point does this tip over from the pursuit of successful self-preservation described by evolutionary biology into a potentially infinite ambition that repeatedly leads into the abyss or into depression? Sexual drives can combine with the desire for success, recognition, and "victory"—as famously seen in Stendhal's *The Red and the Black* or Balzac's *Père Goriot*—but they do not necessarily do so. To put the question yet another way, is ambition a modification of one of Freud's two basic drives, an excess of the ego or sexual drives, or does it constitute a separate "third drive," which would be a bold hypothesis indeed? Given that the drive for self-preservation and the drive to procreate are common to all living things, whereas excessive ambition certainly is not, this "third drive" would be a purely human one. Accordingly, man would be defined as *the ambitious animal*.

---

[8]Alexis de Tocqueville, *Democracy in America*, edited by Eduardo Nolla, translated by James T. Schleifer (Indianapolis: Liberty Fund, 2012), 1090.

28 AMBITION: AN ESSAY ON THE BURNING DESIRE TO RISE

"Salvation in Posterity"

In a chapter of *Democracy in America* that will be discussed separately below, Tocqueville offers a definition of ambition that, according to Pettigrove, concretely unifies the list of various objects named above: it is "a yearning desire to rise."[9] Tocqueville thus conceives of ambition as the will to climb (socially), as career ambition, as the desire to get one or multiple steps "higher." While this vertical conception of ambition comprehends a wide variety of behaviors that are defined as ambitious both in the empirical world and in literature (in Shakespeare's *Macbeth* and *King Lear*, as well as in many of the social novels of the nineteenth century), it by no means covers the entire semantic spectrum. What does the ambition to complete a painting or solve a math problem in solitude, for example, have to do with the will to rise through the ranks of society or the need for admiration? As I will discuss in greater detail in the corresponding sections below, the sociologists Gustav Ichheiser and Karl Mannheim develop this observation into a distinction between *achievement*, which is strictly related to the task at hand, and *success*, which represents a genuinely social category. Furthermore, it does not seem entirely reasonable to describe the ambition of people who already find themselves at the highest of social heights—the ambition of kings from Alexander the Great to Louis XIV—as simply the will to "climb the social ladder." A different form of ambition underlies the desire of kings to attain honor and immortal glory. Tocqueville himself expands upon this divergence in the context of his astute analysis of military ambition, in which he points to the sociological difference between aristocratic and bourgeois officers:

> Among aristocratic peoples, the office, apart from his rank in the army, still occupies an elevated rank in society; the first is almost always in his eyes only an accessory to the second; the noble, by embracing the career of arms, obeys ambition [in the sense of the desire for advancement, EG] less than a sort of duty that his birth imposes on him. He enters the army in order to employ honorably the idle years of his youth, and in order to be able to bring back to his household and to his peers a few honorable

---

[9]Cited in Pettigrove, "Ambitions," 55.

THE SEMANTICS OF AMBITION   29

memories of military life; but his principal objective there is not to gain property, consideration and power; for he possesses these advantages on his own and enjoys them without leaving home.[10]

Thus with respect to the ambition of those who already enjoy a high social rank, we must distinguish heuristically between immanent and transcendent ambition. This is why it does not seem absurd to speak of "religious ambition." Max Weber even jokes about the "unrivaled degree of piety" performed by the English Puritans.[11]—Political usurpers like Julius Caesar exemplify the fusing of immanent and transcendent ambition into an Achillean ambition that strives to rise to immortality, to "godliness." Ancient Roman society famously elevated its emperors to the status of gods after their deaths.

Here we must recall Montesquieu's famous differentiation between the principles that in his view underlay the three classic forms of government. Republics, according to Montesquieu, require "virtue" as an additional driving force in order to ensure social cohesion, while the stability of despotic states is secured by the "fear" that always stands at their disposal. Finally, monarchies are animated by the ideal of "honor," which has a primarily symbolic value, but also serves to motivate action:

> [I]f one spring is missing, monarchy has another. HONOR, that is, the prejudice of each person and each condition, takes the place of the political virtue of which I have spoken and represents it everywhere. It can inspire the finest actions; joined with the force of the laws, it can lead to the goal of government as does virtue itself.
>
> Thus, in well-regulated monarchies everyone will be almost a good citizen, and one will rarely find someone who is a good man; for, in order to be a good man, one must have the intention of being one and love the state less for oneself than for itself.[12]

---

[10]Tocqueville, *Democracy in America*, 1155. See also the section on Tocqueville in Chapter 3 below.

[11]Max Weber, *The Protestant Ethic and the "Spirit" of Capitalism and Other Writings*, edited and translated by Peter Baehr and Gordon C. Wells (New York: Penguin, 2002), 8.

[12]Montesquieu, *The Spirit of the Laws*, edited and translated by Anne M. Cohler, Basia Carolyn Miller, and Harold Samuel Stone (Cambridge: Cambridge University Press, 1989), 26.

30   AMBITION: AN ESSAY ON THE BURNING DESIRE TO RISE

The potentially excessive character of specifically human ambition, touched on above with respect to evolutionary biology, returns here with the idea of immortal glory. The struggle to "rise" to the highest position is characteristic of many animals who live in social groups, but the desire for immortality is genuinely human, as only humans, as far as we know, possess an awareness of their own mortality. Achilles is a lion when he desires to become the most powerful of all warriors; he shows himself to be a human being as soon as he thirsts for immortality. This suggests that there is an intimate connection between human ambition and death, and the desire to overcome it. If we follow the line Tocqueville draws "upwards" toward infinity, we can discern conquering death, becoming a god, as the ultimate goal of human ambition. Hercules's blazing ascent to Olympus is the apotheosis of this utopia of the ambitious; Caesarian megalomania, its shadow. Conversely, the desire for undying posthumous fame in this world can take the place of such fantasies of divine immortality. "The 'full form' of glory," according to Dirk Werle, "encompasses both recognition during one's lifetime and especially the enduring embedment of one's name in cultural memory after one's death."[13] The seal of the Académie Française, founded by Cardinal Richelieu, thus bears the motto: *À l'immortalité*. Henning Ritter gets to the heart of this desire for immortality in the afterword to his German translation of Hérault de Séchelles' *Théorie de l'ambition* (1788):

> The young Séchelles was an atheist as a matter of course, and he evidently possessed sufficient alternative solutions with sovereign certainty. At no point in his *Theory of Ambition* can one sense any doubt that this is the only world. Society is everything, and its future is nothing other than an afterimage of the present. Posthumous fame takes the place of religious salvation, and fame during one's lifetime is viewed as a prerequisite of salvation in posterity.[14]

---

[13]Dirk Werle, *Ruhm und Moderne: Eine Ideengeschichte (1750–1930)* (Frankfurt am Main: Klostermann, 2014), 127.

[14]Henning Ritter, "Nachwort," in: Hérault de Séchelles ed., *Theories des Ehrgeizes*, edited and translated by Henning Ritter (Munich: C.H. Beck, 1997), 107 58 (119f.). Despite what the title (which did not come from Hérault de Séchelles himself) suggests, *Théorie de l'ambition* does not offer a theory of ambition but is rather a kind of shrewd, amoral guidebook for climbing the social ladder in a competitive society. As such, it could just as well be titled *Behavioral Guide for the Ambitious*.

Self-Preservation and Self-Realization

Pettigrove somewhat surprisingly derives a third, directly ethical quality of ambition from Tocqueville's definition. Ambition, he argues, not only concerns acquiring an object, but also involves a change in personality. Tocqueville's definition of ambition as "a yearning desire to rise" points to the acquisition of a "higher" moral competency, to our desire to become "better *persons*."[15] From this proposition we can conclude that there might possibly be something like a "moral ambition," though one in which Nietzsche, Freud, and others would surely see a veiled pursuit of power or latent resentment.

Nietzsche's stylistic and intellectual forebears, the French moralists, themselves raised doubts about the peculiar quality of moral ambitions. Vauvenargues, for example, writes: "No one is content with his status out of mere modesty. Only religion or the constellation of powers can curb ambition."[16] La Rochefoucauld similarly remarks that "[w]hat appears to be noble-mindedness is often only disguised ambition that scorns small advantages in order to pursue greater ones."[17] Even more pointedly, La Rochefoucauld also asserts: "Modesty is made out to be a virtue in order to constrain the ambition of great men and console mediocrities about their poor fortune and meager accomplishments."[18] These and numerous other statements by the French moralists can be summarized, in keeping with the teachings of Machiavelli and Nietzsche (whom Pettigrove does not discuss), to the effect that the social world is permeated and even dominated by ubiquitous ambition. What appears to be morality is, from this perspective, actually ambition, frustrated and effectively restrained by social circumstances or mutually checked and balanced by various social actors.

Niccolò Machiavelli devoted an extensive poem to ambition that begins with an invitation to see the world as it is. According to *Dell'ambizione*, ambition has ruled the world since the beginning of time: it is what drove Cain to kill his brother Abel. Personal virtue (*virtù*) and laws can help keep ambition in check, but enforcing

---

[15]Pettigrove, "Ambitions," 55. Emphasis in original.
[16]Fritz Schalk, ed., *Die französischen Moralisten*, vol. 1 (Munich: dtv, 1973), 166.
[17]Ibid., 68.
[18]Ibid., 74.

32 AMBITION: AN ESSAY ON THE BURNING DESIRE TO RISE

morality ultimately requires more than picking up the Bible. We must instead take up the sword in order to tame an amoral ambition that knows no limits: "tener la spada e non il libro in mano."[19] As Bernd Roeck writes, human beings for Machiavelli are "the creators of their world, but at the same time admittedly bloodthirsty wolves eaten up by ambition."[20]

It is difficult to say exactly how certain objects of ambition, such as wealth, can "change" a person—"[A]nd still you will remain just what you are," Mephistopheles admonishes in Part One of *Faust*.[21] Nevertheless, we can state that accomplishing certain ambitious goals of self-realization provides a certain maneuverability. Further distinguishing between self-preservation and self-realization can thus contribute to better understanding ambition. A person who works his way up from oppressive material circumstances to wealth—an often invoked, textbook example of "healthy ambition"—is better able to realize talents or inclinations that otherwise would have withered away. We can of course count among such inclinations the desire for moral betterment that Pettigrove calls a moral ambition. The pursuit of self-realization in the sense of freedom and self-determination, however, may in turn potentially be subject to a further dynamic that can turn this pursuit of freedom into its opposite. The proposition that one may become enslaved to ambition is found repeatedly throughout the moral philosophical tradition. La Bruyère, for example, writes: "A slave has but one master: An ambitious man has as many as there are people who may be useful to him in making his fortune."[22]

Solitary, Calculated Passion

Tocqueville's definition of ambition implies further qualities of the concept that Pettigrove goes on to elaborate. First, Tocqueville's

---

[19]Niccolò Machiavelli, "*Vom Ehrgeiz/Dell'ambizione*," in: *Niccolò Machiavelli. Dichter – Poeta*, edited by Dirk Hoeges (Köln: machiavelli-edition, 2016), 149.

[20]Bernd Roeck, *Der Morgen der Welt: Geschichte der Renaissance* (Munich: C.H. Beck, 2019), 644. Cf. the section below on Jacob Burckhardt's *The Civilization of the Renaissance in Italy*.

[21]Johann Wolfgang von Goethe, "*Faust*," in: Goethe, *The Collected Works*, vol. 2, edited and translated by Stuart Atkins (Princeton: Princeton University Press, 1984), 47 (line 1809).

[22]La Bruyère, *The Characters*, 124.

THE SEMANTICS OF AMBITION   33

"yearning desire" likewise emphasizes the high, "burning" intensity of this desire. Ambition is directed not toward contingent trifles that one could easily get hold of but rather toward ardently longed-for and thus mostly *distant objects*. So intense is this desire that it repeatedly—powerfully and undeniably—thrusts itself into consciousness. It thus borders on an obsession or life-defining *ideé fixe*. Given the intensity and insistence of the desire, Pettigrove astutely concludes, the object ambition longs for must by definition be difficult to attain.[23] Everyday language again confirms this: we do not consider it an expression of ambition when a person goes shopping, but we do when he wants to attain a fiercely fought-over political or social position.

Moreover, Pettigrove argues, Tocqueville's definition accentuates the necessary connection between ambition and *activity*, the strong, persistent will to fulfill ambition, to realize its aim through action. Ambition is practical. It is clearly distinct from daydreaming, from resigned, inconsequential wishful thinking, from the sterile "life-lie" of Henrik Ibsen's *The Wild Duck* that tends to breed resentment. This suggests the further conclusion that, in order to fulfill ambition, one must pursue it not just persistently, but also methodically, rationally. This quality is registered in everyday language in the term "blind ambition," an insightful turn of phrase that criticizes an ambition that lacks the clear-sightedness of cold-blooded rationality.

Ambition is an intense desire for an elusive object that cannot rest or be extinguished until this object has in fact been seized. "[A]mbition involves a self-disciplined commitment or determination to obtain its object," Pettigrove writes.[24] This is a particularly important insight, as it helps us to better understand the seemingly contradictory aspects of the phenomenology of ambition, the intertwining of heat and cold, passion and calculation. To bring it to the point of paradox: ambition is a *deliberately, rationally pursued passion*, a desire whose fulfillment, given the remoteness of its elusive object, must be pursued with perseverance and elaborated strategies as a long-term project. Ambition is not a short-lived fervor, but a deep-seated passion that can shape or even dominate an entire life. Vincent Cespedes thus describes the evolution of ambition as the

---

[23]Cf. Pettigrove, "Ambitions," 55.
[24]Ibid.

34 AMBITION: AN ESSAY ON THE BURNING DESIRE TO RISE

transformation of a passionate urgency, an "inner scream that can erupt at any moment," into a glowing "holy fire." Cespedes, too, speaks of a paradox:

> Urgency is the essential spark that, after a slow process of maturation, is transformed into a *holy fire* that sets the heart of the ambitious man aglow. It is paradoxical to evoke "slowness" and "maturation" when speaking of urgency, as the concept rather refers to a pressing need, to immediacy [...]. Nevertheless, we must sum up ambition with this forced definition as a *mediated urgency*.[25]

In the light of this conception of ambition as a "mediated urgency," everyday references to both "burning" and "cold" ambition now make sense. The sudden eruptions of passion and "holy fire" from otherwise calm politicians are suddenly less surprising. Already in antiquity, Cicero's notorious inclination toward self-praise was perceived as distasteful and embarrassing.[26] Apparently, on these disconcerting occasions, the *temperantia* that Cicero otherwise so eloquently commended was pierced for a few moments by the flames of the more or less well-concealed ambition of an intellectual in the world of politics. A passage from Plutarch's biography of Cicero, which offers a classic example of dealing pragmatically with ambition and the thirst for glory, is illuminating in this context. The up-and-coming Cicero, having achieved extraordinary things as a quaestor in distant Sicily, returns to Rome proudly assuming that his success must be the talk of the town, that he must have already attained the "prominence" his later career would bring. But he had much to learn about attaining glory in a metropolis:

> Meeting an eminent citizen in Campania, whom he accounted his friend, he asked him what the Romans said and thought of his actions, as if the whole city had been filled with the glory of what he had done. His friend asked him in reply, "Where is it you have been, Cicero?" This for the time utterly mortified and cast

---

[25]Cespedes, *L'ambition ou l'épopée de soi*, 78.
[26]Cf. Manfred Fuhrmann, *Cicero und die römische Republik* (Düsseldorf: Patmos, 2006), 102, 122.

THE SEMANTICS OF AMBITION

him down to perceive that the report of his actions had sunk into the city of Rome as into an immense ocean, without any visible effect or result in reputation. And afterwards considering with himself that the glory he contended for was an infinite thing, and that there was no fixed end nor measure in its pursuit, he abated much of his ambitious thoughts. Nevertheless, he was always excessively pleased with his own praise, and continued to the very last to be passionately fond of glory; which often interfered with the prosecution of his wisest resolutions.[27]

This anecdote elegantly and amusingly confronts the boundlessness of burning ambition with the immensity of the metropolis, which itself vouches for the immensity of the world, into the oblivion of which the ambitious striving of men must sink without a trace. This insight, however—and this is Plutarch's real point, which he weaves into the narrative with great tact—does not induce any actual disillusionment. Cicero, as Plutarch diplomatically puts it, "abates" his ambitious thoughts, but does not ever truly conquer them, which is why his usually prudently managed passion continues to get in his way, repeatedly interfering with the prosecution of his wisest resolutions.

Plutarch's anecdote highlights another aspect of the double-edged nature of ambition that prompted Goethe to identify it as "demonic." Ambition is necessary if one is to be successful in competition, but because of its latent, inherent boundlessness, it all but inevitably clouds one's perception, such that the ambitious man may end up stepping on his own toes. Here Cicero himself experiences what elsewhere he so clearly observed in the case of Caesar, namely that the greatest intelligence, even as it may endow one with the ability to recognize the effective unattainability of ambitious aims and thus soberly renounce them, is yet incapable of protecting against ambition. Instead, it only further inflames it. In his book on obligations (*De officiis*), Cicero, considering the career of his rival, finds it "troubling [...] that the desire for honour, command, power and glory usually exist in men of the greatest

---

[27]Plutarch, *Lives*, vol. 2, translated by John Dryden, edited by Arthur Hugh Clough (New York: Random House, 2001), 412.

spirit and most brilliant intellectual talent."[28] Here Cicero exposes what he himself is afflicted by: the addictive nature of ambition even for the most gifted, who become and remain susceptible to flattery *even though* they recognize it as such. Like any other addiction, ambition eludes the grasp of the intellect, nor can it be cured by the sort of philosophical meditation practiced by a politically sidelined man twiddling his thumbs in withdrawal at his beautiful villa in Tusculum. Manfred Fuhrmann writes in this context of the "compensatory literary activities that made Cicero Rome's most important philosophical writer."[29]

The presumed connection between giftedness and ambition is a result of the need for self-realization mentioned above. In schematic terms, a gifted person is best able to fulfill his potential when he can devote himself fully and unreservedly to his field. In politics, however, only the person at the very top has free rein to fully realize his political program—it is strictly from this that his aspiration to the highest position derives. To say that a politician is ambitious is thus an analytical judgment. Inside every gifted politician beats the heart of a little dictator who, to again quote Montesquieu, must learn—or must not forget—to "love the state less for [himself] than for itself." Francis Bacon makes a similar argument, urging princes and states to "choose such ministers, as are more sensible of duty than of using; and such as love business rather upon conscience, than upon bravery." A politician driven solely by personal ambition, on the other hand, represents the greatest danger to the polity: "But he, that plots to be the only figure amongst ciphers, is the decay of a whole age."[30]

Plutarch's Cicero anecdote also clarifies the distinctive connection between *ambition* and *solitude*. A passionately pursued project must not be "exposed." Once an ambitious goal becomes known to others, its pursuer is all but inevitably subjected to their humiliation, because it "must" be an elusive, "high-flying" goal, one that stands in sharp contrast to the ambitious person's current situation. The concealment of ambition does not necessarily mean that the

---

[28]Cicero, *On Duties*, 11.

[29]Fuhrmann, *Cicero*, 104.

[30]Francis Bacon, "Of Ambition," in: Bacon, *The Major Works*, edited by Brian Vickers (Oxford: Oxford University Press, 2008), 414–16 (414–15).

THE SEMANTICS OF AMBITION

ambitious person, like a Shakespearean villain, is pursuing some criminal aim. Rather, it is rooted in the structure of the phenomenon. The typical discrepancy between the ambitious person's low origins and lofty aims is potentially ridiculous. To pursue one's goals with "blind ambition" and stumble in public is to be laughed at. Ambition is a passion with a considerable drop height, pursued in solitude, that the ambitious person speaks about only rarely and reluctantly, and then only to trusted confidants.[31] But when it is directed at an absurd goal that for whatever reason is forever unattainable, it mutates, as Pettigrove rightly notes, into a "delusional obsession,"[32] or it is swallowed and suppressed. *Ressentiment*, Max Scheler argues, drawing on Nietzsche, is the fermented, frustrated ambition of the "impotent."[33]

Ambition and Morality

In order finally to be able to discuss the *moral dimension of ambition*, Pettigrove expands his argument to examine the social context of ambitious striving and, critically, the psychology of the ambitious person. Ambition is a solitary passion, but one that is pursued in society. Consequently, as a relationship to oneself and to others, it invariably possesses a moral index.

Jacob Burckhardt's great book on the ambition-suffused civilization of the Renaissance in Italy, the famous aphorisms of the French moralists at the extremely competitive absolutist court of Versailles, and of course the great social novels of the nineteenth century thus provide an almost inexhaustible archive

---

[31]Cf. La Bruyère, *The Characters*, 117: "Men are not willing we should discover the prospects they have of their advancement, nor find out the dignity they aim at, because if they do not obtain it, they fancy there is some shame attends the being refuted; and if they do, they persuade themselves it is greater glory to be thought worthy by him that gives it them, then to shew they think themselves worthy by their intrigues and cabals; they would at once appear adorned with their dignity and modesty."

[32]Pettigrove, "Ambitions," 56.

[33]Max Scheler, *Ressentiment*, translated by Lewis B. Coser and William W. Holdheim (Milwaukee: Marquette University Press, 1998), 55. Cf. the section on Gustav Ichheiser below.

38 AMBITION: AN ESSAY ON THE BURNING DESIRE TO RISE

of comprehensive knowledge about ambition in the context of moral and social conflicts. In *Père Goriot*, to cite just one example, Honoré de Balzac's observation of psychological details extends to an amoral theory of social ambition elaborated with all desirable candor by one of the novel's protagonists, the Faustian figure Eugène de Rastignac. In 1819, the young Rastignac makes his way from the wretched boardinghouse in which he lives to the salon of Madame de Beauséant, where "luxury simply look[s] elegant." The tremendous social and aesthetic contrast makes for a dazzling, overwhelming experience, in a passage in which Balzac skillfully weaves in the Machiavellian leitmotif of the importance of seeing the world as it is:

> His imagination, soaring into the upper reaches of Parisian society, filled his heart with a host of morbid thoughts, while broadening his mind and his conscience. He saw the world as it is: laws and morality unavailing with the rich, wealth the *ultima ratio mundi*. […] The transition was too abrupt, the contrast too complete, not to arouse in him cravings of boundless ambition.[34]

Thus it is not just the Mephistophelian criminal Vautrin, but also Madame de Beauséant who imparts some critical lessons to the young social climber in her pink and gray drawing room:

> Well, Monsieur de Rastignac, treat the world as it deserves. You want to get on, I will help you. You will plumb the depths of women's corruption, you will measure the extent of men's miserable vanity. Although I am well read in the book of this world, there were yet some pages unknown to me. Now I know it all. The more coldly calculating you are, the further you will go. Strike without pity and people will fear you. Accept men and women as mere post horses to be left worn out at every stage and you will reach the summit of your ambitions.[35]

The challenge of reflecting on ambition and morality is described here with unmistakable clarity. First, it is evident that many of the

---

[34]Balzac, *Père Goriot*, 74.
[35]Ibid., 71f.

THE SEMANTICS OF AMBITION

objects of ambition—power, money, prestige—are objects of social *agon*. They are fought over and competed for in society. The Latin noun *ambitio* is derived from the verb *ambire* and refers to the process of eagerly canvassing for the votes needed to be elected to a desired office in the *cursus honorum*: ambition has had a social and political dimension since antiquity. Even the man whose lone ambition is to be celebrated necessarily requires the (largest possible) social group who will celebrate him. The celebrators, the poets and historians, "make the celebrated man famous, and in the process, also themselves."[36]

The "competitive quality"[37] of many of the objects of ambition all but inevitably raises ethical questions that primarily concern the relationship of the ambitious person to those with whom he competes as well as the means he chooses to employ to do so. Here it is already clear that to inquire about the moral quality of "ambition itself" is to ask the wrong question. Ambition itself is merely the result of a dynamic complex of drives rooted in evolutionary biology; it is one's choice of objects and the means used to attain them that determine its moral quality. It is bigoted to disparagingly call someone "ambitious," inasmuch as this means nothing more than saying, "He desires self-assertion and self-realization." This is why, as noted in the introduction, when we judge someone for being ambitious, we generally have to add the qualifier "terribly" or "horribly" in order to make our criticism valid. In actuality, our criticism is directed not against ambition itself, but against excessive ambition and the way the other person handles it. Of course, it would be a different story if Hume's theory were to be borne out that the true aim of ambition is power and ever more power. Were ambition by definition identical with the pursuit of power or, more precisely, *lust for power*, then widespread condemnation of it would be understandable. But this equation erases the difference between the thirst for power and the thirst for honor. Not every person who craves power also seeks "honor," nor "glory," nor even public recognition of their actions. The influential

---

[36]Werle, *Ruhm und Moderne*, 28. Cf. the section on Burckhardt's *The Civilization of the Renaissance in Italy* below.
[37]Pettigrove, "Ambitions," 56.

40   AMBITION: AN ESSAY ON THE BURNING DESIRE TO RISE

éminence grise has been a stereotype since the days of Richelieu's agent and confidant François Leclerc du Tremblay.

Nietzsche is not mentioned anywhere in Pettigrove's essay, but his oft-quoted aphorism that "[t]he principal element of ambition lies in coming to *feel* one's *power*" serves as confirmation of its ethical devaluation, particularly coming from one of morality's sharpest critics. David Hume, whom Pettigrove does cite, fundamentally shares this view, writing in one of his political essays that "so great is the natural ambition of men, that they are never satisfied with power."[38] Hence his interest in the balance of conflicting powers.

The passage about ambition as a desire for power that Pettigrove cites appears in the context of Hume's analysis of the pride produced by *physical beauty and strength*, which brings him even closer to Nietzsche's amoral philosophy of health. The strong man, according to Hume, desires to live out his strength, to demonstrate it—this is his ambition:

> 'Tis not the beauty of the body alone that produces pride, but also its strength and force. Strength is a kind of power; and therefore the desire to excel in strength is to be consider'd as an inferior species of *ambition*.[39]

This passage from *A Treatise of Human Nature* makes it clear that Hume also recognizes other forms of ambition beyond just the pursuit of power based on sheer physical superiority. Physical strength is only an "inferior species" of ambition—the finer variant is perhaps the ambition of the scholar, the philosopher, and the priest. Similarly, the full Nietzsche quote also demonstrates a more complex derivation of the notorious "will to power" than the banal explanation of Nietzsche's pop-culture reception that the enjoyment of power causes one to lust for ever more power. In an unpublished

---

[38]David Hume, "Of the Independency of Parliament," in: Hume, *Essays: Moral, Political, and Literary*, edited by Eugene F. Miller (Indianapolis: Liberty Fund, 1985), 42–6 (43f.).
[39]David Hume, *A Treatise of Human Nature*, vol. 1, edited by David Fate Norton and Mary J. Norton (Oxford: Oxford University Press, 2007), 196. Emphasis in original.

THE SEMANTICS OF AMBITION   41

fragment written between the end of 1876 and the summer of 1877, Nietzsche writes:

> The principal element of ambition lies in coming to *feel* one's *power*. Delight in power does not come from enjoying being admired by others. Praise and admonition, love and hate are the same to the ambitious person who wants power. Fear (negatively) and will to power (positively) explain our intense regard for the opinions of other people. *Pleasure in power.*—Pleasure in power is explained by the hundredfold experience of displeasure in dependence, powerlessness. In the absence of this experience, the pleasure is also lacking.[40]

Here Nietzsche first sharply differentiates between the thirst for honor or glory and the pursuit of actual power. To the man who pursues power, the judgment of others matters only to the extent that it has a positive or negative effect on his accumulation of power; the substance of such judgments is irrelevant. "There's no such thing as bad publicity," as the cynical PR cliché goes. But the actual point, further elaborated in the first book of *Daybreak* (1881), is that here Nietzsche gives a *different* explanation for the pleasure we take in power than simply the greedy desire to have power. The "will to power" is not some obscure urge but rather is rooted in our primary, recurrent experience of dependence and powerlessness. Nietzsche's psychological insight, which Alfred Adler would later develop into his theory of the "inferiority complex," is that self-realization is only possible once we have been emancipated from these negative factors and experiences—this is the source of the "delight" or "pleasure" we take in power. As he further explains in *Daybreak*,

> because the feeling of impotence and fear was in a state of almost continuous stimulation so strongly and for so long, the *feeling of power* has evolved to such a degree of *subtlety* that in this respect man is now a match for the most delicate gold-balance.

---

[40]Friedrich Nietzsche, *Nachlaß 1875–1879*, edited by Giorgio Colli and Mazzino Montinari (Munich: de Gruyter, 1988), 425.

42 AMBITION: AN ESSAY ON THE BURNING DESIRE TO RISE

It has become his strongest propensity; the means discovered for creating this feeling almost constitute the history of culture.[41]

From this perspective, Nietzsche's controversial "will to power" is likewise initially nothing more than the will to self-preservation, and then to pleasurable, joyful self-realization. The ambition to feel one's own power, developed in the struggle against one's impotence, first becomes an *ethical* problem the moment self-realization collides with the aspirations of others, when the now-powerful subject's exhilaration or paranoia starts getting out of hand, his moral compass is set spinning, and he begins to lash out destructively. This is the phase that, in a political context, Montesquieu refers to as "the Terror."

Against this background, it would be ill-advised simply to dismiss ambition as morally contemptible, not least because ambition can also apply to efforts to demonstrate one's dignity in competitive struggle through one's choice of noble means. Both the gallant knight and the cunning schemer are ambitious. But while the ambition of one who acts nobly is divided between both his object—victory— and his adherence to a code, the schemer, as exemplified in the works of Machiavelli and Shakespeare, is concentrated solely on victory. The "instinct for power" consists in the talent of being singularly focused. "Realpolitik" in the Machiavellian and Shakespearean sense calculates that everyone involved in a competitive struggle has his own interests and is relentlessly ambitious. The point of the sword with which Laertes wounds Hamlet in their chivalrous fencing bout in the fifth act of Shakespeare's tragedy had been ignobly poisoned before the match—this alone is what makes the wound fatal.

Certain objects of ambition, all of which may well arise from what René Girard calls "mimetic desire,"[42] moreover involve social

---

[41]Nietzsche, *Daybreak: Thoughts on the Prejudices of Morality*, translated by R.J. Hollingdale (Cambridge: Cambridge University Press, 1997), 24.

[42]René Girard famously developed a theory of desire that argues that subjects desire certain objects *because* their rivals also desire them, thus their "own" desire is actually only mimetic: "In desiring an object the rival alerts the subject to the desirability of the object. The rival, then, serves as a model for the subject, not only in regard to such secondary matters as style and opinion but also, and more essentially, in regard to desires." René Girard, *Violence and the Sacred*, translated by Patrick Gregory (Baltimore: The Johns Hopkins University Press, 1977), 145. Against this background, we might also locate and elaborate a further anthropological origin of ambition in the mimetic structure of desire.

THE SEMANTICS OF AMBITION 43

valuations, creating a hierarchy or ranking. Ethical questions thus come into play here, too. In a tournament, usually only one person can win, come in "first," or receive the top prize. The field of other competitors is inevitably "outclassed." If they are "driven by ambition," they may feel humiliated, resentful, or envious. Particularly when competing for honor, "acquiring it requires outdoing one's peers: honor is not accorded to the average, only to the extraordinary."[43] On the whole, objects of ambitions exist in relation to and are dependent on specific social orders that change over time. Ambition at the court of Versailles—where, as Norbert Elias writes, "a never-ending competition for status and prestige kept all participants on their toes"[44]—had a different goal than did ambition after the outbreak of the French Revolution. The central object of desire, the king, whom the members of the court wanted to be as close to as possible, was stripped of his power after 1789. The bourgeois ambition that Tocqueville encountered in the young United States as a "yearning desire to rise" in a society of equals took on a wholly new appearance and set new goals for itself in the name of social mobility, becoming an unfettered ambition to climb the social ladder and advance in one's career.[45] What previously was limited to wrangling for favor and position at court now became the *modus operandi* of the whole of society. La Bruyère's lucid description of ambition at the court of Versailles became the model for competitive bourgeois society:

> At court they go to bed, and rise up only for their interest; it is that which employs them morning and evening, night and day; it is that which makes them think or speak, keeps them silent, and puts them on action; it is for this end they speak to some, and neglect others; that they mount or defend; it is by this rule they measure all their cares, complacency, esteem, indifference or contempt. Whatever steps any person makes by virtue toward wisdom and moderation, the first ambitious temptation carries

---

[43]Pettigrove, "Ambitions," 56.

[44]Norbert Elias, *Die höfische Gesellschaft* (Neuwied: Luchterhand, 1969), 98f.

[45]Jacob Burckhardt depicts the world of the Italian Renaissance as the first experiment aimed at creating a society of equals in the early modern age, which came to an end with the absolutism of the foreign powers (Spain and France) that ultimately conquered the Italian city-states. See the section on *The Civilization of the Renaissance in Italy* below.

44 AMBITION: AN ESSAY ON THE BURNING DESIRE TO RISE

them away with the most covetous, who are the most ambitious, and the most violent in their desires. Can they stand still when every one is on the march, and putting themselves forward?[46]

In historical terms, Stendhal—the founder of European realism in the novel, who served as a young and ambitious lieutenant in Napoleon's army—stands at the threshold of the final transition from the *ancien régime* to the bourgeois society of the nineteenth century in the wake of Napoleon's defeat at Waterloo in 1815. The author of *The Red and the Black*, first published in 1830, is one of the most important witnesses of the European Restoration, in the shadow of which the bourgeoisie first prospered.[47] Regarding Stendhal's early autobiographical novel *The Life of Henri Brulard*, Erich Auerbach writes:

The practically active bourgeoisie with its respectable money-making, inspires him with unconquerable boredom, he shudders at the *vertu républicaine* of the United States, and despite his ostensible lack of sentimentality he regrets the fall of the social culture of the *ancien régime*. *Ma foi, l'esprit manque*, he writes in [...] *Henri Brulard, chacun réserve toutes ses forces pour un métier qui lui donne un rang dans le monde*. No longer is birth or intelligence of the self-cultivation of the *honnête homme* the deciding factor—it is ability in some profession. [...] But how can one take anything like practical professional work seriously in the long run! Love, music, passion, intrigue, heroism—these are the things that make life worthwhile .... Stendhal is an aristocratic son of the *ancien régime grande bourgeoisie*, he will and can be no nineteenth-century bourgeois.[48]

Against the backdrop of the events that followed 1789, Roger Caillois, whose conceptual indebtedness to Montesquieu has since

---

[46]La Bruyère, *The Characters*, 113.

[47]Cf. the section below on Tocqueville, who through the example of the United States describes the transition from a revolutionary ambition that made everything seem possible to everyone to the institutionally regulated career ambition of bourgeois society that so repulsed Stendhal in France.

[48]Erich Auerbach, *Mimesis: The Representation of Reality in Western Thought*, translated by Willard R. Trask (Princeton: Princeton University Press, 2003), 464.

THE SEMANTICS OF AMBITION 45

been recognized, describes "a revolution as a change in the rules of play," in this case from the privileges of birth to competition on the basis of social mobility and professional achievement.[49] The progress of democracy, in Caillois' view, is thus tied to fair competition among equals:

> [D]emocracy progresses precisely through fair competition and equality of law and opportunity, which is sometimes more nominal than real.[50]

Ambition as Fore-pleasure

In the context of Pettigrove's own discussion of competition, he finally addresses the kind of potentially unquenchable, burning ambition that transcends its objects, which up to this point he had ignored. Here he is concerned not just with the social determinants of ambition but also with the ambitious subject himself. In keeping with a long tradition of psychological observation stretching back to antiquity, Pettigrove determines that the quenching of ambition with the attainment of the desired object is by no means the rule, but rather the exception: "there is always more that one could desire."[51] The question to be examined here is thus whether ambition is primarily inflamed by its object or whether ambition itself is unquenchable, a desire that always chooses or must choose a new object as soon as the previous one has been obtained and consumed.

In many cases, continuous, potentially unending increase lies in the nature of the object itself—the quintessential example being money. This is the root of its seductive, addictive allure, producing the infamous *auri sacra fames*, the accursed hunger for gold. Money, like power, gives succor to the proliferation of ambition: "One does not just want to earn a six figure salary, one wants wealth."[52] It is the

---

[49]Roger Caillois, *Die Spiele und die Menschen: Maske und Rausch* (Berlin: Matthes & Seitz, 2017), 91.

[50]Roger Caillois, *Man, Play and Games*, translated by Meyer Barash (Urbana/ Chicago: University of Illinois Press, 2001), 109.

[51]Pettigrove, "Ambitions," 57.

[52]Ibid.

46 AMBITION: AN ESSAY ON THE BURNING DESIRE TO RISE

afflictive, addictive character of ambition—apparent in the German word *Ehrgeiz* (literally, "greed for honor") and even more clearly *Ehrsucht* ("addiction to honor")—that transforms the struggle for self-assertion, already solidly guaranteed by a "six figure salary," into a never-ending process of "wanting to have more" (Plato's *pleonexia*):

> [T]hese accomplishments are stages in a never-ending progression. In such cases ambition's desire may never be fully discharged. The pursuit of the kind of ambition that is never fully discharged could be experienced as a series of partial satisfactions.[53]

With respect to the subject, there are essentially two reasons, according to Pettigrove, for the unqunechability of ambition. First, the fulfillment of one's desire creates an appetite for "more": "the more power or honor or knowledge one gets, the more one wants."[54] Second, the lust for money, fame, and power arises in the context of constant comparison and perpetual competition. As Pettigrove shows, recent empirical studies have demonstrated the motivating influence of the kinds of negative impulses that Roxane Gay points to in describing her own struggle with ambition. Latently envious comparison of oneself against others, the critical judgment of others, insecurity, and particularly fear of failure all repeatedly inflame ambition anew: "ambition brings satisfaction or merely staves off fear for another day."[55]

In a rousing essay titled "Macbeth and the History of Ambition," which Pettigrove cites as corroboration of his theory of the unquenchable nature of ambition, the Renaissance scholar William Kerrigan advances a psychoanalytic interpretation of ambition, in the sense of an insatiable appetite for "more and more," as the perpetuation and boundless growth of fore-pleasure. Following Freud's theory of sexuality, Kerrigan understands the physical experience of fore-pleasure first as an enticing bonus of pleasure that creates a desire for greater physical proximity, the telos of which,

---

[53]Ibid.
[54]Ibid.
[55]Ibid.

THE SEMANTICS OF AMBITION   47

according to Freud, is admittedly the "end-pleasure" of orgasm.[56] As Kerrigan demonstrates through the example of *Macbeth*, however, end-pleasure, satisfaction, or "completion" is "ambition's earliest enemy,"[57] as the satisfied man has forfeited his ambition and wearily ceases his striving. Kerrigan discerns this paradox of an ambition that desires its objective only when it drives the ambitious subject to further objectives, thus leaving him or her perpetually unsatisfied, in the murderous fantasies of Lady Macbeth, who vows even to mercilessly slaughter her own child—which, Freud determines, she will never have[58]—should this be necessary for the sake of her great success:

> Her vow is heavy with decision. The infant smiling at the breast is the pleasure principle's supreme benefactor. She will dash its brains out because another mechanism is to drive their ambitions, and its fuel is blood, not milk. The fantasy strikes at satiety, ambition's earliest enemy.[59]

Kerrigan emphasizes that the fore-pleasure Freud describes not only drives directly toward the end-pleasure of orgasm, but also—and this is the critical point—possesses its own uniquely seductive quality distinct from the offensively simple, mechanical "tension-discharge model."[60] Boldly mapping basic psychological structures onto historical developments, Kerrigan describes the ambition of the Renaissance as impetuously living and abiding in an aura of perpetually suspended fore-pleasure that generates hunger for ever more pleasure, courting the paradox of a "fulfillment" that only further whets the appetite. Shakespeare, according to Kerrigan,

---

[56]Sigmund Freud, *Three Essays on the Theory of Sexuality (1905)*, in: *The Standard Edition of the Complete Psychological Works of Sigmund Freud*, vol. 7: *A Case of Hysteria, Three Essays on Sexuality and Other Works (1901-1905)*, edited and translated by James Strachey (London: Hogarth Press, 1953), 123–246 (210).

[57]William Kerrigan, "Macbeth and the History of Ambition," in: John O'Neill, ed., *Freud and the Passions* (University Park, PA: The Pennsylvania State University Press, 1996), 13–24 (19).

[58]On Freud's famous interpretation, see the section below on Karl Mannheim's theory of success.

[59]Kerrigan, "Macbeth," 19.

[60]Ibid., 14.

48 AMBITION: AN ESSAY ON THE BURNING DESIRE TO RISE

articulates a conception of love that "cannot imagine perfect love without removing satiety from appetite. Love is transformed into unending hunger."[61] Kerrigan elaborates the "paradox of satisfaction and excess"[62] that typifies ambition with reference to numerous Renaissance texts, from Rabelais to Milton, with a view not only to love conceived as insatiable hunger but also to other prominent objects of ambition such as fame and power. In the process, he delivers a psychoanalytical explanation of the urgent desire for "more":

> Fame is like foreplay. When it is not increasing, it leads to the unpleasure of frustration. [...] The career of power is restlessness itself. You gain some. You must then gain more, lest the amount you have be felt as insecure. There's beggary in the power that can be reckoned. To secure itself, power must always be in a state of escalation.[63]

Because Kerrigan is primarily concerned with Shakespeare's grim tragedy, the idea of superlative beauty particularly associated with the Italian Renaissance inevitably fades into the background. But his controversial theory can also be translated to the realm of aesthetics. Freud himself warned against excessively cultivating fore-pleasure, lest the "preparatory act in question [take] the place of the normal sexual aim. [...] Such is in fact the mechanism of many perversions, which consist in a lingering over the preparatory acts of the sexual process."[64] But the dynamic of fore-pleasure can also carve another path, that of sublimation, as Freud explains in his essay "Creative Writers and Daydreaming," in which he conceptualizes aesthetic experience as a positive, productive form of lingering in fore-pleasure. If an artist is able to successfully take away the uncomfortably private aspect from his fantasies and give them a captivating aesthetic form, then the beholder of his work will be rewarded with "an *incentive bonus*, or a *fore-pleasure*" that makes possible "the release of still greater pleasure arising from deeper

---

[61]Ibid., 15.
[62]Ibid.
[63]Ibid., 17.
[64]Freud, *Three Essays*, 211.

THE SEMANTICS OF AMBITION   49

psychical sources."[65] What Freud calls the "failure of the function of the sexual mechanism owing to fore-pleasure"[66] is compensated for by the successful artwork, the aesthetic experience of which entices the beholder into pursuing ever new aesthetic experiences. "Beauty" is thus not a quality possessed by an object, but rather speaks to the desire of the beholder in constant thrall to fore-pleasure.

As Kerrigan's observations suggest, excessive ambition and greed have been conceived of together since antiquity.[67] In the Middle Ages, *avaritia*—and, implicitly, *ambitio* along with it—rose in rank to become one of the seven deadly sins, thus giving rise to the question, particularly in Puritan-influenced America, of how ubiquitous ambition, with all of its positive connotations, could be freed of the stigma of sinfulness and vice.[68] Lust, ambition, and greed overlap in their voraciousness, their insatiability. Against the background of this age-old discourse, in the Age of Enlightenment, the English essayist, statesman, and poet Joseph Addison—one of the most important influences on America's "founding fathers"—published an article in which he assigns three modes of desire to the three stages of life in an intuitively plausible way. He also names the morally good variants of the pursuit of pleasure, success, and property. Thus began the recoding of ambition from vice to virtue in the Anglo-American value system:

[T]he whole Species are hurried on by the same Desires, and engaged in the same Pursuits, according to the different Stages and Divisions of Life. Youth is devoted to Lust, middle Age to Ambition, old Age to Avarice. These are three general Motives and Principles of Action both in good and bad Men; tho' it must be acknowleg'd, that they changed their Names, and refined their Natures, according to the Temper of the Person whom they

---

[65]Sigmund Freud, "Creative Writers and Daydreaming," in: Freud, *The Standard Edition of the Complete Psychological Works of Sigmund Freud*, vol. 9: *Jensen's "Gravida" and Other Works (1906–1908)*, edited and translated by James Strachey (London: Hogarth Press, 1959), 141–54 (153).
[66]Freud, *Three Essays*, 211.
[67]See the section on Sallust below.
[68]As noted in the introduction, this is the question that guides William Casey King's *Ambition a History: From Vice to Virtue* (New Haven: Yale University Press, 2013).

50 AMBITION: AN ESSAY ON THE BURNING DESIRE TO RISE

direct and animate. For with the Good, Lust becomes virtuous; Ambition, true Honour; and Avarice, the Care of Posterity.[69]

Double-Edged Ambition

The second and third parts of Pettigrove's essay consider the moral dimension of ambition with respect to the question, first posed at the beginning, of whether ambition is a virtue or a vice. As noted above, however, this is the wrong question to ask, or at least is misleadingly phrased, inasmuch as it seems to ascribe to ambition, still defined as a "desire," an inherent moral quality. This is also the proposition implicitly advanced by Addison: in the passage quoted above, the quality of ambition depends on who acts it out, the "good" man or the "bad." As a desire, ambition can be morally problematic only if—in accordance with Christian doctrine—desire is conceived of as sinful in and of itself, or if ambition specifically is defined as a desire that is chained fast to a morally dubious object, in other words if ambition de facto turns out to always be hunger for money or power. Pettigrove does not go this far; the latter part of his essay thus deals primarily with the moral quality of the objects of ambition as well as the relation of the subject to his own ambition, which can be affected by conscious decisions. Accordingly, depending on the individual case, "ambition will sometimes be a virtue and sometimes a vice."[70] As Pettigrove explains:

> If it is a bad object that is poorly understood, is motivated by a lack of self-esteem, anxiety, envy, selfishness, or invidious comparison, brings pain to the agent and those with whom she has to do, is pursued by debased means and fails to be meaningful, then [ambition's] viciousness will be apparent.[71]

For Pettigrove, the question of whether ambition constitutes "a crucial virtue" or "a devastating vice"[72] thus ultimately depends on

---

[69]Spectator 120 (January 14, 1710) by Addison, from Joseph Addison and Richard Steele, The Spectator, edited by Donald F. Bond, vol. 2 (Oxford: Oxford University Press, 1987), 209–10.
[70]Pettigrove, "Ambitions," 65.
[71]Ibid.
[72]Ibid., 67.

THE SEMANTICS OF AMBITION   51

factors *beyond* the phenomenon of ambition itself, on "bad objects" or immoral motivations.

Pettigrove adds two further points to his ethical reflections on the phenomenology of ambition that still need to be discussed here. First, he argues that ambition "can give a life structure and significance [...] by enabling an agent to see her life as meaningful."[73] The quasi-pedagogical idea that "healthy ambition" can give direction, structure, and possibly even meaning to an otherwise inert life appears already in classic texts on the sociology of success in the context of philosophical debates about the practical consequences of an active versus a contemplative life, which will be discussed in great detail in the appropriate section below.[74]

In addition to the biographical structure-giving function of ambition in the sense of giving purpose to people with low motivation or a lack of drive, Pettigrove also emphasizes the easily understandable psychological problem, also pondered since antiquity, that ambition all but inevitably intensifies one's egoism and selfishness, generating corresponding moral costs for others, who run the risk of being treated like the horse that Madame de Beauséant runs ragged in Balzac's tragic novel *Père Goriot*.

It was Max Weber who, in his famous essay "The Vocation of Politics," condemned personal ambition as a betrayal of the "ethos of politics as a 'cause,'" thus updating for the twentieth century the guiding difference classically articulated in antiquity by Sallust and later taken up in modernity by the likes of Montesquieu, Burckhardt, Nietzsche, and others:

> The sin against the holy spirit of [the politician's] profession begins where this striving for power becomes detached from the task at hand [...] and becomes a matter of purely personal self-intoxication instead of being placed entirely at the service of the "cause."[75]

---

[73]Ibid., 64.

[74]See the section on Karl Mannheim's critique of contemplation below.

[75]Max Weber, "The Vocation of Politics," in: Weber, *The Essential Weber: A Reader*, edited by Sam Whimster (London: Routledge, 2004), 257–69 (258).

52 AMBITION: AN ESSAY ON THE BURNING DESIRE TO RISE

The agnostic Weber did not shy away from throwing the heaviest sin in Christian theology, the sin against the holy spirit, plus the "ethos" of ancient Greece, plus finally the highest ideals of rationally organized (German) bureaucracy—service to a cause and commitment to the task at hand—onto the scale, in order to have a substantial counterweight against the allures and dangers of personal ambition.

In fact, though it might have been difficult for a cultural Protestant to imagine, here Weber could have explicitly referenced the *Summa Theologica*, in which Thomas Aquinas similarly—but of course not at all "metaphorically"—defines ambition as a sin:

> Ambition is that sin whereby one inordinately desires honor that he either has not earned or that he attributes to his own advantage rather than to God. [...] Ambition is opposed to magnanimity as the inordinate to that which is well ordered.[76]

The guiding difference that Weber updated for a modern audience initially appears in antiquity as the distinction between passionate commitment to the state and the pursuit of purely personal ambition. At the pinnacle of medieval philosophy, Aquinas (who, following Augustine's example, also makes reference to Sallust) in turn distinguishes between the honor due *only* to God and that reprehensible ambition (*appetitus honoris*) with which men sinfully strive to claim honor for themselves alone. Aquinas, too, recognizes the excessive, addictive aspect of ambition through which that which is well ordered is thrown out of balance and magnanimity is gravely damaged. In the twentieth century, Max Weber replaces service to God with "service to a cause."

On the one hand, Weber's rhetorical syncretism of antiquity, organizational rationality, and theology strikingly and rightly underscores the deadly seriousness of his subject matter. On the other hand, the strident Wilhelmine "force" of his writing also reveals the embarrassment of a thinker who of course knows perfectly well that the "intoxication" of the powerful man, the bliss of his addiction, is not at all "detached" from his cause, but

---

[76]Thomas Aquinas, *Summa Theologica*, edited by Joseph Bernhart (Stuttgart: Kröner, 1938), 467. See also the afterword on Montaigne and Augustine below.

THE SEMANTICS OF AMBITION   53

very much a part of it. Reading Weber's sentence once again, one wonders what a "sober striving for power" would even be. Power is pursued by individuals, and therefore the pursuit of power, even if initially in service to a "cause," always carries with it the potential for seduction leading to "self-intoxication," overconfidence, and in extreme cases megalomania. This is the source of the notorious tension between personal and official interests, the confusion of person and office.

Among the classic ancient texts on this fundamental problem is the *Alcibiades* dialogue generally attributed to Plato, in which Socrates makes every effort to discourage the twenty-year-old and alarmingly ambitious Alcibiades from throwing himself into the affairs of the Athenian state without any actual serious preparation or expertise. The aim of this dialogue between philosopher and student is to make it clear to Alcibiades that prosperity, military might, and large masses of land and people are of no benefit as long as the citizens and especially the politicians who lead them are not virtuous and meritorious. For only knowledge of what is virtuous and meritorious will enable them to lead the state rightly in both domestic and foreign affairs. "So what you need to get for yourself and for the city," Socrates says, "isn't political power, nor the authority to do what you like; what you need is justice and self-control."[77] An essential requirement of justice, as it is developed in the course of the dialogue in terms of the relation between body and soul/reason, is the judicious subordination of individual desire and personal ambition to the reasonable interests of the whole. Only then, as Socrates emphasizes throughout, can individual and political conduct be "pleasing to God."[78] Any other path leads to darkness:

> But if you act unjustly, with your eyes on what is dark and godless, as is likely, your conduct will also be dark and godless, because you don't know yourself.[79]

---

[77]Plato, *Alcibiades*, translated by D. S. Hutchinson, in: Plato, *Complete Works*, edited by John M. Cooper (Indianapolis/Cambridge: Hackett, 1997), 594.
[78]Ibid. Translation slightly altered.
[79]Ibid.

54 AMBITION: AN ESSAY ON THE BURNING DESIRE TO RISE

The dramatic biography of Alcibiades, whose political and military career was marked by frequently shifting allegiances, can be seen as a historical confirmation of this Socratic proposition. The notorious tension between personal ambition and the prosperity of the whole led ancient writers from Plato to Sallust to the wise political conclusion that it was imperative to establish identification with the polity as a way of mediating between personal ambition and the interest of the state, to ensure that personal ambition could be fulfilled only *in* service to the state. In antiquity, Weber's "sin against the holy spirit" thus appears as an attack against the state and its order.

2

Eris—Agon—Ambition

Plutarch's *Parallel Lives*

The texts and artifacts passed down from Greek and Roman antiquity comprise a precious library of comprehensive knowledge about ambition. They offer remarkably perceptive insights on many of its aspects that have never lost their validity and thus have profoundly shaped Western understanding of ambition down to the present day, as exemplified by Max Weber's reflections quoted above.

Plutarch's *Parallel Lives*, for example, which we have already consulted multiple times, provides exemplary biographies of ambitious men that have radiated throughout history and, in the cases of Alexander and Caesar—to name but two—led to the ends of the earth and beyond into the unknown: "[I]n his attempt to occupy [the island of Britain] [Caesar] carried the Roman supremacy beyond the confines of the inhabited world."[1] But as the wars dragged on, escalating into a devastating civil war after the crossing of the Rubicon, Caesar's legions, like Alexander's

---

[1]Plutarch, *Lives*, vol. VII, translated by Bernadotte Perrin (Cambridge, MA: Harvard University Press, 1967), 499f.

56 AMBITION: AN ESSAY ON THE BURNING DESIRE TO RISE

Macedonian troops in India before them, began to groan in mortal despair:

> [T]he soldiers [...], since they were now past their physical prime and worn out with their multitudinous wars, murmured against Caesar. "Whither, pray, and to what end will this man bring us, hurrying us about and treating us like tireless and life less thugs? [...] Will not even our wounds, then, convince Caesar that he commands mortal men, and that we are mortal in the endurance of pain and suffering?"[2]

Over the course of the centuries, Plutarch's *Vitae parallelae* became bestsellers many times over, inspiring countless young ambitious men. But they have always also been read as warnings against the inhumane excesses of ambition, as chilling images of the "insatiable love of power" and "mad desire to be first and greatest," as Plutarch says of Caesar in his biography of Marc Antony.[3] Plutarch's aim was to write not heroic legends, but biographies. Hence his focus on psychologically revealing details, for "a slight thing like a phrase or a jest often makes a greater revelation of character than battles where thousands fall, or the greatest armaments, or sieges of cities."[4] Thus we find in Plutarch incisive, pithy anecdotes that retain their linguistic currency among the erudite even today. As Diogenes dozes in the sun, Alexander approaches and asks him if there is anything he wants, to which the cynical Diogenes replies: "Yes, [...] stand a little out of my sun." The punch line of this well-known tale comes when Alexander, paragon of the *vita activa*, recognizes in Diogenes' *vita contemplativa* a model of life equal to his own. "But verily," the former pupil of Aristotle acknowledges, "if I were not Alexander, I would be Diogenes."[5] Another famous story, that of the cutting of the proverbial Gordian knot, illustrates Alexander's

---

[2]Ibid., 533.
[3]Plutarch, *Lives*, vol. IX, translated by Bernadotte Perrin (Cambridge, MA: Harvard University Press, 1959), 153.
[4]Plutarch, *Lives*, vol. VII, 225.
[5]Ibid., 259.

aforementioned coldblooded focus on the goal before him and his refusal to get tangled up in convoluted details, including the delicate network of his own emotions. The ambitious man—of whom, in Freud's estimation, Alexander remains the paradigmatic embodiment—is distinguished by his "self-control"[6] in the face of any and all turbulence and his consistent concentration on his great long-term goal. This is also the source of Alexander's fascinating aversion to "sleep and sexual intercourse,"[7] the loss of control involved in which it is horrifying to the ambitious man. Alexander's ambition also explains his loathing of people speaking ill of him, which he would punish severely and unforgivingly, "since he loved his reputation more than his life or his kingdom."[8] The young king, who was gravely wounded multiple times, demonstrated a corresponding recklessness with respect to his body: "[H]e was eager to overcome fortune by boldness and force by valour."[9]

It was Alexander's horse, the famous Bucephalus, who first provided him with an admonitory reminder of the mortality of all living creatures. Only the young Alexander recognized that the seemingly unmanageable steed was merely afraid of his own shadow and, turning him directly toward the sun, was able to calm him: "What a horse they are losing, because, for lack of skill and courage, they cannot manage him!"[10] Read allegorically, this story of the taming of a wild and fearful animal shows that a successful journey eastward, toward the sunrise, to Persia and India is only possible if one first conquers one's uncontrolled emotions and impulse to flee in fear. At Gaugamela, however, Bucephalus was already so old that Alexander rode another horse into battle. Nevertheless, he continued on to India, where he died either of old age or of wounds received in the final battle against Porus. With the death of his horse, Alexander's journey also came to an end.

---

[6]Ibid., 285.
[7]Ibid., 287.
[8]Ibid., 349.
[9]Ibid., 389.
[10]Ibid., 237.

58 AMBITION: AN ESSAY ON THE BURNING DESIRE TO RISE

Dr. Bucephalus

Bucephalus, whose taming enabled Alexander to assert himself against his ambitious father, lives on in a short story—"The New Advocate"—written with deep knowledge of Alexander's often retold biography by Franz Kafka, another son of an ambitious father with a strong yearning to rise. Kafka's adaptation of the material ostentatiously brings ancient and modern ambition into dialogue; the epitome of modernity is "the new." In the disenchanted world of the twentieth century, there are still "plenty of men who know how to murder each other" and "the skill needed to reach over a banqueting table and pink a friend with a lance is not lacking," but "[n]owadays [...] there is no Alexander the Great,"[11] and "no one points the way."[12] Alexander's "battle charger" returns in Kafka as the attorney "Dr. Bucephalus,"[13] immersed in old law books: "In the quiet lamplight, his flanks unhampered by the thighs of a rider, free and far from the clamor of battle, he reads and turns the pages of our ancient tomes."[14]

The careful observer, with "expertise" in the history of ambition and its metamorphoses, will notice similarities between the new advocate and the old warhorse. A servant of the court, "with the professional appraisal of the regular small bettor at a racecourse," marvels at the powerfulness of the advocate's legs, evidently still fitted with horseshoes, as he "mounted the marble steps with a high action that made them ring beneath his feet."[15] In the name "Bucephalus," modern readers sensitized by Freud to Oedipal situations can still hear the "phallic" erection of sons standing up for themselves. Alexander's ambition likewise lives on in the "iron cage" of the administrated world: *agon* prevails both in the competitive races now organized as mass events and along the tightly regulated career ladder climbed by white-collar professionals working in offices. Kafka's marble steps lead not to the royal palace, but—perhaps

---

[11]Franz Kafka, "The New Advocate," in: Kafka, *The Complete Stories*, edited by Nahum N. Glatzer (New York: Schocken Books, 1971), 414–15 (415).
[12]Ibid.
[13]Ibid., 414.
[14]Ibid., 415.
[15]Ibid.

ERIS—AGON—AMBITION 59

even higher—to the courthouse, the place of judgment. The good fortune one needs to succeed in the competitive struggle to ascend can be heard in the "ringing" of Dr. Bucephalus' horseshoes, known to the superstitious as a lucky charm. "[F]or many," Kafka writes, "Macedonia is too confining, so that they curse Philip, the father."[16] Substitute "Prague" for "Macedonia," and the impartial reader will scarcely be able to miss the ironic autobiographical overtones of this text penned by a trained attorney that first appeared in a 1920 collection of short stories dedicated to his own father. In this programmatic tale, the reading and writing advocate of modernity pursues his ambition by identifying himself not with Alexander, but with the subdued animal that the young king dragged along with him to the bitter end. The plea of the "new advocate" is not directed at that ancient ambition that longs and strives for the deification of man but rather moves in the opposite direction, studying and describing man as an animal. Kafka's texts are full of characters and creatures who, like Dr. Bucephalus, are half man, half beast.

*

Following the poetics of Plutarch's great undertaking, his biography of Caesar, coming directly after the life of Alexander, continually emphasizes the parallels between the two. Alexander's dream of conquering the world matches Caesar's desire to "complete [the] circuit of his empire, which would then be bounded on all sides by the ocean."[17] The transcendental urge that arises in Alexander, traveling through the desert to seek the oracle of Ammon, to subdue "not only enemies, but even times and places,"[18] corresponds to Caesar's bold "adjustment of the calendar."[19] The comparison affords opportunity for irony, as well, as Alexander's daredevilry in war appears in Caesar as the insincere publicity scheme of an ambitious politician: "Now, at his love of danger his men were not astonished, knowing his ambition."[20]

---

[16]Ibid.
[17]Plutarch, *Lives*, vol. VII, 579.
[18]Ibid., 303.
[19]Plutarch, *Lives*, vol. VII, 579.
[20]Ibid., 483.

60 AMBITION: AN ESSAY ON THE BURNING DESIRE TO RISE

An as yet unmentioned aspect of insatiable ambition emerges in Caesar's biography once he has been appointed dictator for life. Having secured the maximal position at the highest height, the fifty-five-year-old Caesar now faces a new problem that Alexander had been confronted with only briefly before his early death: the problem of being peerless. Balancing at the top, he no longer has any competition. With the disappearance of any worthy opponent who would make stabilizing, motivating *agon* possible—Pompey and Cato are both dead—Caesar, having ascended to the lonely peak, is left with no other choice than to jealously *compete with himself*. His ambition is not quenched; his own deeds are the only challenge left that could possibly satisfy ambition's logic of outdoing. The melancholy of the ambitious man, even outside of politics, is the result not only of his having exhausted the objects and goals he has attained, but also of his constant comparison of himself against himself and his own accomplishments, now inexorably receding into the past and thus into oblivion. Nothing is more depressing than failing to live up to one's own great, but now fading past achievements with a new endeavor that may turn out to be a miserable failure—other than, perhaps, tiredly resting on one's rapidly wilting laurels:

> Caesar's many successes, however, did not divert his natural spirit of enterprise and ambition to the enjoyment of what he had laboriously achieved, but served as fuel and incentive for future achievements, and begat in him plans for greater deeds and a passion for fresh glory, as though he had used up what he already had. What he felt was therefore nothing else than emulation of himself, as if he had been another man, and a sort of rivalry between what he had done and what he purposed to do.[21]

Aristotle's Empty Middle

The double-edged nature of ambition evident in Plutarch's *Parallel Lives*—both Alexander and Caesar are remembered not just for

---

[21]Ibid., 577.

their "successes," but also as mass murderers—was an object of reflection for "classical" ancient philosophers, particularly Alexander's teacher Aristotle. To this day, the *Nicomachean Ethics* stands alongside the works of Immanuel Kant as one of the most influential texts addressing this moral-philosophical debate. Here Aristotle develops his theory of the good mean between the bad extremes of various forms of human conduct, in an effort to precisely define and catalogue the individual virtues. "Courage," for example, is the good middle term (*meson*) or best form of conduct (*areté*) between the extremes of "cowardice" and "recklessness."

In the case of "honor," Aristotle names pride or "greatness of soul" as the mean between the extremes of "vanity" and timidity, or "smallness of soul." But "ambition," the longing for this honor, presents him with a problem. Ambition seems almost immediately to disappear from the catalogue of virtues to which Aristotle had just added it. Recalling Pettigrove's reflections on the problematic ethical status of ambition, the fact that Aristotle even conceives of it as a virtue in the first place represents a clear positioning:

> For it is possible to long for honor as one ought and more or less than one ought; the person who is excessive in his longings in this regard is said to be ambitious, the deficient unambitious, while the one in the middle is nameless. And the dispositions are in fact nameless, except the ambition of the ambitious person. This is why people at the extremes lay claim to the middle ground, and we sometimes call the person in the middle "ambitious," sometimes "unambitious"; and sometimes we praise the ambitious person, sometimes the unambitious one.[22]

In the Aristotelian catalogue, all other virtues have their best form, their *areté*. Courage, moderation, liberality, gentleness, friendliness, etc., are all found here as designations of the good mean between two bad extremes. Only the mean between excessive ambition and the lack of ambition has no name of its own.[23] In the intervening millennia, nothing has changed. Even today, as we have indicated

---

[22]Aristotle, *Nicomachean Ethics*, translated by Robert C. Bartlett and Susan D. Collins (Chicago: University of Chicago Press, 2011), 37.
[23]Ibid.

62 AMBITION: AN ESSAY ON THE BURNING DESIRE TO RISE

multiple times already, ambition must be qualified with an adjective, marked with a "plus" or "minus" sign, labeled as "healthy" or "sick." Not only that, but, as Aristotle notes, the disposition toward ambition is simply ambition once again—a shrewd observation, as the desire not to be ambitious likewise betrays a form of ambition that, as Michel de Montaigne reflects,[24] turns back against itself. Moreover, there is a *fight* brewing here: both the ambitious and the unambitious person want to occupy the nameless middle ground, to stand on the pedestal embodying the winning virtue:

> As a result of this linguistic vacuum, the vices of excess, love of honour (*philotimia*) and defect, unambitiousness (*aphilotimia*), seem to be opposed to each other and 'to contend for' the place in between, that of the intermediate state.[25]

And "we"—society, the public, the social community of the *polis*—are incapable of fundamentally resolving this dispute. For depending on our perspective, we sometimes perceive the person in the nameless middle as ambitious, sometimes not. Looming in the background of this ongoing sense-confusing battle is a hydraulic understanding of ambition as a charged, highly flammable liquid that one can either turn up, turn off, or keep at a low flame. Here, too, the moral assessment of "too much" or "too little" ambition comes only from outside. Whether ambition conceived of as a pressing desire counts as a virtue or a vice depends on the situation and one's perspective. The ambitious person himself ultimately risks becoming entangled in "'Corionlanus' paradox': seeking recognition from those one desires to be superior to."[26] One who wishes to be honored, and who has more power and success than those who are supposed to honor him, will never be able to know whether their praise and reverence is actually sincere. The more successful a person is, the more uncertain it becomes whether he deserves the honor bestowed upon him or whether others are only

---

[24]See the afterword on the ambition to forsake ambition.
[25]Paul Nieuwenburg, "Aristotle on Ambition," in: *History of Political Thought* 31/4 (2010), 535–55 (539).
[26]Ibid., 546.

ERIS—AGON—AMBITION 63

flattering him because they fear him or hope to reap certain benefits from him. The isolation ambition thus produces forms the crux of Coriolanus' paradox. Aristotle breaks off his rather unsatisfying explanations in the second book of the *Nicomachean Ethics* with a promise to take them up again later, in exactly the way one diplomatically cuts short a messy debate that is threatening to turn into a fight with an agreement to continue it at a later date, in the hope of arriving at a breakthrough and resolution to the conflict. He resumes his reflections on ambition at the beginning of Book 4, although here one is not initially given the impression that the hoped-for breakthrough has been achieved:

> [W]e blame the ambitious person, on the grounds that he aims at getting honor more than he ought and from where he ought not; and we blame the unambitious person, on the grounds that he chooses not to be honored even in the case of what is noble. But sometimes we praise the ambitious person as manly and a lover of what is noble, and praise the unambitious person as measured and moderate, just as we said in the first discussions as well. Yet it is clear that since we speak of the "lover of such and such" in various ways, we do not always apply the phrase "lover of honor" [or ambitious person] to the same thing; when we are offering praise, we apply the term to those who love honor more than the many do, but when we are speaking in terms of blame, to those who love honor more than they ought. Since the mean is nameless, the extremes seem to dispute over it as if it were unclaimed. But where there is excess and deficiency, there exists also a middle term, and people long for honor both more than they ought and less; and, therefore, it is possible to do so as one ought. It is this characteristic that is praised, then, although the mean with respect to honor is nameless. In relation to ambition, it appears as lack of ambition; in relation to lack of ambition, it appears as ambition; and in relation to both, it somehow appears as both. This seems to be the case also with the other virtues, but here it is the extremes that appear to be opposites of each, because the middle term has not been named.[27]

---

[27]Aristotle, *Nicomachean Ethics*, 81.

64 AMBITION: AN ESSAY ON THE BURNING DESIRE TO RISE

Aristotle's prefatory remarks here about praise and blame presuppose a socio-ethical standard—an "ought"—that he does not more precisely explicate. But it can be assumed that the guiding political distinction between an ambition that pertains only to oneself and one that serves and finds it fulfillment in a cause or the polis is at work here in the background, a conclusion that is substantiated by Aristotle's reference to the blame imposed on the unambitious person who does not wish to be honored even in the case of what is noble. What is objectively noble, however, is that which benefits not just personal ambition, but the polis. Accordingly, Paul Nieuwenburg argues that those who seek honor only emerge from the twilight of morality once there is clear evidence "that what they seek it for is of greater value to them than honour itself."[28]

What is new in this second passage on ambition from Book 4 is, first, Aristotle's tying it exclusively to *manliness* and, second, the conception of ambition as a sense for what is *noble*, for quality, for the best or most virtuous accomplishment. This definition encompasses different objects of ambition as well as achievement and success in equal measure. For both the ambitious solitary work on a work of art and the will to achieve its public breakthrough aim at the realization of that greatest accomplishment that Karl Mannheim aptly calls "total success." It may be that ambition found its way into Aristotle's catalogue of virtues because it represents the uncompromising sense for first-class quality and thus the drive for unsurpassable achievement. In this form, as "moral ambition," it effectively becomes a kind of meta-virtue, inasmuch as it is ambition that drives men to become the most courageous, the most moderate, the most generous, etc. Third, the ambitious person, according to Aristotle, is someone whose drive (for the best) elevates him above the (indolent, unmotivated) masses, but who at the same time, in his (solitary) ascent, risks overextending himself, becoming "hybrid," and burning out.

In the closing section of the passage quoted above, Aristotle not very convincingly attempts to resolve the smoldering dispute over the empty middle that arose in Book 2 and forced the postponement of the debate. He now confirms that one very well might have the impression that there is a dispute over this virtuous mean, over

---

[28]Nieuwenburg, "Aristotle on Ambition," 548.

who or what is the best, who will be placed on the pedestal and win the laurels. Both make the claim: the ambitious person as well as the unambitious (whose own camouflaged ambition consists in his demonstrative defense against ambition). The seemingly empty middle has become a bone of contention. How to resolve the dispute?

From the fact that there is both excess and deficiency with respect to ambition, Aristotle concludes that, as with the other virtues, there *must* be a good middle ground here, even if it is "nameless." Remaining with the language of hydraulics, this third term would be the ideal "water level" of self-assertion and self-realization. Ambition is a *virtue* when it ensures self-preservation and, beyond this, facilitates self-realization precisely to the extent that it does not collide with the claims and aspirations of others. The well-established polis would then be understood as a homeostatic system that "adjusts" all of its participants in such a way that the systems remain intact and function well. In Aristotle's view, the dispute between the ambitious and the unambitious person *only* results from the namelessness of the middle term and therefore is illusory, as the absence of a word does not necessarily indicate the absence of the matter in question.

The reason why these passages on ambition from the *Nicomachean Ethics* have repeatedly and rightly been deemed unsatisfying perhaps lies in the fact that Aristotle, unlike Plato's Socrates, is not inclined to irony and thus does not recognize the punch line that he himself has set up: the virulent element in the dispute over the "empty" space of the glamorous middle, over the gold medal for *areté*, is precisely ambition itself. Though he never explicitly acknowledges it, ambition as Aristotle defines it is profoundly contradictory, inasmuch as it seeks out this dispute in order to achieve the moral triumph of winning the crown of virtue as the ideal form of ambition. Yawning in the "empty" middle is the empty abyss of the will to morality revealed as the will to victory. The two parties Aristotle imagines here evidently only become competitors at the precise moment when they both raise their respective claims and thus unavoidably get into a fight over who represents the virtue shining from the pedestal, thus earning the praise of the polis and the applause of all. Both the ambitious and the unambitious person equally nurture the ambition to emerge from the shadows of moral ambiguity (hubris or indolence) and

66 AMBITION: AN ESSAY ON THE BURNING DESIRE TO RISE

finally be accepted into the posh, exclusive club of the Aristotelian virtues.

On the one hand, though Aristotle, to his embarrassment, is unable to do so, here we can determine what the good middle ground of ambition would consist in, namely a socially acceptable mean of self-affirmation and self-realization with an incorruptible sense for quality. On the other hand, a guiding authority must always intervene from outside and decide whether "too much" or "too little" ambition is at work in a particular situation. The level must always be readjusted, the battle always fought anew. The two parties—one openly ambitious, one covertly ambitious—are involved in a quarrel over the highest position that can be resolved only temporarily. This is not at all a dispute over "nothing," but a real conflict over who here is the best. It is as though an evil fairy or terrible goddess tossed a golden apple onto the empty middle ground of virtue, and both parties are now fighting for victory. The supremely sophisticated discourse of the *Nicomachen Ethics* is haunted by the persistent recurrence of an archaic, violent force, one that is strikingly and spectacularly depicted in the ancient epics of Homer and Hesiod.

Eris in Homer

The name of this "terrible goddess" is Eris, one of the daughters of Night (Nyx), who in ancient Greek mythology serves as the personification of strife and discord. All the gods of Olympus— all except Eris—were invited to the wedding of King Peleus to the nereid Thetis, from whose union sprang the ambitious hero Achilles. Eris came anyway and tossed into the middle of the wedding party a golden apple inscribed with the words *te kalliste*, "for the most beautiful." The hate-filled conflict incited by this infamous apple of discord is world-renowned. The contest between the goddesses Hera, Athena, and Aphrodite for the prize of being named the most beautiful—decided by Paris, to whom the winner, Aphrodite, had promised as a reward possession of Helen, herself already married to Menelaus—led to the Trojan War and thus to the death of Achilles, the final consummation of Eris' revenge. Eris stands at the beginning and the end of Homer's great epic of the Trojan War.

ERIS—AGON—AMBITION   67

In both the fourth and the eleventh book of the *Iliad*, the terrible goddess, sister and comrade of Ares, the god of war, appears among the mortals. In Book 4, the Greek and Trojan armies stand facing each other, prepared for battle, but it is the work of Eris that leads to the eruption of bloody war:

> Ares drove [the Trojans], fiery-eyed Athena drove the Argives,
> and Terror and Rout and *relentless Strife [Eris*, E. G.] stormed too,
> sister of manslaughtering Ares, Ares' comrade-in-arms—
> *Strife, only a slight thing when she first rears her head*
> *but her head soon hits the sky as she strides across the earth.*
> *Now Strife hurled down the leveler Hate amidst both sides,*
> wading into the onslaught, flooding men with pain.
> At least the armies clashed at one strategic point,
> they slammed their shields together, pike scraped pike
> with the grappling strength of fighters armed in bronze
> and their round shields pounded, boss on welded boss,
> and the sound of struggle roared and rocked the earth.
> Screams of men and cries of triumph breaking in one breath,
> fighters killing, fighters killed, and the ground streamed blood.
> Wildly as two winter torrents raging down from the mountains,
> swirling into a valley, hurl their great waters together,
> flash floods from the wellsprings plunging down in a gorge
> and miles away in the hills a shepherd hears the thunder—
> so from the grinding armies broke the cries and crash of war.[29]

Eris' appearance in this scene is clearly described by way of a fiery analogy: slight at first, like the tiny flame of a match, she creeps along, then fans out relentlessly like an out-of-control fire, soon blazing up until her head hits the sky and the flames of hate rain down from her colossal height. With a view to Aristotle's doctrine of the good middle, elaborated several centuries later, it is particularly remarkable that Eris hurls down the flames of strife directly into the "midst" of the two sides, blanketing all involved with pain. The insatiable fire of discord, once sparked, eats its way from regiment to regiment, until the heroes set at each other and "the ground streams

---

[29]Homer, *The Iliad*, translated by Robert Fagles (New York: Penguin, 1990), 160 (IV.510–28). My emphasis.

68 AMBITION: AN ESSAY ON THE BURNING DESIRE TO RISE

blood." The elementary power of the fire of aggression, blazing up from the smallest flame to an uncontrollable conflagration that reaches to the sky, matches that of the metaphorical "stream" of blood that follows it. Here Homer compares the roaring fire of two armies surging into each other with the elementary power of individuality-obliterating water, coalescing from countless small sources into two great streams surging into each other only to then plunge, churning and roaring, into the abyss.

Homer's description of the second appearance of Eris, now sent directly into the fray by Zeus himself, is no less captivating and precise. Book 11 of the *Iliad* begins:

> Now Dawn rose up from bed by her lordly mate Tithonus,
> bringing light to immortal gods and mortal men.
> *But Zeus flung Strife on Achaea's fast ships,*
> *the brutal goddess flaring his storm-shield,*
> *his monstrous sign of war in both her fists.*
> *She stood on Odyseeus' huge black-bellied hull,*
> *moored mid-line so a shout could reach both wings,*
> upshore to Telamonian Ajax' camp or down to Achilles'—
> trusting so to their arms' power and battle-strength
> they'd hauled their trim ships up on either flank.
> *There Strife took her stand, raising her high-pitched cry,*
> *great and terrible, lashing the fighting-fury*
> *in each Achaean's heart—no stopping them now,*
> *mad for war and struggle. Now, suddenly,*
> *battle thrilled them more than the journey home,*
> *than sailing hollow ships to their dear native land.*[30]

It is a grand scene. Now flung down by Zeus, Eris once again positions herself "mid-line," in the exact middle of the Greek horde, holding in her fists the sign of war, and unleashes a great and terrible cry. Eris does not speak, does not debate or seek to persuade: she *cries out*. This terrible cry of power and empowerment takes the place of speech that prudently considers and weighs different arguments. In demythologized terms, one might speak here of a

---

[30]Ibid., 296f. (XI.1-16). My emphasis.

ERIS—AGON—AMBITION 69

"fiery" address whipping up hatred, an inflammatory diatribe that robs the soldiers of their temperance but also takes away their fear, mortifying their natural desire for self-preservation. Every rational consideration among the Achaean army is shouted down. Individual thought is suspended, as the promise of a glorious hero's death suddenly "thrills" the soldiers, now fused into a roaring mass bent on attack, more than the journey home alive that they had previously so deeply longed for.

Hesiod's Two Erises

In Homer, there is only the *one*, grim Eris, as can be seen from the passages from the *Iliad* quoted above. Hesiod, the other epic poet of early Greek antiquity, initially confirms this doctrine in his narrative of the origins of the world and the gods, the *Theogony*. Here Eris is one of the many hated spawn of *Nyx*, the primordial goddess of night, of negativity. Eris in turn promptly unleashes other afflictions on mortal men, who are also subject to the retribution of *Nemesis*, the humiliating process of aging, and other evils besides. One need not already harbor a pessimistic view of the world to read the following passage from the *Theogony* and gain the impression that, for Hesiod, human life—not just from time to time, but constantly and fundamentally—plays out *in sum* under the banner of Eris:

Deadly Night gave birth to [...] baneful Old Age, and she bore hard-hearted Strife. And loathsome Strife bore painful Toil and Forgetfulness and Hunger and tearful Pains, and Combats and Battles and Murders and Slaughters, and Strifes and Lies and Tales and Disputes, and Lawlessness and Recklessness, much like one another, and Oath, who indeed brings most woe upon human beings on the earth, whenever someone willfully swears a false oath.[31]

---

[31]Hesiod, "Theogony," in: Hesiod, *Theogony—Works and Days—Testimonia*, edited and translated by Glenn W. Most (Cambridge, MA: Harvard University Press, 2006), 21f.

70   AMBITION: AN ESSAY ON THE BURNING DESIRE TO RISE

The hardworking farmer Hesiod here presents an image of a world marked by painstaking labor whose yield is so quickly forgotten it is as though it had never been rendered, a meaningless and therefore wretched toiling incapable of fully satisfying one's ever-returning hunger. It is a world of drudgery, hunger, and pain, a world of tormenting lack. Bloody battles over ever scarce resources inevitably arise, in which all available means are deployed, from murder and manslaughter to lies, intrigues, anarchy, and false oaths. Under the banner of hated Eris, there is no order or legal certainty. It is horrible to see that this gruesome world is moreover ruled by nagging squabbles and reckless stupidity, related to lawlessness and encouraging it. Hesiod forcefully unfurls this Schopenhauerian world in just a few short verses. At the same time, against the backdrop of a theory of power such as Machiavelli's, this catalogue of plagues unleashed by hateful Eris that human beings are responsible for reads like an exhaustive list of those immoral capabilities that one must have if one wishes to rule the state with unscrupulous ambition and relentlessly defend that rule: the ability to break the law, to kill, to lie, and to swear false oaths. Machiavellians are students of Eris as she is presented in the *Theogony*.

This world of lawlessness and "utter moral corruption"[32] also forms the backdrop against which Hesiod composed his *Works and Days*, the occasion for which was provided by an evidently ugly inheritance dispute, exacerbated by corrupt aristocratic authorities, between Hesiod and his brother Perses, who is explicitly named in the text. It is Perses at whom this didactic poem is directed and whom it is intended to influence: "One theme is justice and its value; the other is success through hard work. Both stand in opposition to amoral and unproductive strife."[33] Law and right are vouched for by Zeus, whom Hesiod thus calls on for support in the poem's prooemium: "Hear me, Zeus, see me, and harken: let righteousness dwell in thy judgment."[34]

---

[32]Hermann Fränkel, *Early Greek Poetry and Philosophy: A History of Greek Epic, Lyric, and Prose to the Middle of the Fifth Century*, translated by Moses Hadas and James Willis (New York/London: Harcourt Brace Jovanovich, 1973), 114.
[33]Ibid., 113.
[34]Cited in: ibid., 114.

ERIS—AGON—AMBITION 71

Directly following the prooemium, Hesiod offers an astonishing self-correction that has since occupied the minds of scholars and laymen alike and is of the greatest interest for a European "prehistory of ambition." Unlike in the earlier *Theogony*, here there are suddenly *two*, sharply distinguished forms of Eris, the evil and the good, and what is more, the good is supposed to be the *older* of the two daughters of dark Night. Glenn W. Most's prose translation reads:

> So there was not just one birth of Strifes after all, but upon the earth there are two Strifes. One of these a man would praise once he got to know it, but the other is blameworthy; and they have thoroughly opposed spirits. For the one fosters evil war and conflict—cruel one, no mortal loves that one, but it is by necessity that they honor the oppressive Strife, by the plans of the immortals. But the other one gloomy Night bore first; and Cronus' high-throned son, who dwells in the aether, set it in the roots of the earth, and it is much better for men. It rouses even the helpless man to work. For a man who is not working but who looks at some other man, a rich one who is hastening to plow and plant and set his house in order, he envies him, one neighbor envying his neighbor who is hastening towards wealth: and this Strife is good for mortals. And potter is angry with potter, and builder with builder, and beggar begrudges beggar, and poet poet.
>
> Perses, do store this up in your spirit [...].[35]

The correction is profound. First, the evil Eris, who in the *Theogony* was a world-defining power who brought work, hunger, and pain to mankind, here becomes the admittedly also fearful "Eris of war" who "comes upon men from time to time."[36] As Hermann Fränkel emphasizes, this new conception is in keeping with the passages from the *Iliad* quoted above that describe Eris as being sent from the gods.[37] One of the most significant consequences

---

[35]Hesiod, "Works and Days," in: Hesiod, *Theogony—Works and Days—Testimonia*, 87f.
[36]Fränkel, *Early Greek Poetry and Philosophy*, 115.
[37]Cf. ibid.

72 AMBITION: AN ESSAY ON THE BURNING DESIRE TO RISE

of this reinterpretation of grim Eris from a perpetual presence into a momentous act of God, however, is that Hesiod now must establish a new reason for the misery he still sees in the world. Thus he introduces the myth of *Pandora* as a world-changing event. Pandora with her fateful box was sent to the human beings of the former Golden Age as punishment for accepting the gift of fire that Prometheus had stolen from the gods, paving the way for "higher civilization."[38] This was the beginning of the countless evils that persistently embitter the lives of men. Fränkel describes Hesiod's elaboration of the Pandora myth as a "new and peculiar turn."[39] The necessity of this story becomes clear, however, when one recognizes that Pandora takes on—and "must" take on—exactly the same function in the *Works and Days* that Eris, henceforth disempowered and now responsible only for exceptional situations, performed in the *Theogony*:

> For previously the tribes of men used to live upon the earth entirely apart from evils, and without grievous toil and distressful diseases, which give death to men. But the woman [Pandora, EG] removed the great lid from the storage jar with her hands and scattered all its contents abroad—she wrought baneful evils for human beings.[40]

The tremendous effort that Hesiod expends here—rewriting the responsibilities of the gods and inventing or discovering a new goddess—serves to buttress his claim of the existence of a "good Eris" planted deep in the earth by Zeus himself and constantly at work among human beings. This new Eris, Fränkel explains, must still bear the old name, as in Hesiod's time, the Greek language had "not yet coined a word" for the phenomenon that the *Works and Days* now takes into account: "competition."[41]

The effect of the good Eris, of *agon*, is to encourage productive ambition among human beings in all areas of life, to motivate them to work hard, diligently pursue their goals, and thus achieve success.

---

[38]Ibid., 117.
[39]Ibid.
[40]Hesiod, *Works and Days*, 95.
[41]Fränkel, *Early Greek Poetry and Philosophy*, 115.

ERIS—AGON—AMBITION 73

The form of ambition that stimulates productive competition, Hesiod teaches, is not only operative at every level of human society, it is "set in Earth's roots" and thus is divinely ordained, "natural," and all-encompassing. Competition, as a "fundamental" law, shapes the life of the natural world as a whole, as the farmer Hesiod would regularly have had opportunity to observe, in the plants eagerly striving to grow upward toward the sun every spring as well as in the animals fiercely battling over mates and territory. It is easy to recognize in this good Eris—as the young Nietzsche did—the Darwinian "struggle for existence,"[42] an ancient depiction of the natural impulse to survive and assert oneself in a world defined by the laws of evolutionary biology. This struggle for self-assertion rooted deep in the life of the natural world consequently also shapes the lives of both farmers and craftsmen (potters and carpenters) who work with natural materials like clay and wood. It even defines the lives of people on the fringes of society, the rivalrous beggars and poets—whom Hesiod, with a touch of self-mockery, lists directly alongside each other. Nietzsche refers to these verses again in *Human, All Too Human*, with a view to the writers of ancient tragedies:

> The Greek artists, the tragedians for example, poetized in order to conquer; their whole art cannot be thought of apart from contest: Hesiod's good Eris, ambition, gave their genius its wings.[43]

Hesiod's new doctrine of the two forms of Eris ends with an admonition to his brother Perses to, as Fränkel writes, "stick to honest competition in order to make himself the richer." At the same time, however, he should "give up his wicked strife with his brother." Beyond this, Fränkel argues, Hesiod's discovery of the good Eris more fundamentally means access to "a permanent force inhabiting earth, of which we may make use according to our desire."[44] In contrast to the bad Eris, whom we must bow to when

---

[42]Friedrich Nietzsche, *Nachlaß 1869–1874*, edited by Giorgio Colli and Mazzino Montinari (Munich: de Gruyter, 1988), 398.
[43]Friedrich Nietzsche, *Human, All Too Human: A Book for Free Spirits*, translated by R.J. Hollingdale (Cambridge: Cambridge University Press, 1996), 170.
[44]Fränkel, *Early Greek Poetry and Philosophy*, 115f.

74 AMBITION: AN ESSAY ON THE BURNING DESIRE TO RISE

she descends upon us sent from the gods, healthy ambition is the constantly operating and "natural" productive force of personal and social progress that we as human beings can harness for ourselves, although only under the guarantee of a stable legal framework. Productive labor under conditions of fair competition can only bear fruit if Zeus hears Hesiod's prayer and (re-)establishes law and order. Perses should therefore also steer clear of the deceitful machinations of the market and turn away from the corrupt authorities scheming to procure for him something that he did not earn himself through honest work.

Considering these characteristics of good competition, one is inclined to agree with Fränkel's view that Hesiod "should not have derived creative Eris from 'Night'; but he probably did not wish to carry his correction so far."[45] But this is precisely the question that has been raised again and again. The *Works and Days* draw a sharp distinction between the good Eris and the bad, yet they remain sisters born of *one* hateful mother and both bear the same name. Are they really two different figures, or do they represent *one* figure with two faces whose work—to invoke Pettigrove's description of ambition of once again—is "double-edged"?

The question of "good" and "bad," "healthy" and "sick" ambition, which has consistently driven discourse on the topic, is paradigmatically predetermined in Hesiod's mythological doubling of Eris. If we consider ambition from the perspective of the *Theogony*, we find its effective extreme in tyranny, achieved by the harshest of means in a lawless world, one of the repulsive children of the bad Eris. In contrast, if we consider ambition from the perspective of the *Works and Days*, it appears to be the critical productive factor that can bring the life of human beings competing peacefully with each other closer to a good future. In the working world of the *Works and Days*, it is natural and good to be ambitious.

Agon in Burckhardt and Nietzsche

Jacob Burckhardt's *The Greeks and Greek Civilization*, first delivered as a series of lectures and published as a book only after his

---

[45]Ibid., 116, fn.

ERIS—AGON—AMBITION 75

death, offers perhaps the most famous depiction of "agonal man" in Greek antiquity and acknowledges the Hesiod of the *Works and Days* as one of the earliest and most important witnesses of the omnipresence of agon:

In Hesiod we find the agon manifested in civic and rural life, that is to say, a kind of competitiveness that formed a parallel to the aristocratic and ideal form of the agon. *This is associated with his doctrine of the good and the bad Eris (strife), to be found at the beginning of Works and Days. The good Eris was the first to be born (while the bad was only a variant form fostering war and conflict)* and Hesiod seems to find her not only in human life but also in elemental Nature, for Cronos had placed her among the very roots of the earth. It is the good *Eris* who awakens even the indolent and unskilled to industry; seeing others rich, they too bestir themselves to plough and plant and order their houses, so that neighbour vies with neighbour in striving for wealth.

Thus after the decline of heroic kingship all higher life among the Greeks, active as well as spiritual, took on the character of the agon. Here excellence (*arete*) and natural superiority were displayed, and victory in the agon, that is noble victory without enmity, appears to have been the ancient expression of the peaceful victory of an individual. Many different aspects of life came to bear the marks of this form of competitiveness. We see it in the conversations and round-songs of the guests in the symposium, in philosophy and legal procedure, down to cock- and quail-fighting or the gargantuan feats of eating.[46]

Burckhardt's comprehensive, still thrilling account of the agonal principle that permeated every area of ancient Greek life is noted here only in passing. With respect to the question of Hesiod's doubling of Eris, the key point of interest is Burckhardt's reading of the relevant passage in the *Works and Days*. He solves the problem instantly and elegantly here by fusing the supposedly twofold Eris back into a single goddess in a nonchalant parenthetical, interpreting Hesiod as suggesting that the bad Eris who "fosters war and conflict" is only

---

[46]Jacob Burckhardt, *The Greeks and Greek Civilization*, edited by Oswyn Murray, translated by Sheila Stern (New York: St. Martin's Griffin, 1999), 165f. My emphasis.

76 AMBITION: AN ESSAY ON THE BURNING DESIRE TO RISE

a mutated "variant form"—Burckhardt uses the word *Ausartung*, literally: "degeneration"—of the good Eris. He rightly notes that, according to the *Works and Days*, the good Eris was "the first to be born," but he interprets this as meaning that she is the "original" or "actual" Eris. This further implies that the bad Eris is not sent by God, but likewise falls under the purview of human beings, whose responsibility it is to prevent the dangerous and destructive "degeneration" of the natural, good Eris into war and conflict, a manifestation of pathological excess. Adherence to the legal order established by Zeus protects against such excess. The existence of this order, however, at least indirectly confirms human beings' tendency toward "degeneracy"; otherwise, it would be superfluous.

Burckhardt also emphasizes that the firstborn—original, actual—good Eris can be found at work in "elemental nature," and that there exists an organic continuity between this elemental force and human competition. Agon, pervasive in Greek life from lowly cock- and quail-fighting to the lofty verbal sparring matches of Plato's *Symposium*, is thus deeply rooted in and grows out of the life of the natural world. The catch with Burckhardt's elegant solution, which betrays the influence of Goethean natural philosophy, is that the bad Eris inevitably must be conceived of as a "degeneration," as something unnatural and monstrous. If one does not believe in the work of evil goddesses, however, then it must be human beings themselves, in contrast to plants and animals, who bring this "degeneracy" into the world.[47] War and excessive conflict, meaningless strife, hate, the will to destroy—all this is uniquely human, as Burckhardt himself well knows and strikingly describes in his other works, particularly *The Civilization of the Renaissance in Italy*. "Noble victory without enmity" is the exceedingly rare exception in a world of suffering ruled over according to the *Theogony*, by toil, hunger, pain, and jealous competitive struggle. *Philotimia*, love of honor, operates in the historical and political world not only in the form of noble and productive "competition," but also and repeatedly as unrelenting, merciless ambition, divorced from self-preservation and bent on the "total success" of tyranny.

Burckhardt's derivation of organic competition from elemental nature, in keeping with the Hesiod of the *Works and Days* and in

---

[47]Cf. Reichholff, *Warum wir siegen wollen*, 202ff.

ERIS—AGON—AMBITION 77

the spirit of Goethe's *Pandora*, obscures the radical "unnaturalness" of the ancient Greeks, who attributed even to the gods the menacing tendency toward human affect that impels burning ambition. Agamemnon's fear upon arriving home that he will be fatally met by the eye of an envious god as soon as he dons his purple robes is justified.[48] In Burckhardt's *The Greeks and Greek Civilization*, however, the scale clearly tips *not* in favor of the bleak worldview of the *Theogony*, but decidedly in favor of the naturally deep-rooted competition of honest labor that Hesiod recommends to his dissolute brother Perses in the *Works and Days*.

Nietzsche, during his time in Basel, corresponded frequently with his older and much sought-after colleague Burckhardt, particularly about the agonal principle in ancient Greece. His fascinating but problematic short essay "Homer's Contest," written in December 1872 but never published during his lifetime, picks up the debate about Hesiod's twofold Eris, but takes a different path than do the readings of Burckhardt and, later, Fränkel. Nietzsche, too, fuses the two Erises back into one, but his amalgamation is far darker than Burckhardt's; here the bright world of the Greeks devoted to institutionalized agon shines forth against a grim backdrop of hate-filled "pleasure in destruction."[49] For Burckhardt, the good Eris-as-agon represents the refined, civilized continuation of the productive competition of organic nature. In Nietzsche, she embodies the institutionalized management of man's unnatural perversion. Nietzsche inverts Hesiod's image of the good Eris' rootedness in nature in the essay's very first sentences. Here, the good—humanity—is rooted in inhumanity:

> [Man's] dreadful capabilities and those counting as inhuman are perhaps, indeed, the fertile soil from which alone all humanity, in feelings, deeds and works, can grow forth.[50]

---

[48]Cf. Aeschylus, "Agamemnon," in: Aeschylus, *The Oresteia*, translated by Robert Fagles (New York: Penguin, 1977), 139.

[49]Friedrich Nietzsche, "Homer's Contest," in: Nietzasche, *On the Genealogy of Morality and Other Writings*, translated by Carol Diethe, edited by Keith Ansell-Pearson (Cambridge: Cambridge University Press, 2007), 174–81 (174).

[50]Ibid.

78 AMBITION: AN ESSAY ON THE BURNING DESIRE TO RISE

According to Nietzsche, the pessimistic view of earthly existence reflected in the "repellingly dreadful legends"[51] and difficult-to-breathe air of the *Theogony*, in which life is "ruled over by the *children of the night* alone, by strife, lust, deception, age and death,"[52] still applies in the *Works and Days*. He finds confirmation of his thesis in an anecdote he shares in which Pausanius, on his travels through Greece, is shown an ancient copy of the *Works and Days*, inscribed on lead plates that "did not carry that little hymn to Zeus at the head,"[53] but instead began straight with the distinction between the two Eris-goddesses: an entire world subject to ambition *without* a divinely ordained legal order.

In the fragments related to "Homer's Contest," Nietzsche succinctly articulates what he wants to demonstrate in his own competition with Burckhardt. The Greek agon sublimates the elemental human emotions—grievance, envy, hatred, and burning ambition—that define the world of misery and war presented in the *Theogony* and that the Greeks recognized as valid and justified. These dark emotions are further worked out, but within the stable, institutionalized framework of athletic and artistic competitions at various levels. Here Nietzsche does not yet have at his disposal the concept of "sublimation" in the sense of a diversion or "transfer" of mental and emotional energy to different objects that he would later introduce to the vocabulary of cultural theory. Instead, in his early work, he lays claim to the idea of "idealization," later used primarily in psychoanalytic contexts:

> The poet overcomes the struggle for existence by idealizing it as an open contest. Here is the existence that is still fought for, existence in praise, in posthumous fame. The poet *nurtures*: he knows how to translate the Greeks' tiger-like drives to destruction into the good Eris. [...] *Gymnastics as idealized war.*[54]

Beyond the concept of sublimation outlined here, which a generation later would become one of the building blocks of Freud's psychoanalytic theory of culture, this fragment also offers

---

[51]Ibid., 175.
[52]Ibid.
[53]Ibid., 176.
[54]Nietzsche, *Nachlaß 1869–1874*, 398.

ERIS—AGON—AMBITION 79

an explanation for the at times extremely strong emotions that individuals attach to praise and posthumous fame. We—and not just poets—are so deeply concerned about how we will be viewed after we die because we have "transferred" the struggle for existence to the struggle for posthumous fame. This concern lives on today in the idea of "character assassination," which brings with it "social death." Nietzsche, who always prided himself on his philological rigor, is willing to mistranslate Hesiod at a critical juncture in order to establish his perspective on the history of Greek civilization, which is fundamentally different from Burckhardt's; this may have played a role in his decision to leave the text unpublished. It is critical for his argument—aimed at demonstrating the institutionalization, channeling, and defusing of originally destructive emotions into productive agon—that the *bad* Eris be the *older* of the two daughters of Night, and he translates the passage in question accordingly. The inversion of the facts that this mistranslation makes possible ends up changing everything, as Nietzsche, contrary both to Burckhardt and to the text of the *Works and Days* itself, is able to use it as a basis for giving historical primacy to the "bottomless pit of hatred"[55] over commitment to productive work. In the original Greek, the passage in Hesiod (lines 11–19) reads:

Οὐκ ἄρα μοῦνον ἔην Ἐρίδων γένος, ἀλλ' ἐπὶ γαῖαν / εἰσὶ δύω· τὴν μέν κεν ἐπαινήσειε νοήσας, / ἢ δ' ἐπιμωμητή· διὰ δ' ἄνδιχα θυμὸν ἔχουσιν. / ἢ μὲν γὰρ πόλεμόν τε κακὸν καὶ δῆριν ὀφέλ / σχετλίη· οὔ τις τήν γε φιλεῖ βροτός, ἀλλ' ὑπ' ἀνάγκης / ἀθανάτων βουλῇσιν Ἔριν τιμῶσι βαρεῖαν. / τὴν δ' ἑτέρην προτέρην μὲν ἐγείνατο Νὺξ ἐρεβεννή, / θῆκε δέ μιν Κρονίδης ὑψίζυγος, αἰθέρι ναίων, / γαίης [τ'] ἐν ῥίζῃσι καὶ ἀνδράσι πολλὸν ἀμείνω·[56]

Stanley Lombardo's jocular verse translation is in keeping with both Most's and Burckhardt's:

It looks like there's not just one kind of Strife—
That's Eris—after all, but two on the Earth.

---

[55]Nietzsche, "Homer's Contest," 174.
[56]Hesiod, *Works and Days*, 86f.

80 AMBITION: AN ESSAY ON THE BURNING DESIRE TO RISE

You'd praise one of them once you got to know her,
but the other's plain blameworthy. They've just got
Completely opposite temperaments.
One of them favors war and fighting. She's a mean cuss
And nobody likes her, but everybody honors her,
This ornery Eris. They have to: it's the gods' will.
The other was born first though. Ebony Night
Bore her, and Kronos' son who sit high in thin air
Set her in Earth's roots, and she's a lot better for humans.[57]

Now here is Carol Diethe's rendition in English of the young
Nietzsche's German translation of the same passage:

There are two Eris-goddesses on earth. [...] One should praise
the one Eris as much as blame the other, if one has any sense;
because the two goddesses have quite separate dispositions.
One promotes wicked war and feuding, the cruel thing! No
mortal likes her, but the yoke of necessity forces man to honour
the heavy burden of this Eris according to the decrees of the
Immortals. *Black Night gave birth to this one as the older of
the two; but Zeus, who reigned on high, placed the other on the
roots of the earth and amongst men as a much better one.*[58]

It is an initially inconspicuous modification, the full weight of which
only becomes clear once one recognizes that the notion of "two

---

[57]Hesiod, "Works and Days," in: Hesiod, *Works and Days and Theogony*, translated
by Stanley Lombardo (Indianapolis/Cambridge: Hackett, 1993), 23f.
[58]Nietzsche, "Homer's Contest," 176. My emphasis. Compare Nietzsche's text in
German: "'[Z]wei Erisgöttinnen sind auf Erden.' Dies ist einer der merkwürdigsten
hellenischen Gedanken und werth dem Kommenden gleich am Eingangsthore
der hellenischen Ethik eingeprägt zu werden. 'Die eine Eris möchte man, wenn
man Verstand hat, ebenso loben als die andre tadeln; denn eine ganz getrennte
Gemüthsart haben diese beiden Göttinnen. Denn die Eine fördert den schlimmen
Krieg und Hader, die Grausame! Kein Sterblicher mag sie leiden, sondern unter dem
Joch der Noth erweist man der schwerlastenden Eris Ehre, nach dem Rathschlusse
der Unsterblichen. Diese gebar, als die ältere, die schwarze Nacht; die andre aber
stellte Zeus der hochwaltende hin auf die Wurzeln der Erde und unter die Menschen,
als eine viel bessere.'" Friedrich Nietzsche, "Homers Wettkampf," in: Nietzsche, *Die
Geburt der Tragödie, Unzeitgemäße Betrachtungen, Nachgelassene Schriften 1870–
1873*, edited by Giorgio Colli and Mazzino Montinari (Munich: dtv, 1988), 786.

Eris-goddesses," as Nietzsche himself concedes, "is one of the most remarkable of Hellenic ideas and deserves to be impressed upon newcomers right at the gate of entry to Hellenic ethics."[59] But what Nietzsche actually wants to impress on his readers—indeed, what he foists upon them—is his own translation of line 17 of the *Works and Days* that turns the content of the verse on its head. What hangs over the gate of entry to his interpretation of agon is thus not a correctly translated quote from Hesiod, but its Nietzschean reversal of meaning, according to which—and in keeping with the grim verses from the *Theogony* quoted above—life as a whole is dreadfully defined by the bad Eris, and therefore what must be sublimated and overcome in agon is a "pre-Homeric world."

Where do we look if we stride backwards into this pre-Homeric world? "Only into night and horror," say Nietzsche, "into the products of a fantasy used to ghastly things." It is a world of suffering that leads "to nausea at existence, to the view of existence as a punishment to be discharged by serving out one's time, to the belief that existence and indebtedness [are] identical."[60] According to Nietzsche's spectacular insight, constant competition in all areas of life, from physical training to philosophical disputes, is the heroic Hellenic alternative to renouncing the world in profound disgust. In agon, emotions like hatred, envy, and grievance are accepted as valid and justified and are acted out, not as a "struggle-to-the-death," but in the form of the ubiquitous, frequently organized "contest." The agonal principle pervaded the Hellenic world, sublimating the will to destruction and allowing the Greeks to "release [their] hatred" in the safe space of the stadium or theater:[61]

[T]he whole of Greek antiquity thinks about grudge and envy differently from us and agrees with Hesiod, who first portrays one Eris as wicked, in fact the one who leads men into hostile struggle-to-the-death, and then praises the other Eris as good, who, as jealousy, grudge, and envy, goads men to action, not, however, the action of a struggle-to-the-death but the action of the *contest*. The Greek is *envious* and does not experience this

---

[59]Ibid.
[60]Ibid., 175.
[61]Ibid.

82 AMBITION: AN ESSAY ON THE BURNING DESIRE TO RISE

characteristic as blemish, but as the effect of a *benevolent* deity: what a gulf of ethical judgment between him and us![62]

The Greeks' "unfortunately" frequent relapses into savagery confirm for Nietzsche the bitter necessity of this architecture of institutionalized forms of sublimation: "[I]f we take away the contest from Greek life, we gaze immediately into the pre-Homeric abyss of a gruesome savagery of hatred and pleasure in destruction."[63] A sympathetic reading of Nietzsche's essay might construe it as a philologically dodgy effort to resolve the contradiction between the *Theogony* and the *Works and Days*; in this sense, one might understand his mistranslation as an acknowledgment that the bad Eris was effectively "first" in Hesiod's thought anyway, inasmuch as the *Works and Days* refer back to the pessimism of the earlier *Theogony*. Of course, such an approach effaces Hesiod's spectacular self-correction, in which he designates productive competition as the primary drive, rooted in nature, allowing him to posit a more intimate bond between hardworking man and the world around him.

Nietzsche interprets Hesiod's self-correction as a self-misunderstanding, asserting the primacy of bottomless, life-negating hatred over the productive practices that only grow out of its sublimation. He "improves" the *Works and Days* by positioning himself against its author. In mistranslating Hesiod, Nietzsche completes his transition from a philologist to a philosopher who rejects the worldview presented in the *Works and Days* as false and recommits Hesiod to his "older knowledge," which he— Nietzsche, student of Schopenhauer—deems authoritative. Greek agon becomes for him a model of passionate affirmation of a life understood as terrible and meaningless. The warrior here supplants the peasant farmer.

Leaving aside its suspect explanation of the origins of agon, Nietzsche's essay is important in the context of our reflections on ambition because—now in keeping with Burckhardt's more democratically minded interpretation—it conceives of the institution of agon as a cardinal administrative instrument for safeguarding the polis. Nietzsche traces ostracism, the banishment of ambitiously

---

[62]Ibid., 177.
[63]Ibid., 179.

ERIS—AGON—AMBITION 83

"degenerate" individuals, back to the need to preserve productive contest as the *vital essence of democracy*. The "overreaching," "degenerate" individual must leave the polis because he is a threat to democratic competition:

> [Ostracism] is used when there is the obvious danger that one of the great contending politicians and party leaders might feel driven, in the heat of battle, to use harmful and destructive means and to conduct dangerous *coups d'états*. [...] That is the kernel of the Hellenic idea of competition: it loathes a monopoly of predominance and fears the dangers of this, it desires, as *protective measure* against genius—a second genius.[64]

Because the preservation of agon in politics—what one might also call a productive, perpetual balancing of conflicting forces—was considered essential to the flourishing of the polis, young people were brought up to understand that individual ambition could be fulfilled *only in and for the polis*. While "modern educators fear nothing more than the unleashing of so-called ambition,"[65] in the Greek polis, ambition was encouraged beginning in childhood, but in such a way that it would serve "the well-being of the whole." In Nietzsche's reconstruction of Greek antiquity, "selfishness," the pursuit of personal ambition, did not have to be stigmatized as a "sin against the holy spirit of politics," as Max Weber would describe it over 2000 years later, precisely because it could serve the polis as a powerful productive force. The social-psychological basis of this construction was the systematically promoted *identification* of youth with the polis, which fascism would later generate in modern industrial society through hypertrophic, propaganda-fueled nationalism:

> It was not a boundless and indeterminate ambition like most modern ambition: the youth thought of the good of his native city when he ran a race or threw or sang; he wanted to increase its reputation through his own; it was to the city's gods that he dedicated the wreaths which the umpires placed on his head

---

[64]Ibid., 178.
[65]Ibid.

84 AMBITION: AN ESSAY ON THE BURNING DESIRE TO RISE

in honour. From childhood, every Greek felt the burning desire within him to be an instrument of bringing salvation to his city in the contest between cities: in this, his selfishness was lit, as well as curbed and restricted. For that reason, the individuals in antiquity were freer, because their aims were nearer and easier to achieve. Modern man, on the other hand, is crossed everywhere by infinity.[66]

The idea of freedom that Nietzsche outlines here is less paradoxical or "dialectical" than it initially appears. As we have seen multiple times already, succumbing to ambition means bondage, desire, potential addiction, and excess. But if the aims of ambition are clearly defined and can actually be achieved within the framework of the order of the polis, then there is a chance that it will be quenched by victory. Winning then means being freed from ambition. The price of this construction is paid primarily by the losers, whose shame and inconsolability, in Burckhardt's empathetic description, slink along the walls in the shadow of agonal life and splendor. The situation is different, however, when ambition can never be sated, because there are always new aims that stretch into infinity. The person hooked on such boundless ambition remains unfree, an addict, dragged ever further into the future on the leash of passion.

Given this construction of agon as the decisive instrument for preserving Greek democratic culture, we can now understand why Nietzsche describes the relentless, infinitely reaching ambition of Alexander the Great, at the beginning of the text, as a "grotesquely enlarged reflection of the Hellene"[67] and, at the end, also derogatively, as a "rough copy and abbreviation of Greek history."[68] Alexander, the autocrat on the Persian throne with his thirst for the infinite—for "India"—is an odious example of the "degeneration" of ambition in Nietzsche's view, a grotesque relapse into the pre-Homeric world and, at the same time, a decadent.

That the two "overreaching" usurpers of antiquity profiled by Plutarch, Alexander and Caesar, both perished at the height of

---

[66]Ibid., 179.
[67]Ibid., 174.
[68]Ibid., 181.

their power—the one purportedly of malaria, the other as a victim of a political assassination—can be understood as the inevitable fulfillment of what Nietzsche describes as the fate of all those "degenerates" who, in their boundless ambition, dare to finally designate themselves "*hors de concours*" and place themselves "on a lonely pinnacle."[69] From a mythological perspective, Alexander and Caesar both incur upon themselves the envy of the immortals and so must follow the ancient pattern that Nietzsche reconstructs. In the context of this mythological paradigm, Alexander's illness and Caesar's assassins are thus only the instruments of the inevitable fate to which insatiable ambition leads those who attract the eye of an envious god:

> [T]his divine envy flares up when it sees a man without any other competitor, without an opponent, at the lonely height of fame. He has only the gods near him now—and for that reason he has them against him. But these entice him into an act of hubris, and he collapses under it.[70]

The idea Nietzsche traces in "Homer's Contest," that identification with the polis can transform personal ambition from a destructive element into a force that benefits the whole and therefore should be viewed and encouraged as a consequence of the "good Eris," persisted over centuries throughout antiquity. It is found, for example, in the writings of the Roman historian Sallust, whose work Nietzsche greatly admired and whose history of the Catiline conspiracy exposed and thwarted by Cicero elaborates a concise phenomenology of various forms of ambition. To Sallust, then, we now turn our attention.

ambitio in Sallust

In the fall of 1775, the young Johann Wolfgang Goethe—son of a wealthy Frankfurt family, successful lawyer, and star author— arrived at the court of Weimar, driven by what in his autobiography

---

[69]Ibid., 180.
[70]Ibid.

86 AMBITION: AN ESSAY ON THE BURNING DESIRE TO RISE

he calls "the daemonic." There he voluntarily placed himself in the service of a minor prince and even after 1789 remained loyal to the *ancien régime* to the last. 1775/1776 marked the beginning of a decade in which Goethe, soon to be ennobled, assumed a "worldly role" and began "*governing*."[71] He ascended to the highest of public offices. His writing, increasingly relegated to the fringes of his activity, changed during this period, entering a phase of formal experimentation and psychological exploration. Despite the other pressures on his time, he produced some of his most famous poems, which grew to comprise a precious lyrical diary. One of these pieces was integrated into a light opera—*Lila*—that received its first performance in 1777. The poem is supposed to help the depressive title heroine, who spends her days avoiding other people and her nights indulging in her own fantasies, regain her mental health and develop a new sense of self-confidence.

Like a young and sensitive poet who finds himself seriously involved in and responsible to the world of politics for the first time, the deeply dismayed Lila "always" distrusts people. For as she is forced to recognize, "the gods also give power to the unjust and good fortune to the treacherous."[72] Doctor Verazio, disguised as "magus," who hopes to cure Lila (and, at the end of this therapeutic play, ultimately does), becomes close with our disturbed heroine and gains her trust. Following their initial conversation, he sings the now-famous verses intended to encourage Lila not to "lower" her sights beneath what she is capable of.[73] He then leaves her alone so that the poem can have its effect on her. And affect her it does: Lila no longer wants to "pine away" in solitude, but desires to return to "society."[74] Thus begins her healing. The untitled poem about the self-assertion of the sensitive reads as follows:

Feiger Gedanken	Fearful wavering
Bängliches Schwanken,	Of cowardly thoughts,

---

[71]Johann Wolfgang von Goethe, *Das erste Weimarer Jahrzehnt: Briefe, Tagebücher und Gespräche vom 7. November 1775 bis 2. September 1786*, edited by Hartmut Reinhardt (Frankfurt am Rhein: Deutscher Klassiker Verlag, 1997), 19 and 106. Emphasis in original.

[72]Goethe, "Lila," in: *Sämtliche Werke nach Epochen seines Schaffens*, edited by Karl Richter et al., vol. 2.1 (Munich: C. Hanser, 1985), 143.

[73]Ibid., 145.

[74]Ibid.

ERIS—AGON—AMBITION 87

Weibisches Zagen,	Womanish apprehension,
Ängstliches Klagen	Anxious lamentation
Wendet kein Elend,	Will not ward off woe,
Macht dich nicht frei.	Will not set you free.
Allen Gewalten	Persevering in spite
Zum Trutz sich erhalten,	Of all hardship,
Nimmer sich beugen,	Never bending,
Kräftig sich zeigen,	Proving your might,
Rufet die Arme	Summons the arms
Der Götter herbei.[75]	Of the gods.

The initial conversation between Lila and Doctor Verazio alone will surely lead a modern reader to doubt whether the doctor's therapeutic approach is wisely chosen or appropriate for his patient. He calls out to the frightened woman: "Take courage, and everything will work out."[76] But when he further chides her in verse not only for her cowardly thoughts, but also her "womanish apprehension," he locks her into the double bind discussed above in the introduction, which makes on her an impossible demand: namely, that she become a man in order to survive in life. The young Goethe, allowing himself a brief reprieve from the hustle and bustle of politics, himself played the role of Doctor Verazio in *Lila*'s premiere performance. It is thus easy to imagine that, with these words, he was also encouraging himself, admonishing his own feminine side to "man up," so to speak. For Goethe now found himself in a situation that had filled his life with worries and cares—with *Sorge*, also the title of a key poem from this period—and thus required a corresponding level of fortitude.

The harsh tone of the poem, which its subtle arrangement of rhymes and assonances cannot completely erase, gives reason to suggest that we might also be dealing here with an echo of Goethe's reading of Sallust. Even as this poem about the fearful wavering of cowardly thoughts modifies the trope that God or the gods help those who know how to help themselves, its affinity with a passage found in Sallust's chronicle of the Catiline conspiracy is remarkable.

---

[75]Ibid.
[76]Ibid.

88 AMBITION: AN ESSAY ON THE BURNING DESIRE TO RISE

The climax of Cato's speech in the Roman Senate, which culminates in his call for the conspirators to be put to death, articulates the notion that only men of action receive the help of the gods in a surprisingly similar way. What suggests that Goethe might be alluding to Sallust here is the detail that the furious Cato likewise repudiates "womanly entreaties." The passage in Sallust reads:

> non votis neque suppliciis muliebribus auxilia deorum parantur: vigilando, agundo, bene consulundo prospere omnia cedunt. ubi socordiae te atque ignaviae tradideris, nequiquam deos inplores: irati infestique sunt.

> But it is not with prayers and womanly entreaties that we earn the help of the gods; it is by being watchful, taking action, making good policy, that all things succeed. When you have handed yourself over to apathy and lethargy, it would be an empty gesture to call upon the gods; they are angry and hostile.[77]

Goethe's knowledge of Latin was excellent, and it may well be that he consulted Sallust during his early days at the Weimar court because he had discovered in *De coniuratione Catilinae*, traditionally taught in Latin classes of the day, a paradigmatic depiction of political struggle and a classification of various forms of ambition all but unsurpassable in its clarity. Goethe would then be yet another example of the comprehensive reception the Roman historian has found over the centuries, ever since Augustine described the old republicans of ancient Rome, as portrayed in Sallust, as secular exemplars of the pious citizens of the new City of God.[78] Sallust's chronicle of the Catiline conspiracy is not just any account of a random chapter of Roman history, but has been and still today is studied as the paradigmatic portrayal of a conspiracy that heralded the impending collapse of a social system, the end of a republic giving way to a dictatorship. The utilization of Sallust's works, along with the historical constellations and striking characters

---

[77]Sallust, *Catiline's Conspiracy*, in: Sallust, *Catiline's Conspiracy, The Jugurthine War, Histories*, translated by William W. Batstone (Oxford: Oxford University Press, 2010), 41.
[78]Cf. the afterword on Montaigne and Augustine below.

he depicts, as a literary blueprint or even a practical manual for navigating the machinery of politics stretches from Montaigne to Shakespeare, Goethe, Tocqueville, Bismarck, Burckhardt, Brecht, and beyond. Burckhardt offers an exemplary demonstration of this with respect to the politics of Renaissance Italy, where Roman antiquity not only provided a philosophical, literary, and aesthetic standard to live up to; the rulers of the time, "both in their conception of the state and in their personal conduct, took the old Roman empire avowedly as their model,"[79] including the most famous conspiracy in a century of civil wars, uncovered by Cicero, the idol of Renaissance humanists. The conspiracies of the Italian Renaissance, Burckhardt writes, betray "the influence of that worst of all conspirators, Catiline—a man in whose thoughts freedom had no place whatever. The annals of Siena tell us expressly that the conspirators were students of Sallust [...]. Elsewhere, too, we meet with the name of Catiline, and a more attractive pattern of the conspirator [...] could hardly be discovered."[80] When Tocqueville invokes "Sulla and Caesar" as cautionary tales and Bismarck warns against "Catilinarian characters," these political realists are also referencing the personages and events depicted and analyzed by Sallust, which we will therefore examine more closely in the following pages with particular attention to Sallust's haunting propositions about burning ambition.

Goethe arrived at the court of Weimar in 1775/76 as a bourgeois, not unlike Cicero, who began his career as a *homo novus* and intellectual in a Rome ruled by old noble families and rose to the position of consul. One of the thornier aspects of the intrigues surrounding the Catalinarian conspiracy was that Catiline was a patrician descended from an ancient family, while the man who brought him down, Cicero, was an ambitious upstart without noble ancestry, a "new man."[81] In a letter to the Senate quoted by Sallust, Catiline takes aim at this weakness of Cicero's, arguing that his— Catiline's—humiliating loss to Cicero in the consular election of 63

---

[79]Jacob Burckhardt, *The Civilization of the Renaissance in Italy*, translated by S.G.C. Middlemore (New York: The Modern Library, 2002), 42.
[80]Ibid., 43.
[81]Sallust, *Catiline's Conspiracy*, 22.

90 AMBITION: AN ESSAY ON THE BURNING DESIRE TO RISE

BC forced him to take action to salvage what remained of his "dignity."[82]

The ex-politician Sallust saw Catiline's conspiracy as symptomatic in a way similar to how Goethe viewed the "diamond necklace affair" of the mid-1780s, which cast a harsh light on the rotten state of modern aristocratic society. As the German translator of Sallust Wilhelm Schöne explains:

> It was clear to [Sallust] that this conspiracy represented an important episode in Roman history, but he was concerned less with the facts of the event than with its fundamental significance: a handful of ne'er-do-wells had brought a world empire to the edge of the abyss.[83]

Sallust's "brazen" depiction—to use a frequently (and not unjustly) applied epithet—places more weight on presenting clearly hammered-out, "eternal" archetypes than on delivering an exact account, in terms of both content and style, of dramatic events involving protagonists whom he personally knew. He does so to draw our attention to the sociopolitical theories of ambition discussed above in the context of Greek antiquity, which Sallust updates for contemporary Rome and finds reapplied, *mutatis mutandis*, in Roman history and politics. Rome succeeds Greece in this respect, as well, just as Sallust—self-consciously enough, even to the point of borrowing individual ideas and phrases—assumes the legacy of Thucydides.[84]

Jörg Fündling, author of a nuanced biography of Sulla (138–78 BC), has aptly compared the extraordinarily complicated domestic political situation in Rome during the century of civil wars that ended in the establishment of a dictatorship to an extremely dangerous "Mikado play."[85] Sallust immensely simplifies this history, but herein lies not only the artistic purpose that Nietzsche so admired, but

---

[82]Ibid., 27.

[83]Wilhelm Schöne, "Sallust als Historiker," in: Sallust, *Werke und Schriften* (München: Heimeran, 1965), 469.

[84]Cf. Kurt Latte, *Sallust* (Darmstadt: Wissenschaftliche Buchgesellschaft, 1962), 43–7.

[85]Jörg Fündling, *Sulla* (Darmstadt: Wissenschaftliche Buchgesellschaft, 2010), 24.

ERIS—AGON—AMBITION 91

also the will to write something like an early sociology of (political) ambition through the working-out of ideal types that can also be applied to different historical constellations. Bertolt Brecht's *The Business Affairs of Mr. Julius Caesar*, an unfinished novel written in Danish exile in 1938/1939, in which Rome functions as a modern city with politically influential business interests that find themselves in constant conflict with a conservative Senate dominated by 300 old families, is one of the finest testaments to the possibilities of an updated application of this typology.[86] Here, then, let us first consider Sallust's ideal typology of ambition.

Sallust's history of Rome begins with the toppling of a monarchy that had degenerated into "arrogance and domination."[87] Following the expulsion of the last king, the Romans established a republic governed by two consuls, who served one-year terms and during their time in office were overseen by an assembly of elders, the Senate, which maintained the balance of ambitious power. Weapons in hand, the Romans now vigorously defended "their freedom, their fatherland, and their parents."[88] The first, "healthy" form of ambition that Sallust describes is the desire among the Roman people to attain glory for the fatherland on the basis of passionate identification with the Roman city-state: "But competitions for glory were among them the toughest competitions. [...] They were greedy for praise, but with money they were generous: they wanted

---

[86]In Brecht's unfinished novel, Caesar's former banker Mummlius Spicer delivers the records of Caesar's secretary, the slave Rarus, to a young, idealistic historian who desires to write a hagiography of the dictator. On handing over the records, Spicer says: "Don't expect to find heroic deeds described in a classical style, but if you read it with an open mind perhaps you'll find some clues as to how dictatorships are established and empires founded." Bertolt Brecht, *The Business Affairs of Mr. Julius Caesar*, translated by Charles Osborne, edited by Anthony Phelan and Tom Kuhn (London: Bloomsbury, 2016), 49f. Rarus' notes reveal the financial interests of Roman bankers and businessmen as the decisive factors in political developments. Among the sources that Brecht drew on for his novel are not just Sallust's works but evidently also Theodor Mommsen's *History of Rome*, which includes a comment on the tense situation at the height of the Catilinarian conspiracy that surely must have pleased Brecht: "The capitalists hovered in nameless fear." Theodor Mommsen, *Römische Geschichte*, vol. 1, *Könige und Konsuln* (Gütersloh: Bertelsmann, 1957), 768.
[87]Sallust, *Catiline's Conspiracy*, 13.
[88]Ibid.

92 AMBITION: AN ESSAY ON THE BURNING DESIRE TO RISE

glory that was huge, wealth that was honorable."[89] Desire for glory, modesty, tradition, public spirit, and laws ruled undisputed. As an experienced, practical politician, Sallust was well aware of the existence of emotions like "hatred" and "pleasure in destruction," and he emphasizes the wisdom of the Republic in directing these emotions outward as a means of maintaining internal harmony: "The Roman people [...] engaged in quarrels, disputes, competition with the enemy, but among citizens the contest was over manly virtue."[90] Here we find an exemplary expression of the distinction between the bad, destructive Eris—or her Roman equivalent, Discordia—and the good, productive Eris, which lives on in Sallust in modified form: While the Greeks vented their hatred and lust for destruction through athletic and artistic competition, the unartistic Romans of the old Republic turned their aggressions outward, thereby continually expanding their *imperium*.

What happened next, according to Sallust, can be understood as the revenge of the bad Eris, who now returned to the city in the form of *discordia*, undermining its order. For the rise of Rome as the result of a politics of conquest conducive to internal peace, particularly in the wake of the Second Punic War, brought with it a seductive overabundance of money and power, "the root, so to speak, of all evils."[91] Laudable *cupido gloriae*, the desire for glory indifferent to money, now gave way to *avaritia* and *ambitio*, avarice along with a second, *negative* form of ambition that no longer found fulfillment in the commendation of the fatherland, but greedily operated on its own account, becoming self-indulgent and boundless:

> Ambition forced many men to become liars, to hide one thing in their heart and have something else ready on their tongue, to value friendship and enmity according to convenience, not substance, and to put up a good face rather than have a good heart.[92]

---

[89]Ibid., 13f.
[90]Ibid., 14.
[91]Ibid., 15.
[92]Ibid.

ERIS—AGON—AMBITION 93

Here Sallust offers a "classical" formulation of the modern critique of reprehensible social pretense articulated by Jean-Jacques Rousseau nearly 2000 years later. The reordering of society under the banner of lust for money also resulted in the emergence of a new form of rhetoric-as-social-pretense that even today makes certain political slogans repulsive: "[A]fter those times whoever stirred up the Republic with honourable claims, [...] pretending to work for the public good, they struggled for their own power."[93]

But Sallust is subtle. He praises thirst for glory and understands ambition: "For both the good man and the worthless man desire for themselves glory, honor, power." The critical difference for him lies in the means used to achieve these goals, and in their quality. He questions whether "treachery and deception" are decisive or honorable.[94] Here we thus also find an anticipation of the basic contours of the ethical debate posited by Pettigrove. Ambition "itself" is not condemnable, rather it is its methods and aims that are the actual object of moral assessment. Sallust moreover recognizes that certain objects and aims such as money and power, unlike the clearly defined prizes won in competition or the concrete honors bestowed by the city, lead desire along the self-indulgent, never-ending path of "always wanting more": *avaritia semper infinita et insatiabilis est.*[95] A new plutocratic regime emerged in Rome that inverted the "old values." Glory became a matter of money, while poverty was considered disgraceful:

After wealth began to be considered an honour, and after glory, political authority, and power followed in its wake, manly virtue began to lose its lustre, poverty was considered a disgrace, innocence was taken for malevolence. And so, as a result of our wealth, extravagance and greed with arrogance assaulted our youth [.][96]

Scholars have long noted that, in these reflections on the decline of the old order, Sallust is rewriting a famous chapter about the

---

[93]Ibid., 29.
[94]Ibid., 15.
[95]"Avarice [...] is boundless and insatiable." Ibid., 15.
[96]Ibid., 16.

94   AMBITION: AN ESSAY ON THE BURNING DESIRE TO RISE

"barbarization of political morals" that Thucydides had integrated into his history of the Peloponnesian War, shedding light on certain shifts in historical semantics.[97] Sallust's *avaritia* and *ambitio* trace back to Thucydides' pairing of *pleonexia* (desire for more) and *philotimia* (love of honor). During the great war of his own era, Thucydides likewise observed the decline of long-standing ethical standards in favor of a new, "perverse" assessment of human conduct: hesitation came to be thought of as cowardice, decency as an excuse of the fearful, violent temper as manly, guile as clever, treachery as shrewd, etc. "At the root of all this," Thucydides determines, "was the desire for power, based on personal greed and ambition, and the consequent fanaticism of those competing for control."[98] Sallust's adoption of these observations (which now differentiate between love of honor, *cupido gloriae*, and lust for honor, *ambitio*) is less an act of plagiarism than a confirmation of Thucydides' pessimistic worldview that historical events will always unfold in exactly the same way as long as "human nature remains what it is."[99] As Kurt Latte notes, Sallust's reflections only intensify "the impression of gloom and hopelessness that his depiction already arouses, thus contributing to the total picture."[100]

In Sallust's diagnosis, however, the deep rupture that emerged in the stable construction built from the connection between internal peace and aggressive foreign policy was a result of the violent reign of Sulla, who in November 88 BC became the first Roman general to march on Rome with his legions, an act of iniquity that amounted to a desecration of the city. The invasion of Sulla's army brought with it "a newborn idea: that the legitimate authority to delegate state power could be removed from the assembly of the people under supervision of the Senate and transferred to soldiers."[101] The dangerous "new" temptation, according to Sallust, was that Sulla, as a "strong man" in a situation of acute crisis, offered a seemingly attractive alternative to the endless, agonizing debates and altercations that had been become dangerously polarized in

---

[97]Cf. Latte, *Sallust*, 43.
[98]Thucydides, *The War of the Peloponnesians and the Athenians*, translated by Jeremy Mynott (Cambridge: Cambridge University Press, 2013), 213.
[99]Ibid., 212.
[100]Latte, *Sallust*, 46.
[101]Fündling, *Sulla*, 70.

the course of the social conflict between large landowners and impoverished peasants and had escalated into civil war. Sulla "finally put an end" to these enervating controversies, and in 82 BC was appointed dictator for the duration of the state of emergency. With this, he positioned himself "*outside* republican mechanisms"[102] and, through a series of notorious proscriptions, introduced large-scale "cleansing" as a means of terroristic politics. The young Catiline was to serve as "executioner in the hunt for those Sulla had proscribed."[103] The impressive clemency Caesar famously performed in his Senate speech about the Catiline conspiracy was intended to underscore the fundamental difference between him and the vengeful dictator, and to indirectly assure the Roman people that he, likewise a climber with the highest ambitions in the year 63 BC, would never be a new Sulla.

Sulla's tyrannical reign is remembered primarily for the cruelty of his "cleansing" campaign. The revival of proscriptions by the Second Triumvirate was brought to the stage in Shakespeare's *Tragedy of Julius Caesar* exactingly and to terrific effect. With Caesar's murder in Act III, clemency dies, too. In the opening scene of Act IV, Mark Antony, Octavian, and Lepidus sit at a table and coldly draw up the new death lists. The matter-of-fact, bureaucratic calm of the scene stands in extremely sharp contrast to the tumults of Act III, culminating in Antony's cynical proposal to rewrite Caesar's will to the detriment of the Roman plebs, whom he had been able to bring over to his side only shortly before with the aid of this same generous testament.[104]

---

[102]Ibid., 121. Emphasis in original.

[103]Schöne, "Sallust als Historiker," 470.

[104]In his great chronicle of the year 1599, James Shapiro argues that Shakespeare—for various reasons, of course including short-term political considerations—took meticulous efforts in *Julius Caesar* to produce a precise equilibrium between the argument for and against the tyrannicide of an ambitious dictator: "Shakespeare didn't conceive of his tragedy in Aristotelian terms—that is, as a tragedy of the fall of a flawed great man—but rather as a collision of deeply held and irreconcilable principles, embodied in characters who are destroyed when these principles collide." James Shapiro, *1599: A Year in the Life of William Shakespeare* (London: Faber and Faber, 2005), 147. Given this context, the unpleasant proscription scene should thus also be understood as balancing out the tragedy, as it emphasizes the moral dubiousness of the loyal Mark Antony, who in his famous speech in Act III had sought to refute the accusation that "Caesar was ambitious."

96 AMBITION: AN ESSAY ON THE BURNING DESIRE TO RISE

Sulla is also remembered, however, because he demonstrated that the system of the old Republic, strictly organized with respect to the career paths of public officials, was not inviolable, but could be overthrown entirely with raw power. Forms of social advancement that previously were unimaginable now became possible and have remained conceivable ever since. Following Sulla's reign, the Roman Republic dominated by 300 families was just *one* possible option for the political organization of the polity. Sulla broke the spell of the old Republic through the sword. After his death in 78 BC, the dictator who one year earlier had voluntarily resigned and retired to private life left not his restorative body of laws, but "the ambition to match Sulla or to surpass him"[105] as his true legacy. The desire for glory with the aim of being lauded by Rome gave way to the ambition to conquer the city and rule it permanently alone. Sulla's dictatorship ended with a successful restoration, including the disempowerment of the tribunes of the plebs; Caesar's dictatorship would end only with his murder. Thus in the "sewer" of Rome that the patrician Catiline deigned to swim in, "there were many who remembered Sulla's victory" fifteen years after his death:

They saw that some common soldiers had become senators, others so wealthy that they passed their time surrounded by kingly feasts and culture. Everyone expected for himself the same kind of outcome from victory, if it should come to war.[106]

Memories of the dizzying career options that a usurper could open roiled the "sewer"[107] (Sallust uses the word *sentina*, literally: "bilge") that Catiline waded into thus betraying his own class. Profligate and thus debt-ridden upper-class youths, "crowds of vices and crimes,"[108] aging courtesans, even barbarians (Allobroges) and recalcitrant slaves were the clientele who comprised Catiline's following. Crassus, the richest man in Rome,[109] who later avoided any investigation or indictment because so many were "privately

---

[105]Fündling, *Sulla*, 157.
[106]Sallust, *Catiline's Conspiracy*, 28.
[107]Ibid.
[108]Ibid., 16.
[109]Ibid., 18.

ERIS—AGON—AMBITION 97

in debt"[110] to him, may also have been supporting Catiline in the background; Theodor Mommsen goes so far as to staunchly declare Catiline and the other conspirators "tools in the hands of Crassus and Caesar."[111] The social "melting pot" of commoners discreetly supported by financiers and possibly even Caesar himself befits not just the plot "to kill the consuls [...] [and] many senators,"[112] but also the apocalyptic plan to set Rome ablaze and build a new world from the ashes. In the speech that Sallust imagines Catiline delivering to his followers, he shrewdly and accurately invokes the virtues of the old Republic in order to rile up his mob against those segments of the population that in the populist debates of the twenty-first century are often called "the elite." Catiline makes it a point to stoke his supporters' envy and resentment:

All the rest of us, hard-working good men, aristocrats and plebeians, we are a common crowd, without favour and without prestige. We are dependent upon those who would be afraid of us if the Republic meant anything. And so all influence, power, honour, and wealth lie in their hands or where they want it; we are left with dangers, electoral defeats, litigation, and poverty.[113]

Sallust's horrifying depiction of the deaths of the main conspirators— Cornelius Lentulus, for example—who likewise all descended from old families, brings home the image of the "swamp." In the end, those who waded into the muck and mire are strangled to death in a fetid sewer twelve feet under the earth: "[S]qualor, murk, and stench [made] it hideous and terrible to behold. After Lentulus was sent down into this place, the executioners strangled him with a rope as ordered."[114]

But why and how did the "sewer" and the aristocratic scion Catiline come together in the first place? Sallust recognizes or constructs an exact parallel between Catiline's hatred and that of

---

[110]Ibid., 34.
[111]Theodor Mommsen, *Römische Geschichte*, vol. 1, *Könige und Konsuln* (Gütersloh: Bertelsmann, 1957), 766.
[112]Sallust, *Catiline's Conspiracy*, 19.
[113]Ibid., 20.
[114]Ibid., 43

98 AMBITION: AN ESSAY ON THE BURNING DESIRE TO RISE

the have-nots; his characterization of the individual is reflected in his characterization of this social group. The poverty of the dispossessed matches the intemperance and amorality of the "good-for-nothing" Catiline, to whom morality and the order of the state likewise meant "nothing" and who therefore determined, like Sulla before him, that "everything is possible." After Sulla, "everyone began to steal and rob."[115] Those who had nothing allowed themselves to be seduced by a man for whom nothing was sacred; the plan to burn all of Rome to the ground thus became the disturbing symbol of this alliance, which sought to outdo Sulla's restorative politics with an excessive "will to destruction." At the outset of his work, Sallust introduces Catiline, the future conspirator and "master student of Sulla,"[116] as follows:

> L. Catiline was born in an aristocratic family. He was a man of great strength, both mental and physical, but his nature was wicked and perverse. From early adulthood on, he took pleasure in civil wars, murders, plunder, and political discord, and this was where he exercised his youth. His body could endure hunger, cold, sleep-deprivation beyond what one would believe; his mind was an arrogant, clever, unstable. He could pretend or dissemble whatever he liked. He coveted others' property but was profligate with his own; he burned with passionate desires. He had some eloquence, but little wisdom. His mind was vast, always longing for the extravagant, the unbelievable, the things beyond his reach. After the "Domination of Sulla" he was overcome by an extraordinarily powerful desire to seize control of the state. He did not care at all about how he attained his goal as long as he got a "realm" for himself.[117]

Sallust precisely, almost schematically portrays Catiline as the personification of Rome's crisis. A physically powerful Roman of the old school—who even met his ultimate demise fighting bravely on the battlefield—also blessed with rhetorical talent, as a young man he supported Sulla in the civil war of 84–81 BC. From this experience he came to embody *Discordia*, the Roman equivalent

---

[115]Ibid., 15.
[116]Fündling, *Sulla*, 140.
[117]Sallust, *Catiline's Conspiracy*, 12.

ERIS—AGON—AMBITION 99

of the bad Eris, the opposite of *Concordia*, goddess of harmony, the conflict and strife that now once again engulfed the sublime architecture of the Republic. He was the son of an age of pretense, in which dissimulation was honored and endless accumulation of money the only concern. The turning point announced by Sulla's violent reign convinced him that boundless ambition beyond the *cursus honorum* is not absurd if only one ultimately wins. Catiline and the dispossessed found common ground in the promise of Sulla and the career opportunities he opened up. Sallust later describes a corresponding, ideal-typical characteristic of the dispossessed that in his view "always" obtains:

> [F]or it is always the case in a community that the poor despise respectable men, they exalt the disreputable, they hate tradition and call for innovation; they are eager to change everything because they despise their own circumstances; they feed on turmoil and rebellion, and they do not care, since poverty does not cost much and cannot lose much.[118]

In the nefarious scoundrel Catiline, who likewise had nothing to lose and accordingly allied himself with those who had nothing at all, we have our first "C," painted here in garish colors. Mommsen would later also deliver a withering judgment against him: "His knaveries belong in criminal files, not in history."[119] Crassus, by contrast— the second "C"; the personification of faceless, abstract money, of the pure value of exchange; the greedy hoarder who already has everything and therefore also directs everything, the Senate and the plebs alike—remains in Sallust's masterful depiction a shadowy outline in black and white, forever lurking in the background of events. Only his passionate defenders, those who are economically dependent on him, are visible and vociferous. These two great C's join the other three—Cicero, Caesar, and Cato—as towering figures of ambition.

It is decidedly difficult to speak of "humor in Sallust," but there is no lack of entertainment value in studying his oft-noted, oddly

---

[118]Ibid., 28.
[119]Mommsen, *Römische Geschichte*, 764.

100 AMBITION: AN ESSAY ON THE BURNING DESIRE TO RISE

minimizing depiction of the role in this affair of Cicero, who after all was the consul who uncovered Catiline's conspiracy and risked his life multiple times to crush it. It is as though Sallust, a loyal Caesarean partisan, wanted to spite the ambitious *homo novus* and opponent of Caesar, even in death, by belittling him in a work that largely cedes the stage to the sons of old families and pushes the hero of the day to the margins. The repeated branding of Cicero as an upstart is striking; he is and remains "a 'new man'"[120] who efficiently, tirelessly and all too assiduously works for the Optimates. The actual rulers of the city grudgingly suppress their "jealousy and pride" during the crisis and let the new consul operate.[121] Sallust imbues Catiline with character, but offers no characterization of his adversary Cicero, mentioning him only briefly at critical points when he could not do otherwise. He dispenses entirely with any stylized rendition of Cicero's speech against Catiline, who himself was sitting in the Senate at the time, because although it was "brilliant and useful to the Republic," Cicero "later wrote [it] down and published [it]" himself.[122] The point of this seemingly reverential acknowledgment of Cicero's eloquence is not only to note that Cicero delivered not just one, but four famous speeches against Catiline. Sallust also formulates an implicit critique of the ambition of this parvenu whose *index falsi* was his notorious tendency toward self-praise: Cicero himself did enough to highlight his immortal role as the first *pater patriae* ever awarded that title; the historian can thus keep things brief.

Sallust does incorporate the otherwise marginalized hero of the day into the broader framework of his narrative, however, by depicting the scene in which Cicero programmatically assembles the Senate in the Temple of Concordia in order to tighten the rope around Catiline's neck. But he also delivers a harsh historical judgment against him by *denying* him the title of a "great man," that is, a man of *virtus*: virtue, valor, prowess, manliness.

Following the capture of the conspirators who remained in Rome, Cicero retreats into a secondary role, inquiring in the Senate what ought to be done with them. The crucial speeches here

---

[120]Sallust, *Catiline's Conspiracy*, 22.
[121]Ibid.
[122]Ibid., 25.

ERIS—AGON—AMBITION 101

are given one after the other by Caesar and Cato rather than by Cicero, who subsequently becomes the executor hastily organizing the conspirators' deaths. Mommsen, also not exactly an admirer of Cicero's, offers a striking depiction of this cloak-and-dagger operation as a low point in human history:

> Never perhaps had a commonwealth more lamentably declared itself bankrupt than did Rome through this resolution ... to put to death in all haste a few political prisoners, who were no doubt culpable according to the laws, but had not forfeited life; because, forsooth, the security of prisons was not to be trusted, and there was no sufficient police.[123]

In Sallust's view, what distinguished the Romans from the Gauls and the Greeks was that there were always at least a few men who exemplified Roman virtues and advanced the polity as a whole by actively embodying and applying them. In the following remark, we can also see a certain pedagogical intention on the part of Sallust, who here makes the case for a revival of *cupido gloriae*, hoping to ignite in the youth of the day a fervent desire to become one of these distinguished, immortal, virtuous men, and to recognize in themselves the potential to do so:

> And as I considered many possibilities, it became apparent that everything we accomplished was due to the extraordinary abilities of a few citizens. This was the reason that our ancestors' poverty overcame wealth, that a few overcame many. But after the state had been corrupted by luxury and self-indulgence, the Republic still could support the vices of its generals and magistrates because of its sheer size, and, just as when a woman is worn out by childbirth, for a long time at Rome there was hardly anyone great in manly virtue. Still, in my memory there were two men of extraordinary virtue, but different character, [Marcus] Cato and [Gaius] Caesar.[124]

---

[123]Theodor Mommsen, *The History of the Roman Republic*, translated by C. Bryans and F.J.R. Hendy (New York: Scribner, 1889), 382.
[124]Sallust, *Catiline's Conspiracy*, 42.

102 AMBITION: AN ESSAY ON THE BURNING DESIRE TO RISE

While Sallust only points to Cicero's own publication of his great speech, he stylishly reproduces those of Caesar and Cato *in extenso*, giving the impression that the crisis year of 63 BC ultimately was not about the odious swamp conflict between an eager social climber and a failed aristocrat. Both these forms of ambition Sallust brusquely rejects, being rather more concerned with the two modes of being a great Roman that would ensure Rome's viability into the future: the ambition of the conqueror on the one hand and that of the serious and irreproachable man on the other. Rome's virtues of outward aggression and inward competition are here represented in two exemplary personalities who belong to that exclusive stratum of society to whom Sallust's work is addressed. Domestically, the generosity and clemency of Caesar stood in complementary contrast to the frugality and severity of Cato, who kept the city in order: "In one there was refuge for the wretched, in the other death for the wicked."[125]

The direct comparison of these two "great Romans" with each other forms the resplendent climax of Sallust's text, which stands in sharp contrast to the dark depiction of the strangling of the loathsome Lentulus in a stinking sewer that immediately follows it:

> [F]or himself he [Caesar] longed for a great command, an army, a new war in which his excellence [*virtus*] could shine. But Cato's drive was for self-restraint, propriety, moral absolutism. He did not compete with the wealthy in wealth or with the partisans in partisanship; he competed with the fervent in virtue, with the restrained in moderation, with the blameless in abstinence; he preferred to be good than to seem good; and so, the less he sought renown, the more it followed him.[126]

Cato, too, possesses great ambition, as this passage shows, but the laudable ambition of the old style. He embodies the good Eris of productive competition based on *concordia*: to be always more virtuous than the virtuous, more restrained than the restrained, more blameless than the blameless—to be rather than to seem. He attains

---

[125]Ibid., 43.
[126]Ibid.

ERIS—AGON—AMBITION 103

glory because, driven by incorruptible virtue and committed to the common good, he seeks glory not for himself, but only for Rome. Cato's speech before the Senate thus becomes a harsh indictment of derelict morals, of greed and the world of empty semblance ruled by empty money:

> We make no distinction between good and bad men; ambition usurps all the rewards of virtue. And no wonder: when each man of you takes counsel separately for himself, when at home you are slaves to bodily pleasures and here you are slaves to money and influence, this is why the Republic, abandoned by you, has been attacked.[127]

Cato is the only man in Sallust's text about Catiline's conspiracy who upholds those virtues upon which Rome's success was once founded; for Cato, who in Utica chose self-sacrifice over subjugating himself to Caesar, *ambitio* was not about attaining personal glory. His steadfastness made him the epitome of republican ideals through long stretches of European history, as demonstrated by the resounding success of Joseph Addison's 1713 tragedy *Cato*, which inspired the founding fathers of the United States.[128]

Cato's speech is an unrelenting plea calling for the conspirators brought down by *ambitio* to be put to death and prophesying that their coming incarceration in the underworld will be a hellish existence in "places foul, hideous, revolting, and full of fears,"[129] an eternal *sentina*. This is Cato's response to Caesar's more mannered syllogism that "over there" the conspirators would experience neither sorrow nor joy, for which reason the death penalty would actually be an undeserved salvation for them.[130] Of course, idle reflections on the Last Things are not the central focus of these two masterful political speeches. Caesar makes a different argument, declaring his concern that the death penalty will set a dangerous

---

[127]Ibid., 40.
[128]Cf. Dan Poston, *Joseph Addison: An Intellectual Biography* (Charlottesville: University of Virginia Press, forthcoming).
[129]Sallust, *Catiline's Conspiracy*, 40.
[130]Ibid., 37.

104 AMBITION: AN ESSAY ON THE BURNING DESIRE TO RISE

precedent and pointing directly to the terrible example of Sulla, who upon taking power became a butcher:

> Now, I don't fear these consequences from M. Tullius [Cicero] nor do I fear them at this time, but in a great city there are many different temperaments. It is possible that at some other time, when another man is consul and also has an army at his disposal, a lie will be taken for the truth. When this precedent allows the consul by the decree of the Senate to draw his sword, who will stop or restrain him?[131]

That Sallust here puts into the mouth of the future dictator-for-life Julius Caesar an exhortation that can also be read as a warning against himself is still astonishing. And his question has remained an object of intense debate among theorists of sovereignty: Who will stop or restrain the man who decides the state of exception and draws his sword?

Following the assassination of Caesar, who in 44 BC was in fact stopped and restrained by Brutus and his co-conspirators, Sallust himself retreated from politics to private life, dedicating the remaining decade of his life entirely to his work as a historian. Unlike Catiline, Crassus, Cato, Cicero, and even Caesar, he had survived civil war and dictatorship. A wealthy man, he now spent his time writing in one of Caesar's villas, which he had purchased, or in his famous gardens, the *horti Sallusti*. In accordance with Sallust's own self-image, the old form of virtue that in the politics of his age had been almost entirely pushed aside in favor of *avaritia* and *ambitio* also survives in his historical work. Here the good ambition lives on: "[T]he glory of wealth and physical beauty is fluid and fragile; but virtue is held brilliant and eternal."[132] Sallust— who, as he himself freely admits, had in his youth been corrupted by ambition (the source of his ill-gotten wealth, amassed in Africa)— places intellectual and political activity alongside each other as equally worthy of glory:

---

[131]Ibid., 38.
[132]Ibid., 10.

ERIS—AGON—AMBITION 105

It is a beautiful thing to serve the Republic with good deeds; but to speak well is also not without importance. One can achieve brilliance either in peacetime or in war. And many win the praise of others, both those who act and those who write up their actions. As for me, although the glory that comes to the writer is not equal to the glory that comes to the author of deeds, still it seems especially difficult to write history.[133]

In the end, however, even the historian Sallust, of whom Lactantius said that "he would have lived rightly, had he lived the way he wrote,"[134] did not abandon the arena of agon. He, too, desired victory, and now intended to emerge victorious. Although the writer of history usually does not find the same recognition as his hero, in Sallust's view the former stands higher than the latter, for our strength of mind is what we have in common with the gods, "[a]nd so I think it more upright to seek glory with our inner resources than with our physical strength." Sallust, too, is avowedly more concerned with the highest aim of ambition beyond mere self-assertion, with "mak[ing] the memory of our lives as long as possible."[135]

---

[133]Ibid., 11.
[134]Quoted in Schöne, "Sallust als Historiker," 463.
[135]Sallust, Catiline's Conspiracy, 10.

3

Ambition in Modernity

1 A NEW ERA OF AMBITION
Jacob Burckhardt

Plus ultra[1]

Platonic Solids

It has often been remarked that Jacob Burckhardt's famous 1860 essay on *The Civilization of the Renaissance in Italy* does not provide a chronological account of the period from the late thirteenth century through the Sack of Rome. Indeed, it does not simply depict the sequence of historical events from the birth of Dante Alighieri in 1265 through the plundering of the Eternal City by Charles V's troops in 1527, but rather presupposes knowledge of this history of events on the part of its readers. As Philipp Müller

---

[1] "Further beyond," the motto of the Holy Roman Emperor Charles V. William Kerrigan and Gordon Braden say of this imperial ambition: "Charles's personal *impresa* is one of the most resonant of the age: two pillars of Hercules, with the motto *plus ultra*, as if in rising to the standards of antiquity he had surpassed them, on terms that antiquity itself would have acknowledged." While Charles V's political ambitions failed, the "cultural program" of the Renaissance as a reawakening of antiquity exerted a long-lasting influence that has emanated throughout history. William Kerrigan and Gordon Braden, *The Idea of the Renaissance* (Baltimore/London: The Johns Hopkins University Press, 1989), 7.

108 AMBITION: AN ESSAY ON THE BURNING DESIRE TO RISE

notes, Burckhardt's book dismantles the "narrative progression" of the Renaissance, transforming "chronological developments into a textual space."[2] Müller's trenchant comment on the "spatialization" of Burckhardt's presentation is supported by the fact that the art historian Burckhardt divides his essay into six parts, the importance of which he emphasizes by taking the unconventional step of integrating his "Introduction" to the whole into Part I. This dense construction evokes the six sides of a three-dimensional object: a hexahedron, a book block or block of marble, with a front and back, left and right side, and top and bottom. In *The Civilization of the Renaissance in Italy*, Burckhardt chisels this block into a sculpture of the modern individual whose existence is inevitably defined by his or her[3] ambitions.

Newly discovering oneself and others as individuals outside of traditional orders and hierarchies in "[t]he century which escaped from the influence of the Middle Ages"[4] meant, among other things, conceiving of the social world as a competitive society of equals in which the path to success for a person who must fend for himself is paved by personal achievement: "[I]n proportion as distinctions of birth ceased to confer any special privilege, the individual himself was compelled to make the most of his personal qualities."[5] In the Renaissance, the ambition born of modern individuality stretched uncompromisingly, relentlessly, "demonically" toward infinity—"as far as to the stars, no doubt!" Thus, at the level of form, Burckhardt's solid construction with its six sides serves as a stable counterweight to mercurial[6] ambition, a limiting frame, containing and "grounding" it. The hexahedron or cube is one of

---

[2]Philipp Müller, "Jacob Burckhardt, 'Die Kultur der Renaissance in Italien,'" in: Jacob Burckhardt, ed., *Die Kultur der Renaissance in Italien: Ein Versuch* (Frankfurt am Main: Fischer, 2012), 525–7 (526).

[3]In an instructive section on the status of women in the Italian Renaissance, Burckhardt determines that "women stood on a footing of perfect equality with men." Jacob Burckhardt, *The Civilization of the Renaissance in Italy*, translated by S.G.C. Middlemore (New York: The Modern Library), 274.

[4]Ibid., 159.

[5]Ibid., 235f.

[6]Mecury/Hermes is the god of both merchants and thieves as well as of commerce and enterprise of the kind that made Florence and Venice rich. See the section below on David McClelland's theory of motivation.

AMBITION IN MODERNITY   109

the "Platonic solids" of geometry that the philosopher describes in
the *Timaeus* and ascribes to each of the elements—specifically, the
compact shape of the cube is ascribed to *earth* as the densest yet
most malleable of the elements.[7]
During the Renaissance, Plato's *Timaeus*, with its theory of
the connection between geometric figures and the four (or five,
including "aether") elements, was among the most important
reference texts of the Platonic Academy at Florence that Burckhardt
discusses at the very end of his book, and particularly of the great
translator and editor Marsilio Ficino. Ficino—and herein lies the
culmination of Burckhardt's art of tactful allusion—invokes the
authority of the eminently speculative *Timaeus* in the section of
his own *Three Books on Life* (*De vita libri tres*) that considers the
"causes [that] make learned people melancholics."[8] According to
Ficino, the price of the "Faustian" ambition that drives the learned
man to "the investigation [of] the center of individual subjects and
[…] the contemplation of whatever is highest"[9] is melancholy or,
as Burckhardt describes it with an uncharacteristically dramatic
flourish, the "darkening [of] men's whole perceptions of spiritual
things."[10] Those scholars who give themselves over to philosophy
are particularly prone, in Ficino's view, to succumb to leaden Saturn
and the black gall associated with him[11]:

> But of all learned people, those especially are oppressed by black
> bile, who, being sedulously devoted to the study of philosophy,
> recall their mind from the body and corporeal things and apply
> it to incorporeal things. The cause is, first, that the more difficult
> the work, the greater concentration of mind it requires; and

---

[7]Cf. Plato, *Timaeus*, in: Plato, *Timaeus and Critias*, translated by Robin Waterfield
(Oxford: Oxford University Press, 2008), 49f. (55b–55e).
[8]Marsilio Ficino, *Three Books on Life*, edited and translated by Carol V. Kaske and
John R. Clark (Tempe, AZ: The Renaissance Society of America, 1998), 113.
[9]Ibid., 115.
[10]Burckhardt, *The Civilization of the Renaissance in Italy*, 361.
[11]Klibansky, Panofsky, and Saxl go so far as to argue that Saturn "eventually became
the chief patron of the Platonic Academy at Florence." Raymond Klibansky, Erwin
Panofsky, and Fritz Saxl, *Saturn and Melancholy: Studies in the History of Natural
Philosophy, Religion, and Art* (Montreal/Kingston: McGill-Queen's University Press,
2019), 273.

110 AMBITION: AN ESSAY ON THE BURNING DESIRE TO RISE

second, that the more they apply their mind to incorporeal truth, the more they are compelled to disjoin it from the body. Hence their body is often rendered as if it were half-alive and often melancholic. My author Plato signified this in the *Timaeus*.[12]

Burckhardt's ostentatious resistance to philosophical speculation—he leaves the philosophy of the Renaissance largely undiscussed[13] and repeatedly distances himself from theoretical contemplation, refusing to "criticize [...] solely with an eye to [...] intellectual content"[14]—in favor of vivid description of concrete cultural phenomena, including spectacles and fashion trends, arises from his recognition of the melancholic potential of an overly abstract scholarly existence, which he consistently opposes. For Burckhardt, the ambition of the scholar of both philosophy and theoretical psychology necessarily becomes excessive, a view that he found confirmed a decade later in the career path of Friedrich Nietzsche. The following passage on the genesis of modern psychology in literature since Dante, and especially since the poetry of Petrarch, is thus also a commentary on his own procedure, which refrains from excessive theorizing as the ultimate aim of scholarly ambition. Burckhardt dwells in the world of the concrete. He observes and describes, but does not ponder, as deep contemplation has been the mark of the melancholic since antiquity:

> Happily the study of the intellectual side of human nature began, not with the search after a theoretical psychology [...] but with the endeavour to observe and to describe. The indispensable ballast of theory was limited to the popular doctrine of the four temperaments [...].[15]

Burckhardt concludes his theory-resistant essay on the Renaissance with a somewhat mystifying, much-commented-on encomium

---

[12]Ficino, *Three Books on Life*, 115.

[13]Cf. Kerrigan and Braden, *The Idea of the Renaissance*, which seeks to compensate for Burckhardt's "most glaring omission" (xii) with a supplementary discussion of Ernst Cassirer's *The Individual and the Cosmos in Renaissance Philosophy*.

[14]Burckhardt, *The Civilization of the Renaissance in Italy*, 223. Translation slightly modified.

[15]Ibid., 212f.

AMBITION IN MODERNITY 111

to the "Platonic Academy at Florence" and the "circle of chosen spirits" surrounding the great translator and commentator of Plato, Marsilius Ficino.[16] With this, he also closes the circle of his own disquisition; the fluid subject matter and six-part formal structure of his essay finally assume the symmetrical correlation guaranteed by the six Platonic solids. The theism of the Florentine Academy, Burckhardt writes, is capable of harnessing the unleashed ambition of modern subjectivity and integrating it into a harmonious figure, beyond melancholy, composed of soul, God, and earth: "The soul of man can by recognizing God draw Him into its narrow boundaries, but also by love of Him itself expand into the Infinite—and this is blessedness on earth."[17]

David and Perseus

In the Italian Renaissance, we encounter "a boundless ambition and thirst after greatness"[18] as dominant forces in nearly every area of life. Ambition, lust for glory, and often cutthroat competition shaped the politics and art of the Renaissance, its humanism, its voyages of discovery, and its study of nature all in equal measure, in addition to defining the sumptuous festivals of the age and even its fashion, which likewise became an expression of individualism—and the disappearance of which in the realm of men's fashion was lamented even by the reserved, serious nineteenth-century scholar Burckhardt:

> [E]ven serious men [...] looked on a handsome and becoming costume as an element in the perfection of the individual. At Florence, indeed, there was a brief period when dress was a purely personal matter, and every man set the fashion for himself [...]. Our own age, which, in men's dress at any rate, treats uniformity as the supreme law, gives up by so doing far more than it is itself aware of.[19]

---

[16]Ibid., 387.
[17]Ibid.
[18]Ibid., 106.
[19]Ibid., 256.

112 AMBITION: AN ESSAY ON THE BURNING DESIRE TO RISE

In passages such as this, it is clear that Burckhardt always also has his own era in view. Building on Hayden White's assessment that Burckhardt implicitly portrays the Renaissance, "this age of action and splendor," as the antithesis of the "gray world" in which he himself lived, Bernd Roeck argues that the "master narrative" of *The Civilization of the Renaissance in Italy* is that of a "book of longing, written by a man who felt abandoned by God."[20] Burckhardt did indeed view "the Renaissance and the Greco-Roman" world as "far above our own in the sense of beauty"[21]—a sense of beauty that manifested itself in the exemplary depiction of beautiful human forms in sculpture, itself also a monument to great ambitions.

Anyone who visits the Piazza della Signoria in Florence and stands between Michelangelo Buonarroti's *David* and Benvenuto Cellini's *Perseus*—two world-famous statues that programmatically demonstrate the proud ambition of the free city of Florence and the claim to power of the Medicis, respectively, and thus exemplify the power-political confrontation between republicanism and tyranny—will surely acknowledge the cogency of Burckhardt's argument that in the Italian Renaissance, ambition was omnipresent.[22] The two figures also stand in artistic

---

[20]Bernd Roeck, *Der Morgen der Welt: Geschichte der Renaissance* (Munich: C.H. Beck, 2019), 569.

[21]Burckhardt, *The Civilization of the Renaissance in Italy*, 180.

[22]Scholars have repeatedly cast doubt on the cogency of Burckhardt's thesis, however, questioning not the fact that ambition was widespread in the Italian Renaissance, but whether this was "exclusive" to the Italian Renaissance. Johan Huizinga, for example—in *The Waning of the Middle Ages: A Study of the Forms of Life, Thought and Art in France and the Netherlands in the XIVth and XVth Centuries* (London: Edward Arnold, 1924), 59—argues that Burckhardt does not adequately account for the continuities between the Middle Ages and the Renaissance with respect to the prevalence of personal ambition. Dirk Werle, in his monumental work on fame and glory in modernity, further illustrates that, as Burckhardt fails to recognize, the glorification of the "new man" in the Renaissance was not fundamentally new, but rather exhibits certain continuities with the rhetorical tradition dating back to antiquity. He goes on to argue that "Burckhardt's theory of the origins of the 'modern individual' and, with him, 'modern glory' in the Renaissance perhaps says more about the nineteenth century's interest in the great individual and the idea of glory than it does about the unique character of the Renaissance." See Dirk Werle, *Ruhm und Moderne: Eine Ideengeschichte (1750–1930)* (Frankfurt am

AMBITION IN MODERNITY

competition, and not only with respect to the incisive moments they depict (David *before* killing Goliath, Perseus *after* killing Medusa) or the cultural-historical context from which they derive (Old Testament, Greek mythology). The agonal tension between them is also a result of the opposing ideals of masculine beauty they represent. The overexercised, almost insect-like severity of Cellini's *Perseus* stands in sharp contrast to the clear, flowing form of Michelangelo's *David*. Even the materials used by the two sculptors are in competition with each other: white marble versus dark bronze, stone versus metal, precisely corresponding to the two mythic heroes' weapon of choice: the slingshot versus the sword.

Those impressed by these two statues will find further confirmation of Burckhardt's thesis of the fiery ambition of the Italian Renaissance in Cellini's autobiography (translated into German by Goethe), which culminates in a sublime depiction of the fiery, cast-bronze *Perseus*. Burckhardt says of Cellini (indirectly explaining why Goethe chose precisely this furious text to translate): "[H]e lives, such as he was, as a significant type of the modern spirit."[23] With this characterization of the extremely ambitious Cellini as an archetype of the modern man whom we perhaps see in the brutal figure of his *Perseus*, Burckhardt both modifies and deepens his influential and controversial thesis. He conceives of the Italian Renaissance as the age that gave rise to the individual and thus as the beginning of the modern age in Europe, which unleashed a world of relentless

---

Main: Klostermann, 2014), 188f. Finally, Bernd Roeck emphasizes that "the value of the individual and the importance of earthly existence" were first asserted much earlier, during the Middle Ages. With respect to Burckhardt's central thesis, then, one ought to speak of a historical evolution rather than an epochal break (Roeck, *Der Morgen der Welt*, 317). The American Renaissance scholars William Kerrigan and Gordon Braden, on the other hand, are among those who contend that Burckhardt's powerful argument for the "appearance of a newly ambitious individualism" in the Renaissance has withstood its critics, writing that "Burckhardt's thesis receives news like the sea the rain" (Kerrigan and Braden, *The Idea of the Renaissance*, xii). As this book is primarily concerned with certain aspects of the phenomenology of ambition, however, the exposure of historical continuities or the endurance of certain patterns over time is only welcome.

[23]Burckhardt, *The Civilization of the Renaissance in Italy*, 233.

114 AMBITION: AN ESSAY ON THE BURNING DESIRE TO RISE

ambition and tough competition. In this way, he delivers one of the great "origin stor[ies]" of the nineteenth century.[24] In Burckhardt's construction, the particular intensity and ubiquity of ambition in the Italian Renaissance are essentially an expression of the necessarily open-ended process of self-discovery, self-assertion, and self-realization through which the modern age emancipated itself from the previously binding, now questionable structures of the Middle Ages. The decisive factor in this process and progression is thus not the contingent, subjective aspirations of individuals, but rather an objective historical transformation that manifested itself in individual subjects as an irresistible compulsion, a commanding, inescapable "demonic" force:

> In more than one remarkable and dreadful undertaking the motive assigned by serious writers is the burning desire to achieve something great and memorable. This motive is not a mere extreme case of ordinary vanity, but something demonic, involving a surrender of the will, the use of any means, however atrocious, and even an indifference to success itself.[25]

Burckhardt's essay on the Italian Renaissance is therefore particularly relevant for a theory of ambition, as it offers not just a phenomenology of individual ambition but supplements this with analysis of an entire society that at the dawn of modernity conditioned individual subjects *as a whole* to be ambitious, setting them on a path of potentially excessive competition. Martin A. Ruehl pointedly and clearly demonstrates that Burckhardt's characterization of the Renaissance—despite its focus on "culture"—is strikingly similar to Karl Marx and Friedrich Engels' depiction of the competitive capitalist society of the nineteenth century in their *Communist Manifesto*. The economic and social forces first unleashed in fourteenth-century Florence came to a climax in Manchester in the years during which Burckhardt was drafting and writing his own book. Burckhardt, Ruehl argues, understood the Renaissance as a "dress rehearsal" of the capitalism

---

[24]Michael Gamper, *Der große Mann: Geschichte eines politischen Phantasmas* (Göttingen: Wallstein Verlag, 2016), 283.
[25]Burckhardt, *The Civilization of the Renaissance in Italy*, 106.

AMBITION IN MODERNITY   115

of his own era. The "demonic" thus reveals itself as the work of socially enforced competition[26]:

> Burckhardt viewed the Italian Quattrocento [...] meritocratic world of atomized individuals competing with one another on an equal basis, without regard for traditional religious, social and moral constraints. In that respect, Burckhardt's Renaissance Men bore a striking resemblance to the early capitalists described in Marx's *Communist Manifesto*, published twelve years earlier: both were secularizers, rationalizers and demystifiers, pioneering self-made men, as efficient as they were ruthless.[27]

The Six Sides of the Figure

Statues like Michelangelo's *David* and Cellini's *Perseus* could have served as models for Burckhardt's "three-dimensional" arrangement of *The Civilization of the Renaissance in Italy*. In each of the book's six closely related, meticulously constructed parts, he describes one major aspect of the Renaissance: "The State as a Work of Art," "The Development of the Individual," "The Revival of Antiquity," "The Discovery of the World and of Man," "Society and Festivals," and "Morality and Religion." These six titles articulate in condensed form the thetic nexus of Burckhardt's essay, which we must now elaborate in order to bring into view what Burckhardt recognized as the mutually conditional structural connection between individuality and ambition.

The paradigm of the individual was implemented by the *condottieri*, the illegitimate warlords of the early Renaissance: emancipated,

---

[26]Cf. Tocqueville's analogous reflections on the society of equals, discussed in the next section.

[27]Martin A. Ruehl, *The Italian Renaissance in the German Historical Imagination, 1860–1930* (Cambridge: Cambridge University Press, 2015), 64. Kerrigan and Braden elegantly outline the historical transition from the illegitimate *condottieri* to the absolute rulers of the early nation-states. What the *condottieri* were before the demise of the Italian city-states, the rulers of Europe became after: "The *signori* reappear in the established monarchies of France, Spain, and England, their power newly and dramatically strengthened in the political arrangement that comes to be known, at the prompting of Jean Bodin, as absolutism." Kerrigan and Braden, *The Idea of the Renaissance*, 37.

116 AMBITION: AN ESSAY ON THE BURNING DESIRE TO RISE

amoral modern men going their "own way" without regard for tradition.[28] According to Michael Gamper, with this thesis, Burckhardt exposes the "violent beginnings of the *uomo universale*."[29] Burckhardt also presents a quotation from Aeneas Silvius Bartholomeus, the future Pope Pius II (1458–64), that sounds like a distant echo of the age of Sulla's reign of violence that had shaken the foundations of the Roman order: "In our change-loving Italy, where nothing stands firm, and where no ancient dynasty exists, a servant can easily become a king."[30]

This, according to Burckhardt, is the sign of an individual existence: going one's own way, asserting oneself, understanding one's own needs, desires, talents, and aspirations, and insisting on fully developing and realizing oneself. The *condottieri*, as a way of shoring up their otherwise questionable reputations, surrounded themselves with artists and humanists, "the most striking examples and victims of [...] unbridled subjectivity" in the modern age,[31] who in their works depicted, reflected on, and further developed the political and aesthetic idea of modern individualism. For "[t]his keen eye for individuality belongs only to those who have emerged from the half-conscious life of the race [meaning the species, EG] and become themselves individuals."[32] The illegitimacy of the tyrant's rule "isolated [him] and surrounded him with constant danger; the most honourable alliance which he could form was with intellectual merit, without regard to its origin."[33] This brief remark in the first part of Burckhardt's essay hints at something that he later expands on in the fifth, namely the emergence in Renaissance Italy of the first modern society as a society of equals, insofar as what counted was not primarily one's ancestry or origins, but sheer power on the one hand and, on the other, artistic talent, as exemplified by the careers

---

[28]Burckhardt, *The Civilization of the Renaissance in Italy*, 346.

[29]Gamper, *Der große Mann*, 284. Gamper also rightly observes that, in Burckhardt's telling, the modern individual was forged not only by tyranny but also by the radical solitude of exile, as exemplified by Dante. As Burckhardt notes: "The cosmopolitanism which grew up in the most gifted circles is in itself a high stage of individualism." Burckhardt, *The Civilization of the Renaissance in Italy*, 96.

[30]Ibid., 19.

[31]Ibid., 188.

[32]Ibid., 229.

[33]Ibid., 7.

AMBITION IN MODERNITY

of Michelangelo and Leonardo da Vinci. Early in the first part of his book, Burckhardt emphasizes how "awful and God-forsaken"[34] the existence of both the *condottieri* and the artists and intellectuals serving them was, thus drawing a line to the sixth and final part, in which he explains why individuality and evil seem to become one and nearly indistinguishable from one another.

In the realm of poetry, according to Burckhardt, Dante stands at the beginning of the trend toward reflexive individuality. If one studies literature, he writes in a particularly elegant passage, it seems "that throughout the Middle Ages the poets have been purposely fleeing from themselves, and that he [Dante] was the first to seek his own soul."[35] As Kerrigan and Braden note in their concise summary of Burckhardt's section on the genesis of individualism, the modern individual is characterized by his "self-conscious uniqueness," "proud reflexivity," and "the possibility of self-possession offering itself as its own justification."[36] The political power of the early Renaissance warlords mutually depended on and reinforced the growing journalistic power of the equally amoral poet-philologists, who rose to become the ambitious *condottieri* of the intellectual world:

> The new race of poet-scholars which arose soon after Dante quickly made themselves masters of this fresh tendency. They did so in a double sense, being themselves the most acknowledged celebrities of Italy, and at the same time, as poets and historians, consciously disposing of the reputation of others. An outward symbol of this sort of fame was the coronation of the poets [...].[37]

In this way, the prominent and feared satirist Pietro Aretino became "the father of modern journalism,"[38] embodying "the first great instance of the abuse of publicity to such ends" (beggary, extortion, etc.).[39] The Italian poet-scholars had "the fullest consciousness that

---

[34]Ibid., 10.
[35]Ibid., 216.
[36]Kerrigan and Braden, *The Idea of the Renaissance*, 11.
[37]Burckhardt, *The Civilization of the Renaissance in Italy*, 101.
[38]Ibid., 115.
[39]Ibid., 114.

118 AMBITION: AN ESSAY ON THE BURNING DESIRE TO RISE

[they were] the giver[s] of fame and immortality, or, if [they] chose, of oblivion."[40] They were the first public relations agents, fulfilling the ambitious desires of their clients and in so doing becoming famous themselves. Burckhardt describes the Renaissance idea of fame as "modern" not only because it rests on a recognition of the power of media, but also because, on the one hand, it substantiates, cements, and glorifies the kind of "distinction" that is not rooted in tradition but rather is "won by a man's personal efforts"[41] and, on the other hand, establishes and ensures the "immortality" of a man's name beyond Christian notions of the immortality of the soul. The fact that "the Roman authors, who were now zealously studied, are filled and saturated with the conception of fame"[42] contributed significantly to strengthening modern, purely worldly fame through recourse to ancient models and further fueling the ambition of the epoch. Ambition needs fame as its correlate so as not to lose itself in oblivion, and the poet-philologists exclusively delivered this correlate on commission. Burckhardt quotes an insight of Machiavelli's that anticipates the still widely accepted PR rule that there is no such thing as bad publicity:

They [the previous generation of historians, EG] erred greatly and showed that they understood little the ambition of men and the desire to perpetuate a name. How many who could distinguish themselves by nothing praiseworthy strove to do so by infamous deeds![43]

The "reawakening" of antiquity—first of Roman culture, still formative in Italy, and later of Greek culture—depicted in the third part of Burckhardt's essay provided critical momentum as modern individuals differentiated and distanced themselves from the traditional religious, ethical, and social order of the Middle Ages. With the Renaissance reception of antiquity, a second intellectual

---

[40]Ibid., 105. On this entire complex, see Dirk Werle's great study of fame and glory in modernity, *Ruhm und Moderne*.
[41]Burckhardt, *The Civilization of the Renaissance in Italy*, 105.
[42]Ibid., 100.
[43]Cited in ibid., 106.

AMBITION IN MODERNITY 119

and spiritual power emerged alongside the church, becoming a countervailing force:

> The general result of it consists in this—that by the side of the Church which had hitherto held the countries of the West together (though it was unable to do so much longer) there arose a new spiritual influence which, spreading itself abroad from Italy, became the breath of life for all the more instructed minds in Europe.[44]

This is the very aspect highlighted by the term "Renaissance," a beautiful but also controversial designation of the epoch. Burckhardt emphasizes that "it was not the revival of antiquity alone, but its union with the genius of the Italian people"[45] since the late Middle Ages that ushered in the modern age, and he describes the "measureless devotion to antiquity in the fifteenth century" in great detail.[46] Passionate commitment to the most comprehensive possible analysis of the classical tradition and, specifically, the beginnings of "historical criticism"[47] made it possible for Renaissance Italians to now view the Middle Ages from outside as a past era and, at the same time, see themselves as "new": "[I]t was the study of antiquity which made the study of the Middle Ages possible, by first training the mind to habits of impartial historical criticism."[48]

Machiavelli's fundamental insight that what is most essential is to see the world as it really is, to speak only of "things [...] that are true," and to "search after the effectual truth" of matters[49]—an application of the reality principle that epitomizes *realpolitik* to this day—represents an effective summary of the fourth part of Burckhardt's essay, on the discovery of the world and of man. This section begins with an appreciation of Christopher Columbus and Amerigo Vespucci, two great explorers of the *Mundus Novus* who,

---

[44]Ibid., 120.
[45]Ibid., 121.
[46]Ibid., 140.
[47]Ibid., 168.
[48]Ibid., 168.
[49]Niccolò Machiavelli, *The Prince*, translated by Peter Bondanella and Mark Musa (Oxford: Oxford University Press, 1984), 52.

120 AMBITION: AN ESSAY ON THE BURNING DESIRE TO RISE

hailing from different cities (Genoa and Florence, respectively), were also competitors. This is followed by a series of passages—groundbreaking in intellectual, literary, and art history alike—on the discovery of the beauty of *landscape*. The experience and depiction of landscapes in Renaissance literature and panel paintings demonstrate not only that in Italy "nature had by this time lost its taint of sin, and had shaken off all trace of demoniacal powers," but also that there had emerged at this time an awareness of "distance" that illuminates the as yet little discussed affinity between landscape and the wanderlust of the explorers of the age.[50] Manifested in this awareness of distance is the longing of the modern subject to discover himself and the world. Landscape is not an objective assessment of elements in space, but a new form of perception, floating between subject and object as a membrane. As Joachim Ritter writes, with a view to Petrarch's famous ascent of Mount Ventoux, "Landscape is nature that is aesthetically present in the sight of a feeling and sensing observer."[51] Man's experiences of the external world and of his inner world—as exemplified by his experience of landscape—are mutually interwoven and mutually reinforcing. Together, they generate the consciousness of the modern human being who seeks and takes responsibility for his belief or unbelief in purely subjective terms, experiencing the world in its worldliness, as a site of power and of art, to be taken pleasure in and studied:

> These modern men, the representatives of the culture of Italy, were born with the same religious instincts as other medieval Europeans. But their powerful individuality made them in religion, as in other matters, altogether subjective, and the intense charm which the discovery of the inner and outer universe exercised upon them rendered them markedly worldly.[52]

The fifth part of Burckhardt's essay—which bears the rather innocuous title "Society and Festivals," but in fact delivers a microsociology of the Renaissance—describes "the fusion of classes

---

[50]Burckhardt, *The Civilization of the Renaissance in Italy*, 206.
[51]Joachim Ritter, "Landschaft," in: Ritter, *Subjektivität: Sechs Aufsätze* (Frankfurt: Suhrkamp, 1989), 141–63 (150).
[52]Burckhardt, *The Civilization of the Renaissance in Italy*, 345.

AMBITION IN MODERNITY

in the modern sense of the phrase"[53] as a general characteristic of an age in which "early traces of a general society"[54] emerged in part as a long-term consequence of the discovery of a "New World" in 1492: "[I]t might well seem that the age of equality had dawned, and the belief in nobility vanished for ever."[55] Here we find Burckhardt's abovementioned insight that, in a society of equals, constant competition will necessarily become the *modus operandi* of its subjects, as ambition to climb the social ladder inevitably pervades every social context: "[I]n proportion as distinctions of birth ceased to confer any special privilege, the individual himself was compelled to make the most of his personal qualities."[56] Of course, for large swaths of the population in Renaissance Italy, and later in France, social equality remained only a fleeting dream, as Burckhardt himself implicitly acknowledged with his suggestion that it might well "seem"—if only for a moment, in light of the spectacular social ascent of certain individuals—that an age of equality had dawned. Max Horkheimer's great essay "Montaigne and the Function of Social Skepticism," which begins with a long quotation from Burckhardt's *The Greeks and Greek Civilization*, thus emphasizes the social privileges that made possible the ataraxia of a man whose *Essays*, a philosophical summation of Renaissance individualism, give expression to "the Stoicism of the rich."[57] In contrast to the privileged interiority of the philosopher, Horkheimer continues,

[a]t the same time, a kind of interiority developed among the masses that had nothing to do with restfulness. The collapse of the feudal order drove the poor into unaccustomed and arduous work in manufactures. Unemployment and the rising price of food compelled people to hire themselves out at every opportunity. A

---

[53]Ibid., 249.
[54]Ibid., 100.
[55]Ibid., 250.
[56]Ibid., 235f.
[57]Max Horkheimer, "Montaigne and the Function of Skepticism," in: Horkheimer, *Between Philosophy and Social Science: Selected Early Writings*, translated by G. Frederick Hunter, Matthew S. Kramer, and John Torpey (Cambridge, MA: The MIT Press, 1993), 265–312 (272). On Montaigne, see the afterword below on the ambition to forsake ambition.

122 AMBITION: AN ESSAY ON THE BURNING DESIRE TO RISE

new labor discipline became necessary. The comfortable mode of work still dominant in France in the sixteenth century was less and less compatible with modern competition.[58]

The sixth and final section of Burckhardt's essay—a bold work of intellectual history to which I can by no means fully do justice here—describes the transformation of morality and religion in the course of the Italian Renaissance. The dissolution of the traditional medieval order, the discovery of subjectivity and the outside world—the globe—the beginnings of historical awareness and historical criticism, the reawakening of "sensuous antiquity" and the corresponding differentiation of a "sense of beauty," and the advent of modern science and medicine (anatomy) all worked together to give birth to the idea of a decidedly "personal religion"[59] that attained its theological elaboration during the Reformation and, in the course of the sixteenth century, led to the second great schism of the Christian Church. The emergence of individual religiosity, however, was accompanied by a decline in religious substance overall. In Italy, Burckhardt notes with the nonchalance of an Enlightenment thinker spinning a narrative of discovery, "each individual [...] went his own way, and thousands wandered on the sea of life without any religious guidance whatever."[60] At the same time, there was also an "epidemic of religious revivals,"[61] epitomized by the rise of Savonarola in Florence, along with growing interest in astrology and magic. In spite of all assertions to the contrary, humanism "was in fact pagan, and became more and more so as its sphere widened in the fifteenth century," and its representatives were "the advance guard of an unbridled individualism."[62]

Petrarch's *Secretum*, a trilogy of dialogues written between 1347 and 1353, offers an early—and, for the history of modern ambition, eminently instructive—example of the conflict between humanists' concern for their own salvation and their deep love of books, ancient ones to be read and new ones to be written. Here the poet,

---

[58]Ibid., 273.
[59]Burckhardt, *The Civilization of the Renaissance in Italy*, 346.
[60]Ibid.
[61]Ibid., 342.
[62]Ibid., 352.

AMBITION IN MODERNITY

123

plagued by depression while working on what he intends to be his magnum opus, the epic poem *Africa*, engages in a three-day-long debate, under the watchful eye of *Veritas*, with the manifestation of Saint Augustine, who aims to dissuade him from "this pursuit of a false immortality of fame."[63] In the end, Augustine must relent in the face of the defiance of the modern spirit: "You seem inclined to leave yourself derelict, rather than your books."[64] Petrarch ultimately decides to put off worrying about his salvation to some undetermined future date, after he has completed the major work that will make him immortal; he cannot do otherwise. The poet's ambition is stronger than the fear of God that the saintly apparition tries to put into him over the course of three days. Worries about the afterlife will have to wait until Petrarch is finished:

> I confess [that attending to the salvation of the soul is of necessity in light of our certain death, EG]. And I now return to attend to those other concerns only in order that, when they are discharged, I may come back to [this one]. I am not ignorant that, as you said a few minutes before, it would be much safer for me to attend only to the care of my soul, to relinquish altogether every bypath and follow the straight path of the way of salvation. But I have not strength to resist that old bent for study altogether.[65]

Against this backdrop, Martin Luther's preface to the first volume of his German writings, published nearly two centuries later in 1539, reads like a grand revocation of the humanist ambition to achieve immortality by writing books. "I would rather have seen all my books hidden and then disappear,"[66] Luther writes, as to read them means that one is not reading the only book that actually matters, namely the Bible. At least from the perspective of critics of religion such as Nietzsche, the Reformation represents a precarious

---

[63]Petrarch, *Petrarch's Secret or The Soul's Conflict with Passion: Three Dialogues between Himself and Augustine*, translated by William H. Draper (London: Chatto & Windus, 1911), 166.

[64]Ibid., 184.

[65]Ibid., 192.

[66]Martin Luther, "Preface to Luther's German Writings: The Wittenberg Edition (1539)," in: Luther, *The Ninety-Five Theses and Other Writings*, translated and edited by William R. Russell (New York: Penguin, 2017), 194–9 (194).

124 AMBITION: AN ESSAY ON THE BURNING DESIRE TO RISE

effort to restore the Middle Ages under the conditions of modern subjectivity. Humanists and theologians who succumb to authorial pride and the lust for fame are, in Luther's view, nothing but asses destined for hell. He thus sees here primarily the dark side of modern individuality, the hypertrophy of "self-seeking." In Luther, honor is once again due to God alone; ambition, the thirst for honor, is the stuff of the devil:

> [I]f you think you have made it and want to boost your own ego—flattering yourself with your own little books, doctrines, and writings, when you've done it beautifully and preached excellently; greatly pleased when someone praises you in the presence of others; if you perhaps look for praise, and would sulk or quit what you are doing if you did not get it—if you are like that, my friend, then take yourself by the ears, and if you do it right, will find a beautiful pair of big, long, shaggy donkey ears. Then do not spare any expense! Decorate them with golden bells, so that people will be able to hear you wherever you go, point their fingers at you, and say, "Look! Look! There goes that clever beast, who can write such exquisite books and preach so remarkably well." Then you will be blessed way beyond measure in the kingdom of heaven. Yes, in that heaven where hellfire is ready for the devil and his angels.
>
> To summarize: Let us be proud and seek honor in the places where we can. But in this book the honor is God's alone, as it is said, "God opposes the proud, but gives grace to the humble" [1 Peter 5:5]; to whom be glory, world without end, Amen.[67]

With scarcely concealed contempt in the sixth part of his essay, Burckhardt adds to the ensemble of factors that contributed to the epochal transformation leading to the birth of the early modern age, the guilt of the Church, which during the Renaissance recruited its leaders from mafia families like the Borgias and Medicis, prompting Luther to declare that the pope had inevitably "become Antichrist."[68] Burckhardt writes:

---

[67]Ibid., 198f.
[68]Ibid., 196.

AMBITION IN MODERNITY 125

But history does not record a heavier responsibility than that which rests upon the decaying Church. She set up as absolute truth, and by the most violent means, a doctrine which she had distorted to serve her own aggrandizement. Safe in the sense of her inviolability, she abandoned herself to the most scandalous profligacy.[69]

In Burckhardt's dialectical argument, the papacy and, with it, the Catholic Church, undoubtedly would have perished "if the Reformation had not saved it."[70] To him, the weight of the Roman Catholic Church's historical responsibility is extraordinarily heavy. The superlative that Burckhardt employs twice in this critical passage, along with his highly unusual emphasis of the *singularity* of the event—"history does not record a heavier responsibility"—at least seems to suggest that he considers the failure of the *Ecclesia Sancta* to be principally responsible for the emergence of modern subjectivity, although this cannot be stated definitively. But we can understand these sentences to mean that the human beings abandoned by the profligate Church were left with no other alternative than to become individuals and follow their own path. The options presented by these circumstances, as well as the consequences for ethics, which now had to be rethought for modern individuals, form the subject matter of Burckhardt's concluding reflections.

Individuality and Evil

From the perspective of the Church, however corrupted, and indeed from the perspective of any sanctioning regime, a person who insists on taking "his own path," realizing himself along this path, and thus stepping out of line is latently or manifestly "evil." In this way, individual existence, "willfulness," and evil are conflated to the point of being indistinguishable from one another:

[I]t was Machiavelli, who, in one of his most well-considered works, said openly: "We Italians are irreligious and corrupt

---

[69]Burckhardt, *The Civilization of the Renaissance in Italy*, 320.
[70]Ibid., 324.

126 AMBITION: AN ESSAY ON THE BURNING DESIRE TO RISE

above others.' Another man would have perhaps said, "We are individually highly developed; we have outgrown the limits of morality and religion which were natural to us in our undeveloped state, and we despise outward law, because our rulers are illegitimate, and their judges and officers wicked men." Machiavelli adds, "because the Church and her representatives set us the worst example." Shall we add also, "because the influence exercised by antiquity was in this respect unfavourable"? The statement can only be received with many qualifications. It may possibly be true of the humanists, especially as regards the profligacy of their lives. Of the rest it may perhaps be said, with some approach to accuracy, that, after they became familiar with antiquity, they substituted for holiness—the Christian ideal of life—the cult of historical greatness.[71]

Burckhardt in this passage once again significantly deepens our understanding of modern ambition. The success and fame aspired to by the modern individual here take on the function previously possessed by the ideal of the Christian life: *ambition now serves as the organizing principle of the life of all individuals.* The immortality of the soul here gives way to immortal fame as the goal of mortal life, with the classical concept of *gloria* providing the great examples of the likes of Caesar and Augustus. Fame and—to use an anachronistic term—"prominence" are idolized. Burckhardt's concept of ambition differentiates itself not only through its recognition of ambition as a social dynamic that "demonically" infiltrates the individual will of subjects living in a competitive society. It also illuminates why ambition is inevitably met with ambivalence.

Ambition is double-edged because to be an individual is double-edged: free, but at the same time forsaken; longing for and excited about the future, but at the same time empty; asserting a singular identity, but at the same time incapable of ever becoming "one" with this identity that we claim to be our "self." Ambition is latently excessive because the modern individual, incapable of healing the rupture produced by the reflexivity of living for himself alone, even through the greatest successes, is constantly transcending himself.

---

[71]Ibid., 300f.

AMBITION IN MODERNITY

Or put another way, the ultimate object of individual ambition is an answer to the question of the meaning of one's own identity and life, a question to which there can be no answer outside of a revealed religion. Every spectacular success or brilliant triumph thus inevitably rings hollow, because it does not bring with it this secretly longed-for answer and so pulls the individual ever further into a bad infinity. This pull moreover brings a personal, existential poignancy to the constant struggle of competition, which can never attain its ultimate goal of overcoming meaninglessness and conquering death. The seventeenth-century philosopher Blaise Pascal hits on precisely this sensitive point of modern ambition in one of his most famous, edifying *pensées*, where he insists that even a king will be "unhappy" if he begins to "consider and reflect on what he is."[72] Given the chaotic, never-ending competitive battles among men at court and in war, it is evident to Pascal that "man's unhappiness springs from one thing alone, his incapacity to stay quietly in one room."[73]

Burckhardt highlights the double-edged nature of ambition that announces itself as an unbearable tension even in the quiet of one's study in a brilliant chapter on the "fall of the humanists in the sixteenth century," whom he considers to be exemplary exponents, the avant-garde of God-forsaken subjectivity, in the "uncertainty"[74] of whose public existence the uncertainty of existence itself is laid bare. Burckhardt paints the precarious life of the humanists in bold colors as one that "only the strongest characters could pass through [...] unscathed,"[75] a life of "malicious self-conceit," "abominable profligacy," and "irreligion"[76] that frequently ended in "madness" and "suicide."[77] Critically, many of the conflicts Burckhardt depicts were not imposed from without, but flared up among the intellectuals, poets, and professors themselves, who mutually reproached each other as wicked and depraved:

---

[72]Blaise Pascal, *Pensées and Other Writings*, translated by Honor Levi, edited by Anthony Levi (Oxford: Oxford University Press, 1995), 45.
[73]Ibid., 44.
[74]Burckhardt, *The Civilization of the Renaissance in Italy*, 186.
[75]Ibid., 187.
[76]Ibid., 185.
[77]Ibid., 189.

128 AMBITION: AN ESSAY ON THE BURNING DESIRE TO RISE

The first to make these charges were certainly the humanists themselves. Of all men who ever formed a class, they had the least sense of their common interests, and least respected what there was of this sense. All means were held lawful, if one of them saw a chance of supplanting another. From literary discussion they passed with astonishing suddenness to the fiercest and the most groundless vituperation. Not satisfied with refuting, they sought to annihilate an opponent.[78]

The humanists—and this makes the chapter on their downfall perhaps the *punctum* of the entire book *pro domo et mundo*—were sociologically the experimental laboratory of modern individuality, "the most striking examples and victims of an unbridled subjectivity."[79] Invoking Pierio Valeriano's *On the Ill Fortune of Learned Men*, Burckhardt determines that these representatives of the new all suffer from the "modern disease." Their bottomless hatred of others is at bottom self-loathing; their will to destruction, an expression of chronic pain: "Who, after all, is happy? And by what means?"[80] The example of the humanists, who were incapable of joining together in solidarity and instead tore each other apart, offers an exemplary illustration of the problem of ethics and good politics following the disempowerment of Christianity.

While Burckhardt's essay may aptly be described as a "book of longing" that elaborates a brilliant antithesis to the drab everyday world of modernity, it is in no way meant to espouse a modern revival of the so-called "Renaissance man." Rather, it just as decidedly presents an accounting of how the dreary horror of modernity emerged *simultaneously* amidst the splendor of the Renaissance. It does not shy away from depicting the horrors and "profligacy" of the epoch and, unlike more idolatrous writers of the *fin de siècle*, accusing Cesare Borgia, the son of Pope Alexander VI, of taking a "devilish delight" in the "destruction" of his enemies and engaging in "cruelties" that "were certainly out of all proportion to the end which he had in view."[81] Burckhardt's book towers over such

---

[78]Ibid., 185f.
[79]Ibid., 188.
[80]Ibid., 190.
[81]Ibid., 318.

AMBITION IN MODERNITY 129

monstrosities of history as a dignified, vividly rendered reflection on the question of the possibility of an ethics of modernity. Among the consequences of modern individualism, the ethics of Christianity, as a theory of sin, lost its binding force. The contours of a fundamentally new modern ethics began to emerge that neither is able to measure actions according to a Platonic idea of the good nor operates with a concept of sin, but nevertheless differentiates between "good" and "evil":

> Finally, these intellectual giants, these representatives of the Renaissance, show, in respect to religion, a quality which is common in youthful natures. Distinguishing keenly between good and evil, they yet are conscious of no sin. Every disturbance of their inward harmony they feel themselves able to make good out of the plastic resources of their own nature, and therefore they feel no repentance. The need of salvation thus becomes felt more and more dimly, while the ambitions and the intellectual activity of the present either shut out altogether every thought of a world to come, or else caused it to assume a poetic instead of a dogmatic form.[82]

Burckhardt in this passage provides a quasi-aesthetic and even vitalistic answer to the question of good and evil in nascent modernity. Plastic resources set things right again; the answer to a disruption of harmony is beautiful (poetic) form. Herfried Münkler, by contrast, argues that it was Machiavelli who laid the foundations of modern political philosophy outside of any substantive conceptions of good and evil. Burckhardt confirms that the intellectuals of the Italian Renaissance "distinguish keenly between good and evil," but on what basis and by dint of what authority, once the theology of sin and the classical idea of the good have lost their binding force and persuasive power? The historical novelty, according to Münkler, consists in the fact that, in modern political theory, right and ethics, good and evil are recognized as derivative concepts, no longer absolute, but relative, and dependent on the existing state. In Machiavelli, the state and nothing else emerges as the new absolute:

---

[82]Ibid., 345f.

130 AMBITION: AN ESSAY ON THE BURNING DESIRE TO RISE

[Machiavelli's] theory of the perpetual corruptibility of human beings supplies the moral foundation underpinning the rationally calculated absolute norm of the self-preservation of the state by any means and at any cost. The state itself becomes the creator of the good by directing its force and authority against the evil immanent in human volition and conduct. In Machiavelli, right, mores, and morality originate in the state.[83]

For Machiavelli—as Münkler also emphasizes, with reference to the abovementioned poem *Dell' ambizione*—the excessive "ambition and avarice" born of the "uncertain" existence of modern individuality represent the epitome of human corruptibility: "What men pursue *per ambizione* must be constrained and limited by the political order."[84] Burckhardt, for his part, likewise declares "self-seeking" that metastasizes into ambition and greed to be the root of all evil. But he does not endorse the idea that nothing remains following the dismantling of the theological order but Machiavelli's deification of the state. Burckhardt writes:

If therefore egotism in its wider as well as narrower sense is the root and fountain of all evil, the more highly developed Italian was for this reason more inclined to wickedness than the members of other nations of that time. But this individual development did not come upon him through any fault of his own, but rather through an historical necessity. It did not come upon him alone, but also, and chiefly, by means of Italian culture, upon the other nations of Europe, and has constituted since then the higher atmosphere which they breathe. In itself it is neither good nor bad, but necessary; within it has grown up a modern standard of good and evil—a sense of moral responsibility—which is essentially different from that which was familiar to the Middle Ages.[85]

---

[83]Herfried Münkler, *Machiavelli: Die Begründung des politischen Denkens der Neuzeit aus der Krise der Republik Florenz*, 2nd ed. (Frankfurt am Main: Fischer, 2007), 266.
[84]Ibid., 268.
[85]Burckhardt, *The Civilization of the Renaissance in Italy*, 319.

AMBITION IN MODERNITY 131

The evolution of human beings into individuals is by no means, or not only, simply a license to evil. It is also a higher medium, bringing with it what Kant would later call a "moral imputation," meaning that, as an individual, one must personally vouch for what one has done or refrained from doing. Burckhardt is entirely aware that, on this point, Machiavelli would point him to the wickedness of man and the corresponding indifference of figures like Cesare Borgia and his successors. Thus all that remains for Burckhardt in the end is the sublime gesture of turning the concept of ambition in on itself and declaring a *sense of honor* to be the ultimate, fragile ethical authority of modernity. Cesare Borgia and all those who act like him are *without honor*. Reflected ambition would be the ability not to violate one's own sense of honor or that of others. The sense of honor

is that enigmatic mixture of conscience and egotism which often survives in the modern man after he has lost, whether by his own fault or not, faith, love and hope. [...] It has become, in a far wider sense than is commonly believed, a decisive test of conduct in the minds of the cultivated Europeans of our own day, and many of those who yet hold faithfully by religion and morality are unconsciously guided by this feeling in the gravest decisions of their lives.[86]

---

[86]Ibid., 301.

132 AMBITION: AN ESSAY ON THE BURNING DESIRE TO RISE

2 THE AMBITION OF EQUALS
Alexis de Tocqueville

Now I know only two ways to have equality rule in the political world: rights must either be given to each citizen or given to no one.[1]

The Equality of the Bourgeoisie

"[T]his small domestic enterprise absorbs all of his thoughts for the moment and makes him wish to put public agitations off to another time."[2]

With this sentence, the French sociologist and politician Alexis de Tocqueville (1805–59) precisely captured the bourgeois consciousness of the nineteenth century. It probably would have elicited a smile from his contemporaries Stendhal and Balzac, the great chroniclers of the epoch. The bourgeois, concerned about his property and the flourishing of his business, dreads revolution and social upheaval, which is mostly bad for business and might deprive him of his effects: "I know nothing more opposed to revolutionary mores than commercial mores."[3] The catch with the busy bourgeois' request that the revolution be deferred is of course that business is always being conducted; public unrest therefore must always be "put off until later," and so the revolution never occurs. Overcoming the social conflicts and bitter class antagonisms of bourgeois society in the industrial age, the drama of and reasons for which the young Friedrich Engels exemplarily depicts and analyzes in his pathbreaking 1845 study *The Condition of the Working Class in England*, is not something to be achieved through the bringing about of a new socialist order, but rather must be inexorably postponed for the benefit of the status quo:

---

[1]Alexis de Tocqueville, *Democracy in America*, edited by Eduardo Nolla, translated by James T. Schleifer (Indianapolis: Liberty Fund, 2012), 89.
[2]Ibid., 1139.
[3]Ibid., 1138.

AMBITION IN MODERNITY

133

If you attentively consider each one of the classes that compose society, it is easy to see that in no class are the passions that arise from property more ruthless and more tenacious than among the middle class.[4]

The fierce class antagonism between bourgeoisie and proletariat that came to define European history beginning in the mid-nineteenth century remains but a distant storm gathering on the horizon of Tocquesville's monumental and still fascinating work of cultural sociology *Democracy in America*, published in two volumes in 1835 and 1840.[5] Tocqueville—who in 1831 and 1832, under commission by the French government, traversed the vast distances of the young United States, studied its institutions, and detailed the influence of those institutions on the intellect, sentiments, and mores of Americans[6]—comes before Marx and Engels, and not only historically. On a foreign continent, he studied and experienced the first modern republic, where the old European stratification of nobility (from which he himself descended), clergy, and third estate no longer played a defining role, where there were "so to speak no longer any classes"[7] and industrialization, which would produce the fourth estate, was just beginning. Tocqueville visited a country of equals where, at least according to the 1776 *Declaration of Independence*, all human beings were born free, equal, and with inalienable rights and, beginning in 1789, lived in a constitutional republic defined by the US Constitution: "The social state of the Americans is eminently democratic."[8] Compared to Europe, the historical novelty of this young nation constantly expanding to the south and west lay in the fact that it was comprised of immigrants

---

[4]Ibid., 1136.

[5]For an overview of Tocqueville's historical place in his own era, his modern empirical methodology (interviews, etc.), his theoretical and political positions, and his relevance today, see Skadi Siiri Krause's summation of the most recent research on Tocqueville, *Eine neue Politische Wissenschaft für eine neue Welt: Alexis de Tocqueville im Spiegel seiner Zeit* (Berlin: Suhrkamp, 2017).

[6]The first three parts of the second volume of Tocqueville's study are titled "Influence of Democracy on the Intellectual Movement in the United States," "Influence of Democracy on the Sentiments of the Americans," and "Influence of Democracy on Mores Properly So Called."

[7]Tocqueville, *Democracy in America*, 700.

[8]Ibid., 75.

134 AMBITION: AN ESSAY ON THE BURNING DESIRE TO RISE

from many other countries. It was not defined by a "people," but held together by an "idea" that radiated around the world: "It is hardly the happy and the powerful who go into exile, and poverty as well as misfortune are the best guarantees of equality that are known among men."[9]

Tocqueville also ascertained, however, that the already impressive success of this republic of equals, as he extensively details and passionately condemns, rested on racially motivated inequality: the displacement, deportation, and large-scale extermination of the country's indigenous people and the indefensible "evil" of slavery.[10] The equals in America were white people. In light of the specific social situation in the United States, Tocqueville developed a different perspective on a possible revolution in the New World: "If America ever experiences great revolutions, they will be brought about by the presence of Blacks on the soil of the United States: that is to say that it will be not equality of conditions, but on the contrary inequality of conditions that gives birth to them."[11] In the course of his on-site research, he clearly recognized the growing tensions between the Northern and Southern states and foresaw the US Civil War of 1861–5:

> Whatever the efforts of the Americans of the South to keep slavery, moreover, they will not succeed forever. Slavery, squeezed into a single point of the globe, attacked by Christianity as unjust, by political economy as fatal; slavery, amid the democratic liberty and the enlightenment of our age, is not an institution that can endure. It will end by the deed of the

---

[9]Ibid., 50.

[10]Ibid., 549. For a detailed contextualization of these subjects, see Skadi Siiri Krause, *Eine neue Politische Wissenschaft*, 429–73. Krause emphasizes the originality of Tocqueville's arguments on the expulsion and killing of Native Americans and on slavery: "In contrast to contemporary discourse that condemned slavery on moral-philosophical and political-economical grounds, Tocqueville's concern is to analyze racism in a democratic society where social inequality and culturally constructed attributions of difference no longer serve to distinguish between classes and estates. Long before Pierre Bourdieu, Tocqueville succeeds in describing social inequality across multiple dimensions, incorporating into his analysis not only juridical, but also economic, social, cultural, and symbolic resources. Race thus becomes a specific form of symbolic capital examined through the lens of its reproduction and the self-conception of blacks and whites" (ibid., 434).

[11]Tocqueville, *Democracy in America*, 1141.

AMBITION IN MODERNITY   135

slave or by that of the master. In both cases, great misfortunes must be expected.[12]

Democracy and Solitude

As can be seen in this prophetic passage, which upon closer inspection reveals the complexity of this supposedly relatively easy-to-read book, Tocqueville's survey weaves together at least four different projects. First, he delivers a powerful depiction of the American landscape and lifeworld that not only has value as a historical travelogue, but in numerous concrete details is still relevant today. Beyond this, the book is pervaded by the repeatedly explicitly posed question of what sociopolitical consequences the nations of Europe could draw from this study of the American republic.[13] Third, Tocqueville shows himself to be a philosopher of history insofar as he considers the evolution of the modern world in the direction of the universal adoption of democracy—which will then lead to the establishment of equality among not just white people, but all people—to be inevitable. He is "firmly of the opinion that the democratic revolution we are witnessing is an irresistible fact against which it would be neither desirable nor wise to struggle."[14] And as he remarks in the preface to the book's second volume, the critical aspects of his account of democracy—his famous reflections on the "tyranny of the majority"[15] or the tensions between liberty and equality, for example—are simply a result of the fact "because I was not an adversary of democracy [...] I have wanted to be candid about it."[16]

---

[12]Ibid., 581.

[13]Cf. Krause, *Eine neue Politische Wissenschaft*, particularly the section "America as Contrast," 61–7.

[14]Tocqueville, *Democracy in America*, 693.

[15]Cf. ibid., 427–50.

[16]Ibid., 693. Cf. Krause's focused "concluding observations" in *Eine neue Politische Wissenschaft*, 520–31, in which she above all emphasizes that, according to Tocqueville, formal equality in a democracy by no means must necessarily keep pace with the evolution of freedom. The scope of the liberties afforded to all thus becomes the essential benchmark for assessing a democracy: "Accordingly, Tocqueville grouses about liberty when he speaks about the possibilities for self-endangerment present in a modern democracy, including the centralization of administrative government, the tyranny of the majority, as well as the isolation and depoliticization of citizens. These hinder citizens from performing the vital task of leading a self-determined life" (521).

136 AMBITION: AN ESSAY ON THE BURNING DESIRE TO RISE

Fourth, although Tocqueville argues that "[t]here is nothing more unproductive for the human mind than an abstract idea,"[17] he clearly endeavors throughout the book to distill from his study of one, historically specific democratic society ideal types or sociological laws that recur in different periods and therefore could also be useful in analyzing future societies. His survey consistently pursues the goal of articulating "general and constant rule[s]"[18] for political science, coming to the conclusion that the restlessness he everywhere observes is a general structural consequence of equality, which promotes the "competition of all" against all[19]—effectively Hobbes' state of nature in the form of a competitive society that must be tamed through democratic policies and institutions. The subject of Tocqueville's book is democracy in America, but at the time it elaborates a theory of democracy in general.

Consequently, Tocqueville follows a similar line of argument with respect to the phenomenon of American solitude, which has historically specific roots—the severing of Americans' connection with their familial and national origins, extensive mobility within a large territory—but also is supposed to hold true for democratic societies generally, where "each man in particular becomes more similar to all the others."[20] Family ties, social classes, castes, traditions—these possibilities for identification that engender feelings of belonging are diminished in a society of equals as a logical consequence of the abolition of privileges of birth, surviving as conservatism with its traces of snobbery and arrogance: "the thread of time is broken at every moment, and the trace of the generations fades."[21] The coding of intimacy is also subject to change; from the perspective of a writer from Old Europe, personal relationships as a whole seem to grow cooler: "the bond of human affections expands and relaxes."[22] Tocqueville's incisive analysis exposes a paradox against which conservative thought braces itself: While a society that strives for social equality creates greater opportunities

---

[17]Tocqueville, *Democracy in America*, 1096.
[18]Ibid., 1154.
[19]Ibid., 945.
[20]Ibid., 757.
[21]Ibid., 884.
[22]Ibid.

AMBITION IN MODERNITY 137

for individuals to assert and realize themselves, at the same time, "each man in particular becomes more similar to all the others, weaker and smaller" and at risk of disappearing in said society's centrifugal dynamic. "You get used to no longer envisaging citizens in order to consider only the people; you forget individuals in order to think only about the species."[23] Social equalization promotes a form of individualism that terminates in the disappearance of increasingly similar individuals in the crowd: this is the paradox. Democracy, according to Tocqueville, as an ongoing process of establishing equality among subjects, has the effect of also making subjects more isolated. Here he offers a dual portrait of the isolated middle class in the United States and solitude in democracy in general:

> As conditions become equal, a greater number of individuals will be found who, no longer rich enough or powerful enough to exercise a great influence over the fate of their fellows, have nonetheless acquired or preserved enough enlightenment and wealth to be able to be sufficient for themselves. The latter owe nothing to anyone, they expect nothing so to speak from anyone; they are always accustomed to consider themselves in isolation, and they readily imagine that their entire destiny is in their hands.
>
> Thus, not only does democracy make each man forget his ancestors, but it hides his descendants from him and separates him from his contemporaries; it constantly leads him back toward himself alone and threatens finally to enclose him entirely within the solitude of his own heart.[24]

Tocqueville's description of the "restless ambition given birth by equality"[25] also purports to be universally valid beyond the United States as his specific object of study. Here Tocqueville means to offer a phenomenology of ambition as a specific consequence of equality, and here too, he refers to allegedly supra-historical models passed down from antiquity as a way of certifying the dignity of sociological ideal types. He quotes Plutarch when he speaks of the

---

[23]Ibid., 757.
[24]Ibid., 884.
[25]Ibid., 773.

138 AMBITION: AN ESSAY ON THE BURNING DESIRE TO RISE

idea of valor[26] and invokes the unsettling examples of Sulla and Caesar[27] in the context of elucidating why a great army within a democratic people will "always be a great danger."[28] According to Tocqueville, the danger posed by the military is intrinsically connected with the problem of restless ambition in a world of equals. Thus it seems obvious to choose, as an entry point to analyzing Tocqueville's propositions about ambition, this chapter about an "axiom of [political] science,"[29] the enduring relevance of which is attested to by the fact that the modern German military concepts of "citizens in uniform" and practical "leadership development and civic education" follow the exact line of argument provided by the theorist of democracy Tocqueville.

Military Ambition

The tensions that Tocqueville diagnoses between a democratic society and its military have a number of causes. First, a society that strives for social equality promotes broad-based prosperity, allowing the "number of property owners friendly to peace"[30] to grow along with their assets. Consequently, both revolutionary efforts and appetites for war and conquest diminish. Nevertheless, in a world that is still unbalanced and unequal overall, in which war and thus potential foreign threats still exist, maintaining an army is an inevitable necessity for a democratic society. This is a problem, in Tocqueville's view, as he seeks to elucidate first by examining the difference between the position of the military in a democracy and in an aristocracy.

In a stable aristocracy, positions are fixed: "the officer is the noble, the soldier is the serf."[31] There are thus strict limits placed on the ambitions of the simple soldier, while the officer knows that he is likewise part of a strict hierarchy, at the top of which

---

[26]Ibid., 1102.
[27]Ibid., 1160.
[28]Ibid., 1164.
[29]Ibid., 1162.
[30]Ibid., 1154.
[31]Ibid.

AMBITION IN MODERNITY

stands the monarch, thus "temper[ing] the desire of the officer for advancement."[32] As discussed above in Chapter I on the semantics of ambition, according to Tocqueville, the nobleman who embraces a military career pursues not so much "ambition," but rather "a sort of duty that his birth imposes on him,"[33] a (family) tradition. As he already possesses all social privileges, property, esteem, and power, he does not need the military in order to make his career.

Interestingly, Tocqueville does not mention this, but obviously there have been many military leaders throughout history who famously abused their power to launch coups within aristocratic societies. The boundless ambition of these usurpers, who never shrank from toppling the traditional, even sacred institutions they were originally charged with upholding, has drawn the particular interest of poets. The structurally induced, chronic, often vapid ambition of a competitive society is far less attractive as a dramatic subject than a case of sensational, diabolical ambition in a society that does not actually envisage such things. Shakespeare's Macbeth, who kills a king to take his throne, is one famous example of this. Schiller's Wallenstein, who defies his emperor in revolt against the old guard, is another. Henrik Ibsen's great artistic achievement in the late nineteenth century was rooted not least in his ability to turn bourgeois conflicts into high drama, although even he had to rely on theatrically effective extremes like hushed-up crimes (*The Wild Duck*), spectacular illness (*Ghosts*), and revolutionary social changes (*A Doll's House*) in order to break up the stultifying brooding of bourgeois society.

The usurpers change nothing about the analytical force of Tocqueville's argument, however. In a society of equals, in stark contrast to an aristocracy, "all the soldiers can become officers"— here Tocqueville has in mind the meteoric career rises of Napoleon's marshals and generals—"which generalizes the desire for advancement and extends the limits of military ambition almost infinitely."[34] The desire to advance becomes "ardent, tenacious, continual,"[35] as with respect to both income and prestige; promotion

---

[32]Ibid., 1155.
[33]Ibid.
[34]Ibid.
[35]Ibid., 1156.

140 AMBITION: AN ESSAY ON THE BURNING DESIRE TO RISE

is not merely "incidental" to an otherwise already privileged life but defines and gives direction to "existence itself."[36] Tocqueville concludes from this that in a democracy, the military and especially its officers have (and must have) an interest in perpetuating war:

> We thus arrive at this singular consequence that, of all armies, the ones that most ardently desire war are democratic armies, and that, among peoples, those who most love peace are democratic peoples; and what really makes the thing extraordinary is that it is equality which produces these opposite effects simultaneously.[37]

Democratic society, as a society of equals with (ideally) equal chances for advancement, is a society pervaded by ambition; the corresponding "restlessness of heart"[38] is found among both military men and civilians in equal measure. The "ambition" in both spheres is "the same" but in civil society has far more chances of being fulfilled in times of peace. This difference—which is also a financial one—not only gives rise to military dreams of glorious wars but also presents a problem for soldiers and officers: the progressive decline of their prestige in peacetime due to limited possibilities for advancement. The military increasingly becomes a repository for those who have found no success in civil society:

> It is no longer the principal citizens who enter the army, but the least. Men give themselves to military ambition only when no other is allowed. This forms a vicious circle from which it is difficult to escape. The elite of the nation avoids the military career, because this career is not honored; and it is not honored, because the elite of the nation no longer enters it.[39]

The result of this process that Tocqueville so perceptively describes is the growing isolation of the adrift military, who become increasingly resentful and even hostile toward civil society. The military now develops an exclusive internal code of honor, becoming a state

---

[36]Ibid., 1155.
[37]Ibid., 1157.
[38]Ibid., 1158.
[39]Ibid.

AMBITION IN MODERNITY 141

within the state, "a small nation apart, in which intelligence is less widespread and habits are cruder than in the large nation. Now, this small uncivilized nation possesses the weapons, and it alone knows how to use them."[40] The alienation of the military from civil society, according to Tocqueville, leaves the former more susceptible to coup plots, even at the cost of civil war, to "love of revolutions, during which he [the soldier] hopes to conquer, weapons in hand, the political influence and the individual consideration that others deny him."[41]

Among the options available for managing this dynamic, which has emerged repeatedly throughout history, and preventing a putsch by a frustrated military that feels it has been humiliated is the admittedly dicey proposition of "giv[ing] war as a goal for this troublesome ambition."[42] Here Tocqueville is referring to a "classic" move that dates back to antiquity and which was discussed above in the section on Sallust. Sallust praised what he considered to be Rome's political wisdom in providing opportunities for internal tensions to be discharged via outward aggression, preserving *concordia* by directing "hatred" and the "will to destruction" against Rome's enemies, forging them into instruments for the constant, glorious expansion of the empire. "War would only be a remedy for a [democratic] people who always wanted glory," Tocqueville writes.[43] As the use of the subjunctive mood here suggests, Tocqueville does not elaborate this idea of an exportation of aggression that satisfies the military's need for war and prestige into the notion that domestic political problems can be solved via imperialistic foreign policy. To the contrary, he is skeptical of this sort of social imperialism and clear-sightedly argues that foreign wars only defer internal problems, the dangers posed by which later return in "more terrible" form.[44] The extreme possibility would be the seizure of power by powerful generals and warlords, "in the manner of Sulla or of Caesar," but even if a war does not end with a military putsch or the immediate establishment of a military government, the wartime regime with its

---

[40]Ibid., 1159.
[41]Ibid., 1158.
[42]Ibid., 1159.
[43]Ibid., 1160.
[44]Ibid.

142 AMBITION: AN ESSAY ON THE BURNING DESIRE TO RISE

centralized, strictly hierarchical structures will almost imperceptibly lead to tyranny "softly by habits."[45] Continual war in the interest of relieving tensions between the military and society undermines democracy, which according to Tocqueville requires decentralization and on-site citizen participation in order to flourish, and prepares subjects for the despotism of a new Sulla. Expansion of the military is also not a satisfying option, as this leads only to an increase in the number of dissatisfied service members. The political realist Tocqueville therefore comes to the conclusion that "a restless and turbulent spirit is an evil inherent in the very constitution of democratic armies, and that we must give up on curing it."[46] The repression of the military by civil society turns out to be a completely wrong approach, as the measures required would only intensify the abovementioned problems and thus "would favor the establishment of a military tyranny much more than it would harm it."[47]

As the tensions outlined here are structural in nature, the only remaining "remedy" cannot be found within the military itself, but "in the country" from which it recruits.[48] In the final paragraphs of his analysis of the relationship between the military and the people in a society of equals, Tocqueville thus develops the concept of a "citizen in uniform." What is necessary, he argues, is to transform via political education the "natural" aversion of citizens to violence and disorder into a deeply rooted conviction, "into thoughtful, intelligent and stable tastes."[49] This "love of order," which is an identification with the nation's democratic constitution, a conscious "love of this equality,"[50] would then be carried over by citizens "into the career of arms."[51] "Have enlightened, well-ordered, steady and free citizens," Tocqueville writes, "and you will have disciplined and obedient soldiers."[52]

---

[45]Ibid., 1161.
[46]Ibid., 1163.
[47]Ibid., 1164.
[48]Ibid., 1163.
[49]Ibid.
[50]Ibid., 875.
[51]Ibid., 1163.
[52]Ibid. On the identification of Americans with their public institutions and the US Constitution, see Volume II, Part II, Chapter 4 of *Democracy in America*: "How the Americans Combat Individualism with Free Institutions" (ibid., 887–94).

Honor

In order to be able to illustrate the specific, paradoxical form of ambition in a society of equals, which also brings with it the tensions between military and civil society outlined above, Tocqueville first offers a consequential elucidation of the different conceptions of "honor" that emerge in the course of a culture's evolution from an unequal society to a society of equals. Ideas of honor, he demonstrates, originally highlight essentially social distinctions and grow weaker "as these differences fade away."[53] In traditional societies, honor and dishonor are tied to clearly defined codes: "So certain actions that dishonored a nobleman were indifferent on the part of the commoner."[54] In medieval feudal society, for example, honor is associated particularly with *loyalty* to the monarch and *valor* in war. Plutarch notes that, in ancient Rome, "*virtus*, the very noun for virtue [...] in Latin was just like saying valor."[55]

Such traditional notions of honor fade away in a society of equals. "Honor" gradually ceases to be an attribution that defines the identity of a particular group, class, or caste, becoming a general rule according to which "a people or a class distributes blame or praise,"[56] guaranteeing or revoking "civil rights," for example. The concept of honor can never become completely stabilized in a society of equals, however, as—particularly in a multiethnic society like the United States—vastly different notions of honor continually coexist alongside each other. In the New World, the honor of the nobility turned out to be "only one of its forms"; noblemen "gave a generic name to what was only a type."[57] Because honor is "not [...] well defined" in democratic nations, it is "necessarily less powerful."[58] Hence the particular appeal of exclusive, reputedly "ironclad" military concepts of honor in an unstable world—yet another explanation of the tensions between the military and civil society. A similar instability famously arose with respect to the "bourgeois

---

[53]Ibid., 1115.
[54]Ibid., 1097.
[55]Cited in ibid., 1102.
[56]Ibid., 1096.
[57]Ibid., 1105.
[58]Ibid., 1108.

144 AMBITION: AN ESSAY ON THE BURNING DESIRE TO RISE

manners," copied from nobility, that in a society of equals create an unsettling field of uncertainty.

For want of a stable concept of honor for appraising the social status of subjects, Tocqueville brilliantly argues, in the United States, "love of wealth" became the new lowest common denominator. Prestige from wealth acquired through Puritan resourcefulness or in the "pioneer spirit" took the place of traditional notions of honor disempowered by pluralism. Greed, considered shameful in antiquity and a mortal sin in the Middle Ages, was revalued, with financial success now serving as an indicator of social status. The sin of *avaritia* rose to become the cardinal virtue of *ambitio*:

> [T]he passion for wealth has no stigma attached to it in America, and provided that it does not go beyond the limits assigned to it by public order, it is honored. The American calls a noble and estimable ambition what our fathers of the Middle Ages named servile cupidity.[59]

The common scramble for economic success, Tocqueville argues, explains "why the Americans appear so restless amid their well-being": "It is a strange thing to see with what kind of feverish ardor the Americans pursue well-being, and how they appear tormented constantly by a vague fear of not having chosen the shortest road that can lead to it."[60] The society of equals thus finds itself on the path toward plutocracy in which "an eternal movement reigns and [...] no one knows rest."[61]

Tocqueville, too, confirms the nexus between ambition and melancholy. Equality enables universal competition, which consistently produces new inequalities, as not everyone can be equally successful on the "free market" in a world defined by contingency. Because the democratic citizen is "always seeing near himself several points that are above him, [...] you can predict that he will obstinately turn his attention solely in their direction," only further stoking competition: "When all is nearly level, the least inequalities offend [...]. This is why the desire for equality always becomes more

---

[59]Ibid., 1103.
[60]Ibid., 943.
[61]Ibid., 1140.

AMBITION IN MODERNITY 145

insatiable as equality is greater."[62] Money and consumer goods can always be further increased. To use an anachronistic example, there is always a better car and a larger swimming pool. Tocqueville describes the implementation of this breathless race in a society of equals that has become an ambitious competitive society on the road to plutocracy with the corresponding objects of prestige. Equality leads to inequality, which is then equalized only to reemerge yet again. Only "a certain equality" is possible; the equilibrium of a completely tranquil equality free of competition, envy, and the narcissism of small and large differences can never actually be achieved. The "restlessness of spirit" remains, leading Tocqueville to recognize gloom and melancholy as the downside of insatiable ambition:

> It is to these causes that you must attribute the singular melancholy that the inhabitants of democratic countries often reveal amid their abundance, and this disgust for life that sometimes comes to seize them in the middle of a comfortable and tranquil existence.
>
> Some complain in France that the number of suicides is growing; in America suicide is rare, but we are assured that insanity is more common than anywhere else.[63]

Great Ambition and Petty Ambition

The nineteenth chapter of the third part of the second volume of *Democracy in America*, which considers the question of "why in the United States you find so many ambitious men and so few great ambitions," is the Stendhal chapter, so to speak, of Tocqueville's survey, in which he draws a sharp distinction between the ubiquitous, everyday ambition of a society pervaded by perpetual competition and the great, world-changing ambition dreamed of by Julien Sorel, the ambitious but ultimately frustrated protagonist of *Le Rouge et le Noir*, Stendhal's novel set during the Bourbon Restoration in France. Earlier in *Democracy in America*,

---

[62]Ibid., 946.
[63]Ibid., 946f.

146 AMBITION: AN ESSAY ON THE BURNING DESIRE TO RISE

Tocqueville had noted that "[m]ost of those who live in times of equality are full of an ambition intense and soft at the same time."[64] This chapter now expounds upon this assertion, which essentially suggests that, in a democracy, along with so much else, the "great ambition" traditionally reserved only for "exceptional figures"— "great men" like Alexander, Caesar, or Napoleon—ultimately seeps into the consciousness of everyone and, from the perspective not just of figures like Julien Sorel but of the general population, becomes common and mean. The diabolical ambition that reaches for the stars, challenging anything and everything in its path, gives way to ubiquitous restless striving for social advancement and career success. In a society of equals, everyone is a potential leader of men or at least carries a yearning "desire to rise" in his head and heart.[65] "Ambition is the universal sentiment."[66] It thus loses its sensational, exceptional character, its demonic aura, its diabolical sheen, its distinctive association with gloomy solitude, and becomes bourgeois, *prêt-à-porter*. A society of equals is a society of the ambitious. A desire to distinguish oneself is not a distinctive trait, but one shared by everyone. To be ambitious is to be part of the mainstream, leaving ambitious dreamers ashamed of not being special to seek the pathos of distance in seclusion. For Tocqueville and his contemporaries, the obvious archetypes of world-changing ambition were supplied by memories of the Great Revolution of 1789 and the career of Napoleon Bonaparte, as well as of the 1776 *Declaration of Independence* of the thirteen American colonies who successfully fought for their freedom in a war against England and subsequently founded a society of equals.

A revolution, as Tocqueville thus well knew, also results in an outbreak of "almost limitless ambition." In the first rush of victory, "nothing seems impossible to anyone. [...] [P]ower passes so quickly from hand to hand that no one should despair of seizing it in his turn."[67] With the establishment of a new order such as that of the American Union, however, this *esprit révolutionnaire* begins to evaporate, giving way first to a depressing transitional

---

[64]Ibid., 736.
[65]Ibid., 1117.
[66]Ibid., 1120.
[67]Ibid., 1118f.

AMBITION IN MODERNITY 147

phase in which "you see taking fire on all sides disproportionate and unfortunate ambitions that burn secretly and fruitlessly in the heart that harbors them."[68] Ultimately, once the society of equals has become firmly institutionalized, the collective, all-unifying élan for the great cause is superseded by perpetual, wearisome, increasingly petty competition among individual subjects. The liberation of all leads inexorably to the competition of all with all, which, for the reasons established above, can never come to rest and keeps subjects always on the go: "the desire to rise is born at the same time in all hearts; each man wants to leave his place. Ambition is the universal sentiment."[69] The society of equals, in the course of its consolidation, develops fixed structures and institutions that ever more meticulously regulate the advancement to which all alike aspire. Application procedures, qualifying examinations, professional tracks, and career ladders proliferate:

So as men become more similar and as the principle of equality penetrates institutions and mores more peacefully and profoundly, the rules for advancement become more inflexible, advancement slower; the difficulty of quickly attaining a certain degree of grandeur increases. [...] In a well-established democratic society, great and rapid rises are therefore rare; they form exceptions to the common rule. It is their singularity that makes you forget their small number.[70]

In light of the transformation of ambition in a society of equals that Tocqueville outlines here, it makes sense to also speak in this context of the industrial and digital "revolutions," both of which enabled the sorts of exceptional careers that revolutions, in Tocqueville's view, advantage. In the United States, the world-changing scientific and technological innovations of the nineteenth and twenty-first centuries facilitated an increase in "the small number of opulent citizens"[71] in the form of prominent individuals from John D.

---

[68]Ibid., 1120.
[69]Ibid.
[70]Ibid., 1122f.
[71]Ibid., 1121.

148 AMBITION: AN ESSAY ON THE BURNING DESIRE TO RISE

Rockefeller to Jeff Bezos, sensational exceptions who prove the rule that advancement happens slower in an increasingly managed and administrated world. Tocqueville's ultimate point is that ambition in a society of equals becomes polarized. On the one hand, in its ubiquity, ambition becomes toxic—that is, petty, tedious, and depressing. It loses "its impetus and its grandeur."[72] On the other hand, and at the same time, it also becomes dangerous. The "mediocrity of desires"[73] that Tocqueville laments suddenly finds itself confronted with the potential for violence. Precisely because democracy, in Tocqueville's analysis, is characterized by the coexistence and intertwining of restlessness and solitary paralysis, in the dismal context of a life largely spent running in place, the idea of the sudden, meteoric breakthrough takes on a new potential as an object of fascination:

In democratic countries, [ambition] moves usually in a narrow field; but if it happens to go beyond those limits, you would say that there is no longer anything that limits it. Since men there are weak, isolated and changing, and since precedents there have little sway and laws little duration, resistance to innovations is soft and the social body never seems very sound or very settled. So that, when those who are ambitious once have power in hand, they believe they are able to dare anything; and when power escapes them, they immediately think about overturning the State in order to regain it. That gives to great political ambition a violent and revolutionary character[.][74]

It is on the basis of this diagnosis—which precisely predicts Louis-Napoléon Bonaparte's coup d'état of December 2, 1851, in the course of which Tocqueville himself was briefly detained as a defender of parliamentarianism—that the ever-pragmatic Tocqueville develops his concluding argument, again with military ambition in mind. Because ambition is built into the structure of a society of equals, he writes, it does not make sense to try to suppress it. Rather, it seems to him "necessary to purify, to regulate and to adjust the

---

[72]Ibid., 1125.
[73]Ibid.
[74]Ibid., 1124.

AMBITION IN MODERNITY 149

sentiment of ambition."[75] As in the case of military ambition, in a society of equals in general, ambition can at best be *managed* or cultivated. But it can never be completely overcome, as this would mean overcoming competitive society as such. Five years after the publication of the second volume of *Democracy in America*, the young Friedrich Engels—in his 1845 study of *The Condition of the Working Class in England*, based on his experience of Manchester capitalism—would demand exactly this. For he had seen that the ostensibly universal society of equals, to the extent that it was embodied by the bourgeois society of the nineteenth century, oppressed and excluded from equality an entire social class, namely the industrial proletariat. A joint labor strike, in Engel's view, is the appropriate response to the ambition-driven competitive struggle in which all subjects find themselves, including a working class splintered into solitary individual competitors. The strike represents the abolishment of ambition under the banner of a new revolutionary spirit beyond Tocqueville's progressive bourgeois liberalism:

[W]hat gives these Unions and the strikes arising from them their real importance is this, that they are the first attempt of the workers to abolish competition. They imply the recognition of the fact that the supremacy of the bourgeoisie is based wholly upon the competition of the workers among themselves; i.e. upon their want of cohesion. And precisely because the Unions direct themselves against the vital nerve of the present social order, however one-sidedly, in however narrow a way, are they so dangerous to this social order. The working men cannot attack the bourgeoisie, and with it the whole existing order of society, at any sorer point than this. If the competition of the workers among themselves is destroyed, if all determine not to be further exploited by the bourgeoisie, the rule of property is at an end.[76]

---

[75]Ibid., 1125.
[76]Friedrich Engels, *The Condition of the Working Class in England*, translated by Florence Kelley-Wischnewetsky, edited by David McLellan (Oxford: Oxford University Press, 1993), 226.

150 AMBITION: AN ESSAY ON THE BURNING DESIRE TO RISE

3 CRITIQUE OF SUCCESS
Gustav Ichheiser

Anonymity is the fate of the unsuccessful.[1]

Achievement and Success

If, to quote Sallust once again, it is the aim of the ambitious man "to make the memory of [his life] as long as possible,"[2] then a lack of success is his worst nightmare, as to be unsuccessful is to fail, and to fail means to sink into the shadowy world of anonymity, into oblivion. Ambition is the will to success; extreme ambition, the thirst for immortality. Every society the world has ever known, the sociologist Gustav Ichheiser asserts, has been and is structurally divided into an upper class and a lower class. To be successful— which primarily means acquiring money, power, prestige, esteem, and possibly fame and glory—is to climb up; to be unsuccessful is to be laid low.[3] If ambition, as Tocqueville defines it, is a yearning desire to rise, then a study of ambition must concern itself with the question of what "success" consists in and what enables it. in this section, then, we will consider Ichheiser's brilliant 1930 treatise *Kritik des Erfolges (Critique of Success)*, which made him one of the founders of the sociology of success and in which the "pursuit of success" becomes almost synonymous with "ambition." Ichheiser's slim volume is one of those "classic" texts of German sociology that were never reissued after 1945 and to this day remain largely— and unjustly—forgotten.[4] Following the Nazi "annexation" of

---

[1]Gustav Ichheiser, *Kritik des Erfolges: Eine soziologische Untersuchung* (Leipzig: C.L. Hirschfield, 1930), 60.

[2]Sallust, *Catiline's Conspiracy*, 10.

[3]Cf. Ichheiser, *Kritik des Erfolges*, 3.

[4]For a general overview of the various developments in the sociology of success over the years, see Sighard Nickel, "Ehrgeiz, Reputation und Bewährung: Zur Theoriegeschichte einer Soziologie des Erfolgs," in: Günter Burkart and Jürgen Wolf, eds., *Lebenszeiten: Erkundungen zur Soziologie der Generationen* (Wiesbaden: Springer Fachmedien, 2002), 103–18, which includes a brief discussion of Ichheiser (ibid., 110f.). Nickel points out that critiques of meritocracy and an "achieving society" since the 1960s have failed to recall the pioneering achievements of Ichheiser and Karl Mannheim (cf. ibid., 113f.).

AMBITION IN MODERNITY

Austria, the Jewish Ichheiser fled into exile, first to England and then to America. *Memories of Gustav Ichheiser: Life and Work of an Exiled Social Scientist*, an English-language anthology aimed at reconstructing parts of his biography and offering a reassessment of his writings, was published only in 2018.[5]

Ichheiser's *Critique of Success* is particularly relevant for a phenomenology of ambition because here he consistently problematizes and breaks down his preliminary definition of ambition as the pursuit of achievement in order to obtain success. All human beings strive for social success, according to Ichheiser, for two reasons:

> We all strive for social success in order to partake of the *advantages* directly associated with it, whether in the form of political power, a privileged economic position and the comforts that flow from it, ideological interests ("command of hearts and minds"), or whatever else. But it is not only these "advantages" that make success seem desirable to us. We also seek social success for an entirely different reason: because other people's *assessment* of our character turns out to depend on it, and our own sense of self-worth is ultimately dependent on this assessment.
>
> To wit, success is the de facto decisive criterion in evaluating human beings.[6]

---

[5]Amrei C. Joerchel and Gerhard Benetka, eds., *Memories of Gustav Ichheiser: Life and Work of an Exiled Social Scientist* (Cham, Switzerland: Springer, 2018). Markus Wrbouschek's contribution to this volume (ibid., 137–55) combines a reconstruction of the line of argument of Ichheiser's *Critique of Success* with an enlightening discussion of the question of whether and to what extent Ichheiser's theories remain relevant today. Drawing on the work of Sighard Nickel, Wrbouschek shows himself to be skeptical that Ichheiser's proposition that one must constantly demonstrate one's aptitude for achievement is entirely applicable in a new plutocratic age in which the invisible but ubiquitous "power of wealth [...] leaves all rules of the principle of achievement far behind" (151). At the same time, however, the principle of achievement and performance has returned in neoliberalism at the level of individual actors in the concept of constant "self-optimization": "Concepts such as self-initiative and self-responsibility that concern the self-reference of the subject rather than its relation to other economic actors have replaced the justification over performance" (ibid.). Under neoliberalism, the ambition of individuals in competition with each other is thus primarily directed toward constant self-optimization.
[6]Ichheiser, *Critique of Success*, 38. Emphasis in original.

152 AMBITION: AN ESSAY ON THE BURNING DESIRE TO RISE

Accordingly, success possesses an objective and a subjective component. Objective success means the accumulation of money, power, prestige, etc. But even apart from the fact that a lack of success deprives subjects of the comforts that a privileged position in many ways bestows on the successful, it is difficult to prevent negative assessments on the part of others from devastating one's sense of self-worth when one is unsuccessful. Material (economic, social) limitations are almost inevitably joined by humiliating experiences of exclusion, shame, and feelings of inferiority.[7] The obvious question of whether it is possible or desirable to *emancipate ourselves from the idea of success* and its severe socio-psychological effects will thus be taken up below in the section on Karl Mannheim's contribution to the sociology of success. As we shall see, Mannheim reminds us that there is a venerable religious and philosophical tradition behind radically renouncing the idea of success along with its standards and values—embracing the *vita contemplativa*—and good reasons for doing so.

As a way of illustrating the "effective omnipotence of success in motivating human behavior,"[8] Ichheiser, ironically enough, cites a scene from Thomas Mann's novel of decline *Buddenbrooks*, which in 1929, one year prior to the publication of *Critique of Success*, had earned its author the Nobel Prize in Literature and, with it, worldwide success. The scene, from near the end of the novel, plays out in the frightening Wilhelmine "institution" of a German school and itself calls the concept of success into question.[9] The students are being orally quizzed on their knowledge of Ovid. They all cheat, effectively demonstrating no achievement, and everyone is aware of this except the hapless teacher Dr. Mantelsack. Hanno Buddenbrook's classmate Timm successfully fools the teacher and receives an undeserved good grade. "The remarkable thing," Thomas Mann writes,

---

[7]Nina Verheyen discusses the repercussions of these depressing effects in the present day in *Die Erfindung der Leistung* (Berlin: Hanser Verlag, 2018), 25–8. She also notes that in Wilhelmine Germany, "a person's value was directly tied to his achievement" (ibid., 31).

[8]Ichheiser, *Critique of Success*, 44.

[9]On the serious psychosocial effects of Wilhelmine schooling—including a significant increase in student suicides around the turn of the twentieth century—see Verheyen, *Die Erfindung der Leistung*, 34–41.

AMBITION IN MODERNITY 153

was that in that moment not only the teacher but Timm himself and all his classmates, too, were honestly convinced that Timm was truly a fine, hardworking student who had indeed earned a good grade. Even Hanno Buddenbrook was unable to resist this impression, although he sensed something deep inside rebelling against the idea.[10]

When Hanno likewise manages to fool Dr. Mantelsack, he notices the same incredible effect in himself: "In that moment he was truly of the opinion that he was a somewhat untalented but hardworking student [...]; and he clearly sensed that his classmates [...] all held the same view."[11] The students are not proud of the "achievement" of having successfully tricked their teacher. Nor are they pleased with themselves for having finagled a success without achievement. Rather, they "honestly" believe—and herein lies the subtlety of Thomas Mann's observational skill—that they are good students who know their Ovid, delivered solid performances, and thus *earned* their good grades. They are proud of their success, the irresistible magic of which has here worked its charms. Although they cheated, "almost all the gains of [their] success accrue to the account of an imagined aptitude for achievement."[12] The magic of success generates the illusion of achievement with such intensity that all involved are convinced the achievement is real.

Among many other things that will be discussed below, Ichheiser's account of this scene from Thomas Mann establishes, first, the *distinction between success and achievement* in the very simple sense that the former can be obtained without the latter. This fundamental difference between success and achievement in turn forms the basis of the sociology of success.

"Achievement" consists in adequately or even perfectly executing a given task, producing an object, competently performing one's job, etc. Criteria for appraising the genuineness of the achievement are determined strictly with regard to the matter at hand, the

---

[10]Thomas Mann, *Buddenbrooks: The Decline of a Family*, translated by John E. Woods (New York: Vintage International, 1994), 702. Cited in Ichheiser, *Kritik des Erfolges*, 46f.

[11]Mann, *Buddenbrooks*, 704. Cited in Ichheiser, *Critique of Success*, 47.

[12]Ichheiser, *Critique of Success*, 39.

154 AMBITION: AN ESSAY ON THE BURNING DESIRE TO RISE

task performed. Karl Mannheim, in his own contribution to the sociology of success, proposes the term "realization" to characterize the effects of achievement. Franz Kafka's three novels were "realizations" or "achievements" produced in solitude; only after Max Brod's publication of them did they become successful and world-famous. Ichheiser invokes the example of the shoemaker in order to illustrate the difference between achievement related to performing a task and the purely social category of success. It sometimes happens that two shoemakers who manufacture comparably good shoes attain different levels of success in their occupation. An aptitude for achievement must be accompanied by an aptitude for success, through which achievement achieves its *social breakthrough*. Achievement turns into success only when it becomes socially established and honored. This basic distinction has two points. First, a certain aptitude for success is *always* required for an achievement to break through socially. Second, the relation between aptitude for achievement and aptitude for success is eminently variable. A bad shoemaker can be more successful than a good one, for example if he is talented at marketing his shoes. Success is not inherently related to achievement, but rather is the result of a particular social competence, the basic forms of which Ichheiser enumerates and which finds its purest embodiment in the figure of the fraud or confidence man, who attains success without any achievement whatsoever:

> Probably every action that is apt for success ultimately occurs in these basic forms: influencing the entities that determine success, generating a favorable opinion about oneself, an unfavorable opinion about all potential competitors.[13]

The well-known and oft-lamented fact that achievement does not "automatically" lead to success, whereas a consistent orientation toward success can at times make up for a lack of achievement to an astonishing extent, does not mean, however—and herein lies a further psychological challenge for those playing the social game of success—that in pursuing success, one can dispense with achievement *entirely*. Achievement in the sense of realized material competence is

---

[13]Ibid., 13.

AMBITION IN MODERNITY 155

not necessarily reliant on finding a social echo, but recognized as skill, it does enjoy high social esteem. Accordingly, the ability to generate at least the *impression of achievement* is among the conditions of an aptitude for success. One who strives for success "must be *considered* to have an aptitude for achievement. And he is apt for success only so long as he is *considered* apt for achievement."[14]

There is moreover an equally well-known asymmetry in the relation between aptitude for achievement and aptitude for success, inasmuch as those who possess a great talent for a particular activity or occupation often lack the ability to develop the necessary aptitude for success on top of this. The extraordinary, life-defining talent that makes one capable of great achievements can potentially stand in the way of developing an aptitude for success:

> As a characterological attitude, aptitude for achievement— perhaps especially in the intellectual realm—is very often associated with a number of qualities that make it impossible to develop behaviors apt for success: a heightened sensitivity that avoids the brutality that propels success, a certain pride that disdains blatantly advertising one's own achievement; an aversion to cliquishness; an internal resistance to putting time and energy toward the purportedly meaningless business of pursuing success that could otherwise be spent on more sensible pursuits [...].[15]

From this point on, the divide between the person apt for achievement and the person apt for success grows ever wider. Initial success facilitates further achievements, not least because one who attains a certain "position" has more opportunities to flourish as a result than does his competitor who is less apt for success.[16] Success breeds success, just as, according to Karl Marx, under capitalism, money breeds money. Further, success also has a positive psychological effect on one's ability to perform, whereas experiences of failure are disheartening and can diminish further achievements.[17] Finally,

---

[14]Ibid., 21.
[15]Ibid., 21f.
[16]Cf. ibid., 59.
[17]Cf. ibid.

156 AMBITION: AN ESSAY ON THE BURNING DESIRE TO RISE

in a success-oriented society, success has the sort of irresistibly enchanting effect illustrated in the abovementioned scene from *Buddenbrooks*. Success *vindicates* the successful person (including to himself), and the question of whether one's success is "legitimate" in regard to one's achievement fades into the background.[18] This, in Ichheiser's view, is one of the reasons why sociology of success, which emphasizes the variable relationship between aptitude for success and aptitude for achievement, has little hope of being met with more than limited interest, both within the academic establishment and outside it. It is all but inevitable that successful people will confront this sociological "exposure" of their success with skepticism or discomfort:

> *Prestige*, which is ultimately one of the key primary sources of all social *power* and all *authority*, is—as we should never forget—deeply rooted in our *consciousness of its legitimacy*. The *social upper class* cannot be satisfied with the *mere fact of being on top*. In order to *solidify* itself, it must moreover also be considered *entitled*.
>
> But precisely the sociology of success, like perhaps no other perspective, is well-suited to shatter the legitimacy and our consciousness of the legitimacy of being on top or at the bottom. By calling into the question the legitimacy of the social "upper" class, it destroys prestige and thus ultimately undermines the *socio-psychological foundations* of the existing system of social power.[19]

The Enchantment of Success

Here already, we can extract from the groundwork Ichheiser lays for his sociology of success certain ideas that augment our conception of ambition. First, we can differentiate between cause-

---

[18]Verheyen makes a similar argument with respect to the self-image of "elite achievers," who are convinced that they have reached the top "because they are good, because they are better than others," a belief that obscures real inequalities of opportunity. Verheyen, *Die Erfindung der Leistung*, 195.

[19]Ichheiser, *Kritik des Erfolges*, 58.

oriented ambition and success-oriented ambition. The leading difference between operating in the interest of a cause or in the interest of oneself, which we have traced from Sallust to Francis Bacon to Max Weber and beyond into the realm of politics, here returns in a generalized form. Ambition can be directed exclusively at manufacturing perfect shoes or be divided between craftsmanship and marketing or—as is of course also conceivable—be aimed at both. Finally, in a modern society based on the division of labor, there is also the option of hiring an agent to "hype up" one's achievements and turn them into a "smashing success."

Ichheiser's distinction also allows us to further refine the ethical debate over ambition led by Pettigrove. Cause-oriented ambition is morally indifferent as long as it does not have any negative effects on the acting subject or its environment, such as when a chemist, say, blows himself and his house to pieces. Ambition aimed at success, by contrast, inevitably has a moral valence from the beginning, insofar as it not only bears on the extremely variable relation between aptitude for achievement and aptitude for success, but also affects the set of measures one chooses to accomplish one's aim, all of which—at least in Ichheiser's inventory—are ethically problematic: manipulating the relevant authorities, forming cliques, bluffing, cultivating "connections,"[20] defaming or otherwise neutralizing one's competition, etc.

The precarious status of ambition, our ambivalence toward it, is thus also a result of the fact that we prefer to equate it with a consistent orientation toward success that, at least in Ichheiser's view, all but necessitates engaging in morally dubious actions. Our judgment of an ambitious person becomes "unfair" the moment we conclude that, because he is committed to ensuring the social breakthrough of his achievement, he is insufficiently committed to the cause itself. This conclusion is fed by the admittedly obvious-seeming assumption that an ambitious person is not satisfied by the joy of achievement alone and longs for applause, prestige, and glory on top of this. The pursuit of and craving for recognition, which will be discussed below in the section on the psychology of ambition in Freud and Adler, here comes into play. From a "purist" perspective, recognition of an achievement may be dampened by

---

[20]Ibid., 12.

158 AMBITION: AN ESSAY ON THE BURNING DESIRE TO RISE

the bothersome impression that said achievement was carried out primarily for the sake of personal success. Karl Mannheim, by contrast, as we shall see in the next section, takes a more sober, realistic view of success as an important incentive for achievement in a socio-psychologically diverse world.

Here we must also mention a psychological fact that is attractive to individuals who strongly crave recognition or are highly narcissistic: the widespread tendency to assume that an achievement carried out in a specific field and exploited for success is indicative of "some sort of universal, mysterious 'greatness of personality.'"[21] This assumption is generally misguided. In a society enthralled with success, the passions-exciting "spread of success"[22] far beyond one particular segment of the lifeworld creates a halo that leads to "universal recognition," to "celebrity, " and thus to a general overestimation of the successful person. As Ichheiser shows, the "spread of success" does not even spare the self-assessment of the successful person, who risks increasingly forfeiting his capacity for self-criticism and self-irony and himself coming to believe that he is "important," "significant," or—to borrow a relevant term from Jacques Lacan—"the thing." In the case of "confusing the office for the person," the egomaniacal officeholder, fed by his total identification of himself with his outsized social role, experiences severe identity crises after the expiration of his term in office, such as the "bankruptcy of retirement" described by Freud. Increasing vanity and complacency are almost inevitably accompanied by artistic or intellectual regression, unless the subject's burning ambition prevents him from "resting on his laurels" by leading him to perceive his accomplished goals as disintegrating into ashes. Extremely ambitious individuals may well be vain, but they are rarely complacent, as comfortable complacency stands in contradiction to the cardinal psychological roots of ambition, which include—as Alfred Adler argues—tormenting feelings of inferiority that must be compensated for over and over.

In the context of his phenomenology of the kind of rampant success that generates a new, corrupt form of enchantment in a disenchanted world, Ichheiser cites his contemporary Karl

---

[21]Ibid., 54.
[22]Ibid., 55.

AMBITION IN MODERNITY
159

Otto Erdmann, who in 1930 argued that success breeds a form of naivete: "[B]ecause Hindenburg is a great field commander or Gerhart Hauptmann an outstanding poet, they must therefore also be important statesmen and born presidents."[23] The grave historical consequences of this "naivete" became clear shortly after the appointment of Adolf Hitler to Chancellor of the German Reich, when on March 21, 1933—the so-called "Day of Potsdam"—Hitler and now-President Paul von Hindernburg, the representative of the right-wing conservative, militaristic old Reich, came together in a publicly celebrated display of solidarity.

One of the most well-known, still-relevant examples of the overestimation of successful people is that product of the culture industry known as the "star," described by Roger Caillois, in the context of his elaboration of the cultural implications of his theory of play, as a glittering alternative to the drab everyday experience of steadily climbing the career ladder. The fascinating improbability of the "shooting star" gives those whose lives and careers are stuck in a rut the opportunity to dream of a brilliant meteoric rise against all odds. "The star," Caillois writes

> symbolizes success personified, victory and recompense for the crushing and sordid inertia of daily life, a triumph over the obstacles that society sets in the way of valor. The inordinate glory of the idol is a continuous witness to the possibility of a triumph which has already been of some benefit to, and which to some extent is due to, those who worship the hero. This exaltation, which seemingly consecrates the hero, flouts the established hierarchy in brilliantly and drastically obliterating the fate imposed upon all by the human condition. One also imagines such a career to be somewhat suspicious, impure, or irregular. The residue of envy underlying admiration does not fail to see in it a triumph compounded of ambition, intrigue, impudence, and publicity.[24]

As Ichheiser shows, this suspicion that a successful career must somehow be illicit, bearing the stain of intrigue or impudence,

---

[23]Ibid., 54.
[24]Roger Caillois, *Man, Plays and Games*, translated by Meyer Barash (Urbana/Chicago: University of Illinois Press, 2001), 122f.

160 AMBITION: AN ESSAY ON THE BURNING DESIRE TO RISE

is not just an expression of envy, but always has some basis in reality, however weak. Herein lies the "tragic" aspect of successful biographies, which in a competitive society can scarcely exist without ambition in the sense of the capacity to assert and establish oneself. Propaganda thus has to work hard to raise the halo so high that the stain is outshined and the illusion can be maintained: *A star is born*.

Our criticism of ambitious people ultimately devolves into resentment when we conclude that their success implies a lack of achievement, or that they are guilty of some moral transgression and therefore should be condemned out of hand. Max Scheler, in his study of *ressentiment* in the construction of morals, demonstrates that one of the reasons for the emergence of *ressentiment* in a success-oriented society lies in the cruel frustration of markedly high career hopes. This is why, according to Scheler, "*ressentiment* man" not only is effectively an "expert" when it comes to society's orientation toward success, but moreover proves to be compulsively, even "magically" attracted to "such phenomena as joy, splendor, power, happiness, fortune, and strength," remaining forever in thrall to the never-forsaken objects of his desire:

> He cannot pass by, he has to look at them, whether he "wants" to or not. But at the same time he wants to avert his eyes, for he is tormented by the craving to possess them and knows that his desire is vain.[25]

This conglomerate of intense emotional reactions to success also explains why ambition is so often considered shameful, appearing only rarely in people's descriptions of themselves, and why as a rule so much value is placed on giving the impression that one's success is—counterfactually—the result of "achievement alone." Ichheiser also argues, however, that criticism of success-oriented ambition tends to be bigoted or hypocritical, glossing over a systemic problem on which Ichheiser's treatise seeks to shed light. It is not supposedly repulsive ambition itself that is morally dubious, but a system that chiefly rewards success, which it relentlessly declares to be the central goal "toward which all human action is oriented" in

---

[25]Max Scheler, *Ressentiment*, translated by Lewis B. Coser and William W. Holdheim (Milwaukee: Marquette University Press, 1998), 54f.

AMBITION IN MODERNITY 161

"every sphere of society."[26] Against this backdrop, achieving success is virtually identical with maintaining one's dignity.

Thus admitted, as a devoutly longed-for supreme value, into the order of a society that is primarily oriented around it and even fetishizes it, "legitimate," self-justifying success that is also socially justified by universal admiration inherits a central function of religion, that of offering the ruling class a "theodicy of happiness." In the introduction to his collection of essays on the economic ethics of the world religions, Max Weber had shown that, for the happy man, merely possessing good fortune is not enough; his happiness must also be theologically "legitimate." Ichheiser cleverly adapts this proposition to argue that success should be the result of achievement alone and not due to any other machinations, just as, in traditional societies, good fortune was supposed to be owed to mastery and divine providence. The happy man, Weber writes,

> needs to also have a *right* to his happiness. He wants to be convinced that he has earned it, particularly in comparison with others. [...] Happiness desires to be "legitimate." If we understand the general concept of "happiness" to include all the benefits of honor, power, property, and pleasure, then this is the most general expression of the service of legitimization that religion had to offer to the external and internal interest of all ruling, propertied, victorious, healthy—in short, to all fortunate men: the theodicy of happiness. It is rooted in the most grave ("Pharisaical") needs of men and is thus easily understood, although sufficient attention has often not been given to its impact.[27]

Machiavelli as the Father of the Sociology of Success

The next step that Ichheiser takes comes into view with respect to the sociopolitical connection between happiness and success. Having

---

[26]Ichheiser, *Kritik des Erfolges*, 5.
[27]Cited in ibid., 45, fn. 7.

162 AMBITION: AN ESSAY ON THE BURNING DESIRE TO RISE

demystified the first "myth of success"[28]—that it is the capable and industrious who break through and establish themselves—he now proceeds to dismantle the second: that "honesty is the best policy." More than a generation before clinical psychiatry would develop the theory of the double bind in the context of schizophrenia therapy, Ichheiser—though he doesn't use the term—elaborated his own concept of the crucial "double bind" confronting modern "western" societies, an examination of which will help to further differentiate our understanding of ambition. Ichheiser writes:

> The order of social life confronts us with a double demand: we should act in accordance with norms and we should be successful, for social success serves as a sign, a symptom of having inwardly proven oneself.[29]

Ichheiser pointedly emphasizes that, with this dual demand to *simultaneously* adhere to norms *and* be successful, subjects "are faced with an *impossible task*."[30] Just as we cannot fully do justice here to the detailed analysis and critique of techniques of success that Ichheiser offers, we do not have the space to devote an appropriate level of attention to the significant psychological costs that the "*antinomy between norm-bound and success-oriented behavior*" that he identifies entails.[31] Above all, what is relevant in the context of a study of ambition is Ichheiser's identification of one of the reasons why even ambitious people are sometimes haunted by a "bad conscience," namely because being oriented toward success all but inevitably implies violating norms. The ambitious individual, too, is subject to the workings of this double bind.

Ichheiser's exposure of the antinomy of success-oriented societies that glorify success while at the same time enforcing ethical norms with harsh sanctions prompts him to call into question an upbringing oriented primarily or exclusively toward imparting high ethical standards that sends children out into the world "burdened with norms that then prove to be unworkable."[32]

---

[28]Ibid., 6.
[29]Ibid., 61.
[30]Ibid., 62.
[31]Ibid., 23.
[32]Ibid., 62.

AMBITION IN MODERNITY

Recognition of the double bind between this normative system and the imperative to be successful, according to Ichheiser, forms "the *core* of a *second life crisis*" following puberty[33]—a crisis that famously serves as the blueprint not only for the European bildungsroman, but for countless coming-of-age stories and films worldwide. Ichheiser urgently identifies the danger that, faced with the shock of confronting the "antinomy" described above, young people may suffer a mental breakdown if they do not manage to overcome this "second life crisis" in a "healthy" way, through robust repression, irony, cynicism, resignation, affectation, identification with the pursuit of success, adaptation, and other measures that are euphemistically treated as essential aspects of "maturity" or coming to grips with "reality." The socially programmed double bind forces a splitting of one's personality, for example into a "loving father" on the one hand and, on the other, a ruthless businessman who "plays hardball" "out there" in competitive society. In Ichheiser's conception, then, the sociology of success articulates aspects of a critical theory of society.

Considering the discrepancy between ethical norms and the pressure to succeed, Ichheiser argues, Niccolò Machiavelli turns out to be the actual "father of the sociology of success,"[34] inasmuch as his famous treatise *The Prince* is the guide book for proving oneself in modern, success-oriented competitive society. With this, Ichheiser confirms Burckhardt's description of the Italian Renaissance as a "dress rehearsal" of modern capitalism. But Ichheiser is not only interested in Machiavelli's demand that we approach reality without any illusions and recognize that "there is a world of difference between the *actual* laws of social advancement and that officially intended ideal state in which socially valuable conduct is inextricably linked with social success, while conduct that contravenes society's values necessarily leads to social failure."[35] Nor is Machiavelli, in Ichheiser's view, merely the teacher of the notorious art of "hypocrisy" that promises success by integrating "*the officially authorized and the unofficially effective conditions of success into an optimal whole.*"[36] It was first and foremost

---

[33]Ibid., 34.
[34]Ibid., 49f.
[35]Ibid., 29.
[36]Ibid., 32.

164 AMBITION: AN ESSAY ON THE BURNING DESIRE TO RISE

Machiavelli who classically illustrated the seemingly paradoxical fusion of passion and planning, ardent ambition and instrumental rationality, for "*it is the instrumentally rational consideration of success* [...] *that is decisive.*"[37] As we saw clearly through Pettigrove's characterization of ambition as a "long-term project" pursued with instrumental rationality, barring some miracle, only sober recognition of the inextricable connection between aptitude for achievement and aptitude for success, along with the rationally and patiently planned application of the appropriate social techniques, actually leads to success, which in Ichheiser's view also requires suspending one's conscience. Of course, in a society governed by norms and laws, flagrantly violating those norms is indicative only of a lack of skill and finesse. Only a "*highly specific*, in a way '*instrumentally rational*' disregard for and violation of social norms has a favorable effect on one's chances for social success."[38]

The success-oriented person's need to maintain the impression that he has actually achieved something, established in the first part of Ichheiser's *Critique of Success*, here corresponds to the fact that successful actions always require the skillful combination of ostensible normativity and well-concealed violation of norms. Ichheiser cites Herbert Spencer's account of a London tailor, active during Karl Marx's years in the English capital, who "did not want to participate in the 'lax' measurement and calculation of material in the manufacture of clothing semi-officially authorized by local 'customs'" and as a result went out of business three times.[39] Machiavelli had already demonstrated the "superiority of the (instrumentally rational) 'immoral' man in attaining success,"[40] and not only in the realm of power politics:

A *lack of principles—principles* here understood as a mental attitude rooted in value-rational or emotional considerations, independent of any momentary constellation of interests—is and must constitute an *advantage* in the competition of life by dint

---

[37]Ibid., 31.
[38]Ibid., 24.
[39]Ibid., 28.
[40]Ibid., 33.

AMBITION IN MODERNITY   165

of the of the persistence of sociological laws of success; it means
being *unbound* by those social norms that are designed to curtail
one's freedom of (instrumentally rational) movement. Of course,
only an actually existing, but at the same time *disguised* lack of
principles is apt to increase one's chances of success.[41]

The ambitious individual, if he wants to have success, must obtain
what Ichheiser aptly calls "freedom of movement" for himself in
at least three respects. His talent—his commitment to his cause—
must not cloud his sober view of the facts of social life. His aptitude
of achievement and aptitude for success must be harmoniously
intertwined. And he must develop a realistic relationship to the
discrepancy between the pressure to succeed and the normative
system, so that his quest for opportunities to expand or, if possible,
circumvent the normative system in the interest of his own
success is not paralyzed by pangs of conscience. An instinct for
power can thus be understood as the ability to procure "freedom
of movement" for oneself within the framework of a normative
system, as a "*disguised* lack of principles is apt to increase one's
chances of success."[42]

Winners vs. Losers

Toward the end of his treatise, Ichheiser cites the virtually "all-
powerful" evaluation model of modern mass society as one of the
key motivations for decidedly success-oriented actions. The rapid
pace of the lifeworld and the fleeting nature of contacts make it
necessary to apply an undifferentiated evaluation model to social
interactions: "In general, people are evaluated only '*positively*'
or '*negatively*' (or possibly '*neutrally*')."[43] In an accelerated
society involving countless interactions, it is impossible to make
differentiated, nuanced assessments of others. The opposition
"successful"—"unsuccessful" has thus come to be incorporated

---

[41]Ibid., 32.
[42]Ibid.
[43]Ibid., 40.

166 AMBITION: AN ESSAY ON THE BURNING DESIRE TO RISE

into the positive/negative formula—evolutionarily rooted in the age-old pattern of distinguishing between "dangerous" and "harmless" encounters—that defines our interactions. In Ichheiser's incisive structuralist analysis, the contrast between the successful and the unsuccessful is so acute because it fits into ancient, fundamental, readily available stimulus-response patterns that have all but inevitably come to define the modern lifeworld:

> There is at most one further step toward differentiation in the sphere of everyday life beyond this utterly undifferentiated assessment, as our *one-dimensional rating scale* ("positive"—"negative") splits into a *two-dimensional* scale, the poles of which might be called "capable"—"inept" on the one axis and "good"—"bad" on the other.[44]

Ichheiser's insight into the incorporation of the "successful"—"unsuccessful" scale into the otherwise unnuanced universal "positive"—"negative" model of social perception allows him to derive not only the motivation for the ambitious pursuit of success, but also the shame of the unsuccessful from the fundamental patterns of perception of a fast-paced lifeworld that unrelentingly operates on the distinction between *winners* and *losers* and to which has accrued, through the opposition "good" and "bad," a supposedly moral "added value" of the sort that Sallust lamented with his observation that, as Rome became increasingly plutocratic, poverty came to be considered a "disgrace":[45]

> It is *not* our internal disposition, but our *need for approval*, our need to be evaluated "positively" by "spectators," that generally tends to determine the nature and direction of our conduct. Against this need for approval, our (in some cases) differently oriented disposition mostly turns out to be powerless. Most of the time, we are afraid not of (internal) guilt, but only of "disgrace."

---

[44]Ibid., 40f.
[45]Sallust, *Catiline's Conspiracy*, in: *Catiline's Conspiracy, The Jugurthine War, Histories*, translated by William W. Batstone (Oxford: Oxford University Press, 2010), 16.

AMBITION IN MODERNITY 167

And in cases of conflict between the two, our disposition almost always ends up the victim.[46]

A critique of success that engages in this sort of analysis of the patterns of perception and assessment that define our behavior ultimately becomes a critique of society—which in Ichheiser's view ought to proceed not from the individual and his particular motivations, but from the collective of spectators that generates these chains of motivations and perpetuates itself via continual observation and assessment of others and itself. Such a critique would need to scrutinize and potentially dismantle the uncritical rewarding of success along with all of the consequences and double binds that Ichheiser inventories. Its aim: "to liberate the spectator from his delusional, success-oriented assessment of his fellow men and deepen his insight."[47]

---

[46]Ichheiser, *Kritik des Erfolges*, 63f.
[47]Ibid., 64.

168 AMBITION: AN ESSAY ON THE BURNING DESIRE TO RISE

4 CRITIQUE OF CONTEMPLATION
Karl Mannheim

Bred to Strive for Success

Karl Mannheim's comprehensive essay *Über das Wesen und die Bedeutung des wirtschaftlichen Erfolgsstrebens* (*On the Nature and Significance of the Pursuit of Economic Success*), based on a 1929 lecture and also published in 1930, forms a necessary supplement to Ichheiser's study. Mannheim—one of the founders of the sociology of knowledge—likewise presents an exacting ideal-typical, hierarchical classification of "success" and the pursuit of it, but in contrast to Ichheiser, he highlights the various historical transformations of the pursuit of success as well as significant differences in its contours and aims in various social realms (power politics, economic life, bureaucracy). Conversely, Ichheiser's treatise in turn forms a necessary supplement to Mannheim's inquiry: although Ichheiser's stated aim is to work out "basic transhistorical constellations,"[1] in the course of this ahistorical generalization he also articulates an extremely pointed critique of success and of Machiavellian techniques for attaining it, the accuracy and specifics of which can surely be confirmed by many people who find or have found themselves locked in fierce competitive struggles. In Mannheim's essay, by contrast, any critique of success remains largely obscured. Not only that, he ventures a staunch and, for a studied philosopher, surprising apologia for the pursuit of success that, in the name of (the new) objectivity, rejects a "morality shaped largely by contemplative subjects (by religious geniuses and philosophers) or, put another way, by people who have experienced the economy only from the side of consumption" and thus "perceive something

---

[1]Ichheiser, Kritik des Erfolges.

AMBITION IN MODERNITY

suspect in the pursuit of success."[2] The tone of Mannheim's essay is almost optimistic, and as a blueprint for a "sociologically oriented pedagogy," it aims "to push the present form of social life beyond itself."[3] In 1930, one year after the onset of the Great Depression, faced with rising mass unemployment and the rise of National Socialism, and with the Stalin-led Soviet Union in the background, Mannheim rather euphemistically describes the era as an "age of evolutionary transformation."[4] His faith in the progressive objectification—that is, rationalization—of all conditions of life and interpretations of the world as a whole goes so far that he can claim that "a society that is rationally calculating in its essential structure is gradually becoming increasingly foreseeable even in its 'irrational' impulses":[5]

> The more the irrational becomes an "enclave" within the element of the increasingly rational overall structure, the more even this enclave can be reckoned with. The ramifications of a stock market panic, for example, are now just as calculable as the possible sites and ramifications of the irrational reactions of déclassé groups in the process of social struggle. [...] This means, however—to put it less harshly—that the modern economic society (precisely because economic inevitabilities are increasingly pervading even the individual business of everyday behavior) can "afford" to increasingly let "ideologies" loose.[6]

Looking back in the light of National Socialism and the singular German crimes resulting from it, these disturbing misjudgments of the situation in the Weimar Republic at the turn of the 1930s read like something taken from a memo recommending that democratic powers neutralize the Nazis by "containing" and "restraining" them, as though this were a real option. Just three years later, Karl Mannheim had to learn the hard way that the modern, supposedly

---

[2]Karl Mannheim, *Über das Wesen und die Bedeutung des wirtschaftlichen Erfolgsstrebens*, in: Mannheim, *Wissenssoziologie: Auswahl aus dem Werk*, edited by Kurt H. Wolff (Neuwied: Luchterhand, 1965), 625–78 (637).
[3]Ibid., 629.
[4]Ibid., 630.
[5]Ibid., 647.
[6]Ibid.

170 AMBITION: AN ESSAY ON THE BURNING DESIRE TO RISE

thoroughly rationalized economic society could not in fact afford to "let ideologies loose." As a consequence of the enactment of the infamously anti-Semitic and thus fundamentally irrational Law for the Restoration of the Professional Civil Service on April 7, 1933, Mannheim lost his professorship of sociology in Frankfurt and had to go into exile in London, where, incidentally, he was able to find some short-term work for Gustav Ichheiser, who had fled there from Austria before moving on to the United States.

In exposing Karl Mannheim's erroneous diagnosis of the times, my intention is not to cast doubt on his keen observations about the pursuit of success as a whole, which remain relevant today, nor to call into question the sociology of knowledge. Rather, the aim of my reading of Mannheim's work here and below is to show that, in his apologia for the pursuit of success, he overshoots his goal when he rejects, pathologizes, and devalues the *vita contemplativa* that is strictly antithetical to this pursuit as unsuited to his time. I thus want to call attention to a deep contradiction that runs through Mannheim's essay, one that is also instructive beyond this specific context for understanding the contours of ambition: if Mannheim hopes to elucidate the pursuit of success, then he needs contemplation, its conceptual counterpart. It is contemplation that Mannheim casts aside as pathological and therefore null and void, but in so doing, it becomes impossible for him to define and critique the pursuit of success itself.

The unfettered, predatory pursuit of economic success in a competitive society, Mannheim writes, is "an unceasing disturbance, the most radical disruption of any and all contemplativeness,"[7] which simply put means nothing other than that there is no longer any opportunity for anyone to call a moratorium in which they could quietly and open-endedly reflect on and freely decide whether they even want this unceasing disturbance in the name of ambition as a life-defining power for themselves and society. The destruction of any opportunity for contemplation in an accelerated world also entails the loss of any ability to recognize the irrational, excessive aspects of the pursuit of success. Said pursuit becomes "total," and all must succumb to it. Mannheim's ratification of the effective eradication of contemplation under capitalism at the conceptual

---

[7]Ibid., 667.

AMBITION IN MODERNITY

level—his argument that contemplation is only pathological, and thus not a real or good alternative to ambition—leads him to uncritically identify with the pursuit of success, inevitably resulting in his misdiagnosis of the times. Nevertheless, *à contre cœur* or "deconstructively," we can take from Mannheim's essay the insight that the kind of profound *distance from everything* that can only be achieved through serious contemplation is capable of revealing and making one conscious of "the radical questionability of being"[8] and, more specifically, the questionability of the pursuit of economic success at any price—"ruthlessness, ambition, greed"[9]— that dominated Mannheim's era. Distancing contemplation can raise questions "about the 'meaning' of success" that Mannheim explicitly disregards for heuristic and other reasons.[10] Sociology forfeits its critical potential when it is no longer capable of conceiving of itself as social philosophy and devolves into the didactic teaching of social techniques that lead to success. As mentioned above, Mannheim's aim is in fact to outline a pedagogy appropriate for the age of industrialization that assimilates the "society-shaping power"[11] that the economy of capitalist society effectively exerts on its members. Reading Mannheim's essay from the perspective of the present, one could easily show that he anticipates and preformulates numerous elements of the behavioral expectations that neoliberalism places on subjects today: "The quantitative abstractness [of economic thought] tends to pose, in place of the question of who one is, the question [...] of how much one is worth."[12]

The Concept of Success

Mannheim studies the pursuit of success from two different perspectives. Having resolved the question of what "success"

---

[8]Ibid., 665.
[9]Ibid., 671.
[10]Ibid., 653.
[11]Ibid., 632.
[12]Ibid., 665. On the origins of this semantics, see Verheyen, *Die Erfindung der Leistung*, 122.

172 AMBITION: AN ESSAY ON THE BURNING DESIRE TO RISE

actually is, he proceeds to develop a powerful phenomenology of the pursuit of success in general that draws on studies specifically of the pursuit of economic success that radically and definitively shapes society and the lives of subjects under late capitalism. Very much like Ichheiser, Mannheim first differentiates between achievement related to performing a task and the social category of success. While achievement is "*a form of objectivization, realization in a particular field*," success is "*a form of realization in the social realm*."[13] Unlike Ichheiser, however, Mannheim has no problem with the idea of a subject "leveraging his achievement to obtain success"[14] and refers to the "basic fact of life" that ambition can be *primary* and "first finds its way to achievement through the subjective pursuit of success."[15] This nuance already suggests a concept of the pursuit of success that is contrary to Ichheiser's, inasmuch as here, ambition itself creates achievement and not only subsequent success.

With respect to success itself, Mannheim distinguishes between *objective success*—the accomplishment of a task or realization of an achievement—and *subjective success*—the prevailing and self-assertion of the achieving subject.[16] The combination of both aspects can be called "total success,"[17] the ultimate goal of extreme ambition. Excessive ambition never rests until success is "total," and even then, the greedy eye remains on the lookout for ever new objects and aims. Mannheim thus also recognizes the absolute, insatiable ambition, so strikingly described even in antiquity, that is "dynamic through and through and constantly pushes the person possessed by it beyond himself."[18]

Mannheim further adds to his instructive classification the distinction between *precarious success* and *relatively stable success*. Recognition, prestige, fame, and glory are all subject to various fluctuations, to changing moods, tastes, and fashions; they are thus eminently precarious and can be influenced by personal achievements only in limited ways. A person who "takes up,

---

[13]Mannheim, *Erfolgsstreben*, 634.
[14]Ibid., 637.
[15]Ibid., 638.
[16]Cf. ibid., 635f.
[17]Ibid., 636.
[18]Ibid., 671.

AMBITION IN MODERNITY 173

seizes on, or is guaranteed opportunities to make an impact and exert control," however, can stabilize his success, although only "relatively" within the framework of an existing system.[19] Later in his essay, Mannheim examines career success—specifically in the context of established career paths in the public sector, which follow different laws than competition in the world of free enterprise—as a special type of stable success.[20]

Mannheim identifies a number of characteristics of modern capitalism based (at least in theory) on free competition. First, with the strengthening of public opinion in bourgeois society, the precarious success of fame becomes increasingly important, potentially affecting or—in cases of negative publicity—haunting even traditionally rooted exponents of society.[21] Second, and critical for Mannheim's further argument, is the confirmation of Werner Sombart's observation that "the wealth power is increasingly superseded by the power of wealth."[22] Economic success that can be quantitatively measured solely in terms of sums of money "is least of all attributable to class status"[23] and thus increasingly dissolves traditional relations, leading to a fundamental change of mentality in the name of the "rule of money" that Tocqueville so powerfully studied in the young United States. Economic thinking "gradually begins to take hold of all human activities and, sooner or later, to define even those individual modes of acting and reacting that do not have anything directly to do with economic activity."[24] Here Mannheim describes the evolution of the *homo oeconomicus*, whose conduct and behavior correspond to a world in which "the economy tends to become the primary factor of socialization":[25]

A fully developed economic society functions better, so to speak, when the activity it requires has been emptied of all sentiment or principle. To the same extent that economic rationality pervades the structure of social life, we see in the disappearance

---

[19]Ibid., 638.
[20]Cf. ibid., 650ff.
[21]Cf. ibid. 643.
[22]Ibid., 642.
[23]Ibid., 644.
[24]Ibid., 645.
[25]Ibid., 646f.

174 AMBITION: AN ESSAY ON THE BURNING DESIRE TO RISE

of ideological commitments a disappearance of the enforcement of attitudes or principles. This is the social genesis of the modern idea of tolerance.[26]

Where Ichheiser saw a Machiavellian lack of principles unleashed, Mannheim sees the origins of the idea of tolerance as an emancipation from the enforcement of principles, thus opening up a controversy that has endured into the present, including via various theories on the genesis of fascism. Moral restrictions are very much ambivalently assessed in Mannheim. Here we must therefore further differentiate between the "ethics of economic activities" themselves and non-economic "values" that nonetheless have economic effects. A person who does not allow unmarried or homosexual couples to stay in his hotel out of "religious conviction," for example, must do without the profit he would have earned and instead hope for recompense from his god. According to Mannheim, the purely objective "rule of money" fundamentally promotes the "democratization" of societies, at least as long as "the overall economy is based more on free competition than on systematically controllable, monopolistic regulations."[27]

The Pursuit of Subjective Success (Ambition)

Having thus classified the basic forms of success, Mannheim turns to an analysis of the *pursuit of subjective success* that is particularly instructive for the theory of ambition. He frames his analysis as a debate "between two fundamentally different possibilities of being"[28] known in the philosophical tradition as the *vita activa* and the *vita contemplativa*. One of the most astonishing aspects of Mannheim's essay is that, in the section "On the Pursuit of Success in General," he initially matter-of-factly distinguishes between "the path of action, of praxis and the path of renunciation, of meditation

---

[26]Ibid., 648.
[27]Ibid., 644.
[28]Ibid., 656.

AMBITION IN MODERNITY

and contemplation."[29] He points to the venerable tradition that contemplation commands, stretching from ancient India to Greek and Roman philosophical schools to medieval mysticism, and from there to Schopenhauer, Dostoevsky—whom Mannheim invokes with great admiration[30]—and beyond. And accordingly, he emphasizes that he does not want to decide here which of the two paths is the right one.[31] Yet when it comes down to specifics, Mannheim clearly and polemically votes in favor of the goal-oriented pursuit of success; the supposed "'living for the moment' that characterizes the vagabond, the bohemian, and the mendicant in equal measure," meanwhile, apparently yields an existence that is "only sporadically bright and cheerful," tending overall "to cloak life in an impenetrable darkness."[32]

According to Mannheim, deciding against contemplation and in favor of unleashing ambition has a sevenfold effect on the structure of one's personality.[33] First, ambition produces a stable *experience of time and oneself*, as the active life—as Pettigrove also points out—brings continuity to daily life through purposefulness and "perseverance," and a rationally pursued plan functions as a kind of handrail leading to the future that one can always cling to when one fails or experiences the occasional setback. In the language of neoliberalism, high motivation is "expedient" and "productive," pushing one toward one's goals. Second, being oriented toward success has the effect of modifying or simplifying one's *relationship to others* insofar as one does not encounter others in their confounding difference to oneself—which only love, according to Mannheim, can fully discover and endure—but only as teammates or adversaries in the plan one is pursuing. Being oriented toward success means standing in the middle of the fight between competing interests and necessarily developing the kind of heightened psychological acuity that characterizes the human observational prowess found in social novels. Mannheim, too, acknowledges Stendhal as exemplary in this respect. Third, one's *relationship to oneself* is likewise subject

---

[29]Ibid., 654.
[30]Cf. ibid., 657.
[31]Cf. ibid., 656.
[32]Ibid., 660.
[33]On what follows here, see ibid., 654–62.

176 AMBITION: AN ESSAY ON THE BURNING DESIRE TO RISE

to the "orientation toward influencing and having an effect" on others that having a plan demands; self-examination in this context is thus absolved from oversensitive introspection.[34] The fourth modification, *attentiveness to one's actions*, brings into view the instrumental rationality discussed above and thus an understanding of the world as "rationalized" or at least "rationalizable" that, in instances of failure, places blame not on *fate* (or the organization of society), but—anticipating the neoliberal demand for constant self-optimization[35]—on oneself. Fifth, an orientation toward success is supposed to *suppress feelings of anxiety*, a highly attractive promise in social-psychological terms. Anxiety, for Mannheim, is not an existential condition; its root is not—as it is in Heidegger—being-in-the-world as such, rather it results from wantonly cutting oneself off from a life that is open to rational management. It is not bourgeois ideology, in Mannheim's view, but the vagabonds, bohemians, and mendicants who cloak life "in impenetrable darkness."[36] An ambitious, instrumentally rational orientation toward success in life amounts to a "liquidation of the space of anxiety,"[37] an awkward, unfortunate turn of phrase that presages the actual liquidation of "contemplative vagabonds" in totalitarian regimes. For according to Mannheim, the space of anxiety grows as soon as one withdraws from life rather than successfully mastering it, whereupon the world falls into eerie darkness. Mannheim's treatise on the pedagogy of ambition teaches that those who take action, who tirelessly strive for success, will develop a sense of optimism, whereas pessimism and fatalism, from a sociological perspective, tend to be found in powerless groups:

Feelings of anxiety about external threats and the abyss of one's own soul disappear to the extent that one manages to successfully orient oneself on the predictable pathways of the internal and external world. This is what unlocks the optimism of one's consciousness, while an opposing constellation, such as

---

[34]Ibid., 658.
[35]For a balanced analysis that also advances the philosophical discussion of this issue, see Dagmar Fenner, *Selbstoptimierung und Enhancement: Ein ethischer Grundriss* (Tübingen: UTB, 2019).
[36]Mannheim, *Erfolgsstreben*, 660.
[37]Ibid.

AMBITION IN MODERNITY   177

the actually identifiable powerlessness of a group, unlocks their pessimism and fatalism.[38]

Although Mannheim occasionally endeavors to also identify negative aspects of the pursuit of success—restless striving can become "mere restlessness";[39] ambition "can be associated with ruthlessness"[40]—he ultimately argues that the pursuit of success is better suited overall to "philosophically pervade the world" than passive contemplation and meditation. Mannheim's claim that Nietzsche and Stendhal's "privileging of the clear, rigorous, unillusioned intellect in the realm of philosophy has one of its origins in the pursuit of economic success"[41] reads like a sociological derivation of Machiavelli's highly influential theories drawn from the world of rationally operating Florentine bankers in the early modern age. In this context, Mannheim is also one of the few scholars before Henning Ritter to refer to Hérault de Séchelles' *Théorie de l'ambition*, which was conceived of as a detailed guidebook for social success and contains "perhaps the most incisive observations (in terms of being attentive to one's actions)."[42] The remaining two personality-changing aspects arise easily from those outlined thus far: The active, success-oriented person is able both to adapt and to make decisions—what today we would call "flexible"—and, finally, develops a heightened sense for the realities of political and economic life.

Devaluation of Contemplation

The grave consequences that the *vita contemplativa* supposedly has for the subject stand in sharp contrast to this success story of ambition designed to serve as a pedagogy for the industrial age. The contemplative person has a fluctuating, oscillating experience of time and may also experience a disastrous, psychotic loss

---

[38]Ibid., 659.
[39]Ibid., 656.
[40]Ibid., 659.
[41]Ibid., 657.
[42]Ibid.

178 AMBITION: AN ESSAY ON THE BURNING DESIRE TO RISE

of self (if he is not able to elevate this loss of self to a religious aim, as in Buddhism). From the absence of any mention of the contemplative life in Mannheim's section on relationships to others, we can conclude *ex negativo* that an existence turned away from the world and other people is not capable of being attentive or conforming to the "rules of play and commitments" that, in the struggle for success between competing interests, can be more rigorous "than the strictest morality."[43] In terms of one's relationship to oneself, the person who renounces the world, if he is not a mystic, runs the risk of succumbing to "narcissism."[44] The full passage on coping with anxiety finds Mannheim describing the life of the contemplative person as nearly indistinguishable from that of the severe neurotic in an effort to discourage the next generation from dreaming:

> In passive and powerless people, the uncertainty and proliferation of feelings of anxiety stems not only from the realm of what is actually dark in all human existence, but often also from their cluelessness with respect to all those relationships and worldly things that an analytic and attentive consciousness masters rationally and willingly from the beginning. There thus arises in the unworldly person who renounces success a tendency to perceive "profundities," "mysteries," and "destiny" where there are simply things to be mastered. In such contexts, he also conjures well-deserved irony on the part of the worldly man, for the mystification of connections that one doesn't recognize because of one's own inability to do so is deserving of reproach. The faltering character of the worldless person who never comes to a decision and is incapable of adapting then degenerates into a convulsion, the inner mechanics of which have recently been adequately described by psychoanalysis.[45]

Whereas perhaps "only death" is capable of limiting the ambition of the individual who pursues and realizes success according to the

---

[43]Ibid., 657.
[44]Ibid., 658.
[45]Ibid., 661.

AMBITION IN MODERNITY   179

model outlined above,[46] the contemplative life is a narcissistically powerless existence, a convulsion agitated by an effectively objectless anxiety that at best may be tranquil, if it is lived luxuriously in the "forms of the apathetic ecstasy of work of the absolved aristocratic classes."[47] To the apathetic aristocrats, the Brahmans, the world appears static; its actual processual character is revealed only to the ambitious, to those "fixated on success."[48] In Mannheim, the contemplative life gradually devolves from an equally worthy *alternative* to the pursuit of success into an expression of the mere pathology of ultimately lazy people who deserve the reproach of the "worldly man" and in some cases, if they cannot bear success, may need to be cured through psychoanalytic therapy. Here Mannheim briefly refers to an essay by Theodor Reik on "Success and the Unconscious Anxiety of the Conscience" that builds on Sigmund Freud's brilliant reading of Shakespeare's masterful tragedy *Macbeth*.

Freud argues that *Macbeth* remains insufficiently understood as long as the play "is regarded only as a tragedy of ambition,"[49] as such a reading does not explain what the motives may have been that "in so short a space of time could turn the hesitating, ambitious man into an unbridled tyrant, and his steely-hearted instigator into a sick woman gnawed by remorse."[50] For Freud, Shakespeare's tragedy represents the paradigmatic portrayal of one of the character-types met with in psychoanalysis: the subject who is wrecked by success, a figure that the playwright splits into two dramatis personae, Macbeth and Lady Macbeth. This divided figure's long fervently sought-after success—Macbeth's perfidious ascension the throne through the murder of King Duncan—is initially tolerated by the ego as a harmless daydream. But as soon as it is actually attained,

---

[46]Ibid., 660.

[47]Ibid., 662.

[48]Ibid.

[49]Sigmund Freud, "Some Character-Types Met with in Psycho-Analytic Work," in: Freud, *The Standard Edition of the Complete Psychological Works of Sigmund Freud*, vol. 14: *On the History of the Psycho-Analytic Movement, Papers on Metapsychology and Other Works (1914–1916)*, edited and translated by James Strachey (London: Hogarth Press, 1957), 309–33 (319).

[50]Ibid., 321f.

180 AMBITION: AN ESSAY ON THE BURNING DESIRE TO RISE

a previously latent, unconscious conflict of conscience erupts that "forbid[s] the subject to gain the long hoped-for advantage from the fortunate change in reality."[51]

Mannheim's devaluing and pathologizing of contemplation now prompts a simple question: If the pursuit of success loses its equally worthy opponent—that is, if the ambition that effectively dominates society also becomes "total" at a *conceptual level*—then how can one possibly formulate an outside perspective on the pursuit of success in the abstract or demand a substantive alternative to ambition in practice? In Mannheim's reasoning, the economy's accession to power in social and individual life is reflected in the fact that his praise of the pursuit of success devours any alternative to it. The social philosopher turns into a social engineer who can still see and describe the course of things but is no longer capable of critiquing it, because the critic has been devalued as a mere neurotic who does not care to play along in the great game for total success. Thus in the sketch Mannheim draws here, the figure of the "striver" or *arriviste* stands out in sharp contrast to the vagabonds, bohemians, and mendicants—a figure that Max Scheler had provided a justly famous phenomenology of in his study of ressentiment:

> An *arriviste* is not a man who energetically and potently pursues power, property, honor, and other values. He does not deserve this name as long as he still thinks in terms of the intrinsic value of something which he actively furthers and represents by profession or calling. The ultimate goal of the *arriviste*'s aspirations is not to acquire a thing of value, but to be more highly esteemed than others. He merely uses the "thing" as an indifferent occasion for overcoming the oppressive feeling of inferiority which results from his constant comparisons.
>
> If this type of value experience comes to dominate a whole society, then the "system of free competition" will become the soul of this society. [...] No "place" is more than a transitory point in this universal chase. The aspirations are intrinsically *boundless*, for they are no longer tied to any particular object

---

[51]Ibid., 317.

AMBITION IN MODERNITY 181

or quality. The objects have become "commodities," destined for exchange and defined by their monetary value.[52]

The Drowsing of Power

In the next sections of Mannheim's essay, he precisely describes how the pursuit of economic success seized power, from the age of artisanry and craftsmanship to that of mercantilism and liberalism on up to the age of late capitalism. For the striver with an opportunity, calculating reason has become an "*organ of combat*" and, eventually, an "organon for orienting oneself in the world."[53] As noted above, the question, "Who are you?" has given way to the question, "How much are you worth?" The pursuit of success tends "to obscure, to ban the productive questionability (the questionability of being) that lurks in every existence."[54] The banning of this thought produces, however, a new kind of empty narcissism that quantifies rather than "penetrates the world," converting it into money and consequently appropriating the world to its own will.[55] As Ichheiser also argued, the unbridled pursuit of success bets on "maximally exploiting" one's own chances and "ruthlessly exploiting" the disadvantages of others, on "taking advantage" in the interest of profit.[56] The result is a restless turmoil, "the most radical corrosion of every form of contemplativeness."[57] The phase of free competition has unleashed a disinhibited ambition that is "dynamic through and through, constantly driving the person possessed by it beyond himself,"[58] and knows no end in this world. A Faustian "inability to dwell in the

---

[52]Scheler, *Ressentiment*, 38f. Verheyen, however, has convincingly argued that this famous critique of the *arriviste* can also be read "as a critique of social climbers" and thus as a caricature of the struggle for social mobility in the German Empire. Verheyen, *Die Erfindung der Leistung*, 45.
[53]Mannheim, *Erfolgsstreben*, 663.
[54]Ibid., 665.
[55]Ibid.
[56]Ibid., 666.
[57]Ibid., 667.
[58]Ibid., 671.

182 AMBITION: AN ESSAY ON THE BURNING DESIRE TO RISE

present moment" has emerged, a constant "outdoing of oneself," dominated by the "vices of battle" that have been well known since antiquity: "Ruthlessness, greed, ambition, and a total dissolution of all contemplative elements from here on out."[59] Finally, late capitalism has given rise to the formation of trusts and monopolies, such that, as Mannheim strikingly puts it, economic social space now resembles a "fluid," silently administered and largely devoid of conflict, "in which only a few large, pyramid-like corporations fight against each other."[60]

It is illuminating to see how Mannheim, with this dramatic depiction of the global dominance of capitalism, now takes recourse to—and must take recourse to—the very concepts whose world-disclosing dignity he had previously denied: the questionability of existence, penetration of the world, contemplation, ability to dwell in the moment, being with oneself, silence. Mannheim's text thus deconstructs itself, becoming unreadable. The question of whether contemplation, the complete destruction of which brought about unbridled economic ambition, is now the purview only of vagabonds, bohemians, and mendicants, or the moral authority before which predatory capitalism reveals itself as such, remains unanswered. The conceptually jagged essay does not culminate in a depiction of the *gigantomachy* of a few large trusts, but rather ends with a series of reflections on the increasing bureaucratization of the world, on the working life and leisure time of the officials who exemplarily represent the administrated world (as well as of the employees of large, state-like corporations, who have also come to increasingly resemble such officials), and finally with a classification of the pursuit of success in terms of social differentiation and stratification. The contrast is astounding, as Mannheim's striking, almost apocalyptic description of the few remaining giants fighting with each other in a hazy fluid gives way to matter-of-fact information on the reification of the world. The effect is as stupefying as if a blockbuster movie were to set up a spectacular showdown between giant monsters only to abruptly roll the mundane closing credits as soon as the battle began.

---

[59]Ibid.
[60]Ibid., 672.

AMBITION IN MODERNITY 183

To Marxists, of course, it is obvious that Karl Mannheim cannot bring himself to depict the culminating crisis of capitalism that, according to *Das Kapital*, inevitably must follow here, namely the revolution that is supposed to engender widespread social solidarity by overthrowing the regime of merciless competition in favor of social ownership of the means of production. Moreover, it is clear why the disastrous destruction of reflection repeatedly emerges as a central theme in the work of many contemporary writers—Rainer Maria Rilke, Robert Musil, Walter Benjamin, Franz Kafka, and others—who have become known as theorists and advocates of contemplation in modernity.

Mannheim's phenomenology of the lives of those "minor functionaries" whose existences degenerate into monotonous work and empty leisure time to be filled with hobbies reads like a brilliant commentary on Kafka's analysis of the tired and tiresome power of all-pervading bureaucracy. The working world of the civil servant, fed into an incomprehensible, highly compartmentalized machine and tasked with managing a "field of activity devoid of meaning"[61] until his longed-for retirement, is characterized by vacuous *drowsing*. The "deficiencies of [his] professional life" inevitably produce a sluggish "lack of volition" that appears to "extend even into [his] leisure time."[62] "Senselessly drowsing in taverns and bars becomes a necessity,"[63] because it creates continuity between the meaningless tediousness of the workplace and the vacuousness of leisure time. The life of the functionary thus forms a gloomy "whole." As Kafka's novels teach, however, it would be a grave mistake to interpret this irresistible drowsing—such as that of the castle functionary Klamm, observed by K. through a hole in the wall—as a weakness of the system. The individual bearers of bureaucratization—which, according to Mannheim, "is in a way our destiny"[64]—are sick and tired, but the overall machine is relentless, refusing to allow those who protest against it to ever really rest, as the craftsman of the preindustrial age yet could.[65] The story of the land surveyor K. is

---

[61]Ibid., 679.
[62]Ibid., 680.
[63]Ibid., 679.
[64]Ibid., 675.
[65]Cf. ibid., 679.

184 AMBITION: AN ESSAY ON THE BURNING DESIRE TO RISE

a story of constant sleep deprivation and the fatigue that follows from it. Power, exhausted, lies dozing in bed; the intruder is refused any bed at all. Contemplation, previously destroyed, returns in the administrated world as the vacuous drowsing of power, drawing all under its numbing, enervating spell.

5 THE AMBITIOUS SPOILSPORT
Roger Caillois

One who views reality as a game, who helps establish this lofty disposition that puts avarice, avidity, and hatred in their place, enriches the work of civilization.[1]

The School of Competition

Jacob Burckhardt and Friedrich Nietzsche's theories of agon as a civilizing institution of ancient Greece find confirmation in one of the twentieth century's most elegant contributions to a general theory of culture, Roger Caillois' 1958 treatise *Man, Play and Games*. Like Burckhardt and Nietzsche before him, Caillois describes the great competitions of Greek antiquity as a form of "compensation," a "safety valve," and moreover as representative events in which the polis could enthusiastically recognize itself: "[I]t is clear that in Ancient Greece, the stadium games illustrate the ideal of the city and contribute to its fulfillment."[2] The strictly regulated contests of the Olympic, Isthmian, Pythian, and other great games not only facilitated the channeled and controlled discharge of aggression and the harmless satisfaction of the "will to victory," but also served as a model for civilized behavior in general, which itself likewise followed a particular set of rules:

> Stadium games devise and illustrate a rivalry that is limited, regulated, and specialized. Stripped of any personal feeling of hate or rancor, this new kind of emulation inaugurates a school of loyalty and generosity. At the same time, it spreads the

---

[1] Roger Caillois, *Die Spiele und die Menschen: Maske und Rausch* (Berlin: Matthes & Seitz, 2017), 17.

[2] Roger Caillois, *Man, Play and Games*, translated by Meyer Barash (Urbana/Chicago: University of Illinois Press, 2001), 66.

186 AMBITION: AN ESSAY ON THE BURNING DESIRE TO RISE

custom of and respect for refereeing. Its civilizing role has often been stressed.[3]

This last remark can surely be read as an implicit allusion to Burckhardt and especially Nietzsche, who emphasized not only the cathartic, but also the pedagogical function of agon, and whose writings Caillois was introduced to by, among others, his friend Georges Bataille. Caillois' observations on competition in ancient Greece in turn are an integral component of a general theory of social development that he derives from his theory of play and games.

Caillois' elegant classification of games is widely and rightly considered a paragon of intellectual precision and clarity. But this clarity grows murky once he moves away from the phenomenology and classification of games toward "laying the foundations for a sociology *derived from* games."[4] This murkiness is not due to any "error" in Caillois' classification, but rather is primarily a result of the excessive dynamics of ambition, which occupies a central, but ultimately uncontrollable and continuously problematic position in Caillois' book and reveals itself to be a true spoilsport that ruins the game. It is this insight into the insurmountably double-edged nature of ambition in Caillois that I would like to pursue here, which will first require a brief recapitulation of his theory of play.

Theory of Play

Play—participation in a game, as opposed to, say, participation in life—is voluntary, a "free" activity. If the players in a game were forced to participate, it would "at once lose its attractive and joyous quality as a diversion"[5] and become serious. Play is moreover a "separate"[6] activity that takes place within particular limits in time and space—on a stage, for example, or on a soccer field. Third, play is an "uncertain"[7] activity. Among the appeals of a game is the tension

---

[3]Ibid., 108.
[4]Ibid., 67.
[5]Ibid., 9.
[6]Ibid.
[7]Ibid.

AMBITION IN MODERNITY

arising from the fact that the players do not know how long it will last or how it will end. Fourth, play is unproductive. It creates "neither goods, nor wealth, [...] except for the exchange of property among the players."[8] Fifth, play is governed by rules, by certain agreements that are binding for the duration of the game. Finally, play is a "make-believe" activity, "accompanied by a special awareness of a second reality or of a free unreality, as against real life."[9]

Caillois supplements this inventory of the formal qualities of games with a famous system of classification, still used today, that distinguishes between four broad categories of human games. The rubric *agon* covers all competitive games, which as such are characterized by rivalry and generally acknowledge only one victor or winner. The point "is for each player to have his superiority in a given area recognized."[10] Agonistic games—the true playground of ambition in the world of play—are distinct from aleatic games, "in which winning is the result of fate rather than triumphing over an adversary."[11] *Alea* (the Latin word for "dice") "signifies and reveals the favor of destiny."[12] Inasmuch as winning such a game depends primarily on luck, it "seems an insolent and sovereign insult to merit."[13] Aleatic games are thus diametrically opposed to agonistic games in which, at least ideally, the best player wins. Games that combine both *agon* and *alea*—card games like skat or bridge, for example, in which one's success is determined by one's skill as well as by getting "good cards"—are widespread. Caillois' third category, *mimicry*, comprises all those kinds of games in which the participants become something else for the duration of the game, whether animals or cowboys and Indians. The decisive factor in mimetic children's games, for Caillois as for Freud, is children's ambitious desire to be *big*, "to imitate adults."[14] Finally, the category *ilinx* describes those games that are about losing oneself in a frenzy, whether through dancing or even just spinning around, that satisfy the desire "to momentarily destroy the stability of perception and

---

[8]Ibid., 10.
[9]Ibid.
[10]Ibid., 15.
[11]Ibid., 17.
[12]Ibid.
[13]Ibid.
[14]Ibid., 21.

188 AMBITION: AN ESSAY ON THE BURNING DESIRE TO RISE

inflict a kind of voluptuous panic upon an otherwise lucid mind."[15] Games, played in the spirit of freedom, begin with sheer (childlike) joy, what Caillois calls *paidia*, as opposed to what he calls *ludus*, the working out of mandatory rules, hurdles, and artificial obstacles: that is, the actual game.[16]

Spoilsports

With respect to the self-contained world of human games, Caillois recognizes two kinds of *spoilsports* who announce the intrusion of reality into the world of play. On the one hand, there is the one "who denounces the rules as absurd and conventional, who refuses to play because the game is meaningless. His arguments are irrefutable."[17] Distinct from this spoilsport, who does not take the game seriously precisely because it is *just a game*, is the one who takes the game *too seriously*, particularly the one who cannot stand to lose, who knocks over the whole gameboard in a rage and thus ruins the game for everyone. This is the truly ambitious person, who is incapable of understanding that it was all "just a game." For him, it is not about the game, but about winning. Victory and success belong to the world of games *and* the world of the real in equal measure. To win at a game means that one can be renowned in reality. Against this backdrop, one's distance or lack of distance toward a game becomes a test of the scope of one's ambition, a diagnosis of "healthy" or excessive, "unhealthy" ambition:

> [Games] oblige the player to put everything on the line in order to win and yet keep their distance. What will be won can, indeed must be lost again. How one wins is more important than the win itself and in any event more important than the stakes. Accepting failure as simple adversity, welcoming victory without overexuberance or conceit: this standing back, this mental reservation with respect to one's own conduct is the law of play.

---

[15]Ibid., 23.
[16]Cf. ibid., 27.
[17]Ibid., 7.

AMBITION IN MODERNITY   189

One who views reality as a game, who helps establish this lofty disposition that puts avarice, avidity, and hatred in their place, enriches the work of civilization.[18]

Here we can clearly see why Caillois believes that games can have a salutary, moralizing effect on society: they allow people to engage with their latently excessive ambition in a positive way, develop a healthy distance to it, and above all sublimate their rage and hate by exhibiting sovereignty in failure. A person who knows how to lose gracefully will not develop any resentments, whereas one who cannot grasp that a game is just a game is apt to destroy it by blowing open the closed world of play. Conversely, the lofty attitude of distance finds its consummation in viewing all of reality as a game—what is not a frivolous or cynical position, Caillois argues, but rather an expression of noble courtesy toward the world. The social function of games, according to Caillois, consists in the fact that, first, they facilitate a controlled discharge of potentially destructive drives. Second, they promote "disciplining" one's drives, dealing with them in a civilized way that, third, serves as a model for the flourishing of the great social game that is society. Finally, Caillois' four categories of games exemplify four basic human attitudes toward the world: struggle (*agon*), hope (*alea*), accommodating submission (*mimicry*), and intoxication that dissolves the divide between the world and one's consciousness (*ilinx*).

Social Games

Caillois' brilliantly drawn insights lead the way to a sociology built on a theory of play. As we have seen, learning to respect the rules of a game is useful for navigating social life "outside," which demonstrates that social institutions, too, function "partly like a game."[19] Given these evident structural parallels, Caillois concludes that

play is correlated with culture, the most remarkable and complex manifestations of which are closely allied to the structure of

---

[18]Caillois, *Die Spiele und die Menschen*, 17.
[19]Ibid., 91.

190 AMBITION: AN ESSAY ON THE BURNING DESIRE TO RISE

games, or else the structure of games is diffused to reality and institutionalized in legislation, becoming imperious, constraining, irreplaceable, preferred—in a word, rules of the social game, norms of a game which is more than a game.[20]

While participation in an actual game is voluntary, social games and institutions are not optional events. They are "more than a game," which is to say they are systems willing and able to impose penalties, in which subjects find themselves socialized from birth. From the perspective of an existing system, then, a new form of social spoilsport now comes into view: the revolutionary, inasmuch as revolution can be understood as "a change in the rules of play"[21] or their wholesale replacement by other rules. A society in which positions and privileges are distributed according to accidents of birth (aristocracy) can thus be superseded by a society in which positions and privileges are subject to open competition (democracy). Or, translated into the categories of Caillois' theory of play: in the social game, *alea* can give way to *agon*.

Following Caillois' hypothesis, those revolutions that transform or abolish historically established systems and replace them with others are themselves historically preceded by an *original revolution*, a chaotic transitional phase from nature to culture that ends with the implementation of rules as such, which compensate for the atrophying of instinct in the human species. In this way, modern anthropology confirms the ancient Roman adage "Ubi societas, ibi ius."[22] The institution of a dynamic body of rules, the enforcement of the idea that there *are* binding rules, establishes an order of things, founded by this original revolution, through which "society itself begins."[23] An "undirected ambition" is thus introduced into history, and "thanks to these fortunate choices the authority of

---

[20]Caillois, *Man, Play and Games*, 64.

[21]Caillois, *Die Spiele und die Menschen*, 91.

[22]Cited in ibid., 126. ("Where there is society, there is law.")

[23]Ibid. Caillois might well have also borrowed this insight from Nietzsche, who in the sixteenth aphorism of the first book of *Daybreak*, in view of the seeming absurdity of archaic rules, declares the first proposition of civilization to be: "[A]ny Custom is Better than No Custom," in: Friedrich Nietzsche, *Daybreak: Thoughts on the Prejudices of Morality*, edited by Maudemarie Clark and Brian Leiter, translated by R.J. Hollingdale (Cambridge: Cambridge University Press, 1997), 15.

AMBITION IN MODERNITY 191

the past ceases to paralyze the power to innovate and progress—heritage replaces obsession."[24] In athletic or artistic competition, ambition is "directed" by the rules and ultimately is quenched in victory. Ambition pressed into the service of progress by the rules of society, by contrast, is "undirected," because it can be aimed at every possible thing in the world, measured against endlessly many aspects of life, and potentially fulfilled in any number of different contexts. The world is no longer that all-surpassing authority of overpowering nature to which "petrified" man fearfully submits by either accommodating himself to it to the point of becoming unrecognizable (*mimicry*) or losing himself in the intoxication of dedifferentiation (*ilinx*), but rather has become man's opponent in the *agon* of civilization:

> The reign of *mimicry* and *ilinx* as recognized, honored, and dominant cultural trends is indeed condemned [in ancient Greece, EG] as soon as the mind arrives at the concept of the cosmos, i.e. a stable and orderly universe without miracles or transformations. Such a universe seems the domain of regularity, necessity, and proportion—in a word, a world of number.[25]

The world-as-cosmos is conceived of as orderly and predictable, as a world that human beings are constantly processing, studying, and changing, that they measure themselves against, that they wrestle with in order to advance into an open future under the banner of domination of nature. Agonistic society

> engages in an audacious and creative venture, which is linear rather than periodically returning to the same point—experimental, exploratory, endless: the very adventure of civilization.[26]

In this model, "undirected" ambition develops within the framework of an existing system of rules or prevailing laws and thus remains productive in accordance with Hesiod's good Eris. Against the backdrop of his four categories of games, Caillois formulates a bold

---

[24]Caillois, *Man, Play and Games*, 127. Translation slightly modified.
[25]Ibid., 107.
[26]Ibid., 127.

192 AMBITION: AN ESSAY ON THE BURNING DESIRE TO RISE

theory of history according to which "the transition to civilization as such implies the gradual elimination of the primacy of *ilinx* and *mimicry* in combination, and the substitution and predominance of the *agon-alea* pairing of competition and chance."[27] "The competitive spirit," he writes elsewhere, "has indeed become dominant."[28] According to Caillois, the "modern societies" of the western world based on the discoveries of the ancient Greeks endeavor in their principles to minimize as much as possible the social effects of chance, constantly expand the "domain of regulated competition, or merit," and thereby establish a stable meritocracy.[29] In the addenda appended to the main text of the book, Caillois writes of *agon* and *alea* as the complementary principles of modern societies:

> [A]*gon* and *alea* no doubt represent the contradictory and complementary principles of a new social order. Moreover, they must fulfill parallel functions which are recognizably indispensable in one or the other situation. *Agon*, the principle of fair competition and creative emulation, is regarded as valuable in itself. The entire social structure rests upon it. Progress consists of developing it and improving its conditions, i.e. simply eliminating *alea*, more and more. *Alea*, in fact, seems like the resistance posed by nature against the perfect equity of human institutional goals.[30]

This is an astonishing view of modernity, inasmuch as here only the good Eris is invoked as the supposed basis of the social order—fair, creative competition and emulation—the productivity of which is impaired only by the occasional ricochets of fortune and misfortune. Caillois is thus able to affirm that "[t]he new social *game* […] is defined in terms of the debate between birth and merit, between victory through proven superiority and the triumph of the luckiest."[31] The "natural law of competition" that he analyzes

---

[27]Ibid., 97.
[28]Ibid., 110.
[29]Ibid., 114.
[30]Ibid., 157.
[31]Ibid., 125.

AMBITION IN MODERNITY   193

elsewhere in his essay, along with the sort of relapse into "brutality" that frustrates the legend or ideology of the principle of fair competition, here fades far into the background. The success story of a society defined by good, fair competition contradicts and stands in stark, unreconciled contrast to the idea—also articulated by Caillois—that the ambition at work in *agon* by no means functions solely as an agent of linear progress toward an open, potentially more fair and just future, but rather *at the same time* also represents a threat to any and all progress. The *dialectic of enlightenment* is here revealed: *alea* is not the only adversary of *agon*—*agon* is also constantly in competition with itself.

Boundless Ambition

Caillois' schematic account of agon as a phenomenon that has played a critical role in the history of the human species classifies the various forms of sport as exemplary *cultural forms of play* "found at the margins of the social order"; economic competition and competitive examinations and selection procedures, meanwhile, are listed as corresponding *institutional forms* "integrated into social life." Finally, Caillois identifies violence, trickery, and the will to power as detestable forms of "corruption," the renewed unleashing of primary forces within the world of play and social institutions.[32] Here he thus shows himself to be in agreement with the propositions put forth by Gustav Ichheiser in his *Critique of Success*. For in Ichheiser's melancholy view, only those who pursue the will to power, who ably and artfully violate the rules of the game—who, in the language of a theory of play, manage to cheat without getting caught—meet with success in social life. From Caillois' perspective, the person who is successful in real life, outside of those village communities that remain united in solidarity despite any and all competition, in accordance with the good Eris of Hesiod, is therefore by definition a cheat and thus

---

[32]Ibid., 54.

194 AMBITION: AN ESSAY ON THE BURNING DESIRE TO RISE

a spoilsport, living out his never-satisfied ambition with ruthless consistency.

In the real world, competition is effectively "a law of modern life,"[33] one that at its core precisely does *not* purport to establish a fair contest, but rather indicates that the confining rules of games have been suspended, that what prevails is once again the "law of nature," the excessively and "obsessively" exercised right of the stronger—the bad Eris, the "degeneration" (Burckhardt) of the good one. For the moralists of games, as for the likes of Hobbes or Nietzsche, human nature is a kind of un-nature, a "true perversion," from which it necessarily follows that the calling of human beings is play. For Caillois, too, human beings are only free, only freed from their original obsessiveness and avidity, when they play:

> Outside of the arena, after the gong strikes, begins the true perversion of *agon*, the most pervasive of all the categories. It appears in every conflict untampered by the rigor or spirit of play. *Now competition is nothing but a law of nature.* In society it resumes its *original brutality*, as soon as it finds a loophole in the system of moral, social, and legal constraints, which have limits and conventions comparable to those of play. That is why mad, obsessive ambition, applied to any domain in which the rules of the game and free play are not respected, must be denounced as a clear deviation which in this case restores the *original situation*. There is no better example of the civilizing role of play than the inhibitions it usually places upon *natural avidity*.[34]

Human ambition, as conceived of by Caillois as a dynamic of archaic instincts, is continually oscillating between the spheres of play and reality. It is equally at home in both realms, for as a primary and boundless drive to self-assertion, it is older than the distinction between them. Seething in the container of play, ambition consistently eats through institutional frameworks like an acid, pushing with all of its power into social reality, which lures it with its promise of real rewards: it is only in reality, beyond the world of play, that the ambitious person actually receives the prize

---

[33]Ibid., 50.
[34]Ibid., 46. My emphasis.

AMBITION IN MODERNITY 195

of fame and glory. Play is free: "freedom is [...] its indispensable motive power."[35] Nothing is at stake in a game; once it is over, it vanishes. Victory, success, fame, and money, however, are social categories, the seductive factors that draw ambition out of the world of fiction and play and into reality. The ambitious person seeks real fame and glory from unreal games, as Caillois concedes: Games "would quickly lose [their] capacity to amuse if there were no competitors or spectators, at least potentially. [...] [E]veryone tries [...] [to reap] glory from a performance difficult to equal,"[36] thereby taking the momentous step from the closed world of games into social reality. The public and the prizes—the business with fame and glory—have formed the bridge between games and reality since time immemorial. Not even the classic balance of the ancient Greek games, which constrain and successfully sublimate ambition, could be preserved forever; the great panhellenic games were unable to prevent the catastrophe of the Peloponnesian War and the resulting "barbarization" so strikingly described by Thucydides. The lesson Caillois takes from such historic catastrophes is that these elementary impulses should have been continuously subjected to the attentive regime of an institutional existence.

Any understanding of Caillois' equally pro- and anti-agon argument stands and falls with the recognition that he ascribes an excessive, *unnatural* potential to the exclusively human phenomenon of ambition. Human ambition does not expire in self-assertion; it is inherently "perverse," boundless, destructive. Human ambition for Caillois is primordial, "degenerate" in comparison to other species and thus a sign of the unnaturalness of precultural man, the "not yet determined animal" who needs games and institutions to safeguard him against his own boundlessness and "obsessiveness." A collapse of social structures and the structures of play thus does not signify an "emancipation" or a return to an originally "good nature," but rather signifies a regression into a precultural, "perverse" avidity that wants to constantly and ruthlessly act out its destructive potential:

Left to themselves, destructive and frantic as are all instincts, these basic impulses can hardly lead to any but disastrous

---

[35] Ibid., 27.
[36] Ibid. 37.

196 AMBITION: AN ESSAY ON THE BURNING DESIRE TO RISE

consequences. Games discipline instincts and institutionalize them. For the time that they afford formal and limited satisfaction, they educate, enrich, and immunize the mind against their virulence. At the same time, they are made fit to contribute usefully to the enrichment and the establishment of various patterns of culture.[37]

In the sociological part of his book, Caillois thus finds himself constantly confronted with the double-edged nature of ambition that has always already arrived in reality. On the one hand, as we have seen, he defines ambition as a critical productive force of social development: "Nothing is more creative than such an ambition,"[38] he says of competitions and contests. On the other hand, he sees in ambition a merciless "will to success" that leads to "total war." The ancient distinction between the good and bad Eris, first established by Hesiod and repeatedly rethought and reflected upon since antiquity, thus returns in the work of this twentieth-century French philosopher and sociologist in his differentiation between productive and excessive, "corrupt," or "degenerate" ambition. In 1958, in the light of the devastation of the Second World War and the Germans' genocide of European Jews, the antifascist Caillois, whom the Nazis had driven into exile in South America in 1939, writes:

Transposed to reality, the only goal of *agon* is success. The rules of courteous rivalry are forgotten and scorned. They seem merely irksome and hypocritical conventions. Implacable competition becomes the rule. Winning even justifies foul blows. If the individual remains inhibited by fear of the law or public opinion, it nonetheless seems permissible, if not meritorious, for nations to wage unlimited ruthless warfare. [...] War is far removed from [...] regulated combat in an enclosure, and now finds its fulfillment in massive destruction and the massacre of entire populations.[39]

---

[37]Ibid., 55.
[38]Ibid., 77.
[39]Ibid., 54f.

Ambition is profoundly double-edged. It is one of the great motive forces of both actual games and social games, yet it is also always capable of producing those who mercilessly destroy games by shattering their immanence. For Caillois, one who is wholly and uncompromisingly committed to success, who consistently realizes his ambition in this way, always keeping its ultimate aim in mind, is a spoilsport in the context of both agonistic games *and* the social game. The person who employs illicit, performance-enhancing means in minor games for the sake of victory and success—the cheat, the swindler, the hustler, the destroyer of illusions—corresponds, in the great game of the real world, to the talented, amoral student of Machiavelli, who does not shy away from employing any possible means in an entirely different game with the highest stakes, and who merits Caillois' disdain, as he considers this a regression to mere, "degenerate" human nature under the natural law of absolute competition. For Caillois, too, in this productive-destructive dynamic there is only the *one* ambition at work that both fuels play and society and at the same time potentially destroys it. An ambition that, in the language of Karl Mannheim, desires "total success" is acted out "linearly," in fact and to its logical conclusion, when it declares "total war." Ambition is both the motive force of play and *at the same time* its potential destroyer, as it is constantly, greedily searching for "loopholes" that will allow it to circumvent the rules of the game and wring success through trickery, power, and violence. In this construction, the human species is an unnatural creature of nature, a spoilsport who must suffer pain in order to learn not to be one.

6 HESIOD'S RETURN IN THE ACHIEVING SOCIETY
David McClelland

Hesiod [...] is very conscious of man's achievement strivings.

DAVID MCCLELLAND[1]

Ambition and Motivation

The influential American psychologist David McClelland's 1961 book *The Achieving Society*, published in translation in the economic wonderland of West Germany in 1966, provided an entire era with a key concept for understanding itself and society. In the wake of the Second World War, the industrial states of the western world could now conceive of themselves—at first affirmatively, then, beginning in the late 1960s, more critically—as "achieving societies." In contrast to Max Horkheimer and Theodor W. Adorno's *Dialectic of Enlightenment*, written and published during their American exile, McClelland does not describe the individual as but an element in an elaborate, thoroughly organized system of domination whose seamless operation pulls subjects along and drives them to be constantly achieving in an administrated "civilization of employees."[2] His critique is instead directed at a sociology that heretofore has "begun with society and tried to create man in its image."[3] He would rather profile personal *agency*, the importance of individual potential and initiative:

If our study of the role of achievement motivation in society does nothing else, perhaps it will serve to redress the balance a

---

[1]David C. McClelland, *The Achieving Society* (New York: The Free Press, 1961), 120.
[2]Max Horkheimer and Theodor W. Adorno, *Dialectic of Enlightenment*, translated by John Cumming (London/New York: Verso, 1997), 153.
[3]McClelland, *The Achieving Society*, 391.

AMBITION IN MODERNITY 199

little, to see man as a *creator* of his environment, as well as a creature of it.[4]

McClelland's work shows how the ambivalent concept of "ambition" has given way in psychological and overall social discourse to the supposedly more neutral term "motivation," to the point that "ambition" as a discrete problem scarcely appears anymore in modern clinical psychology. At the very beginning of his standard reference work *Motivation and Action*, for example, Heinz Heckhausen illustrates the difference between external and internal reasons to act—self-motivated and situationally motivated actions—by recounting an instance of intrinsic motivation that in everyday language would most likely be described as a matter of ambition or pretension:

> The first occasion [to examine the question of motivation] arises when individuals behave differently in certain situations than most people do or (what is the same thing) than seems customary or appropriate. For example, one student is more eager to learn than normal, not just in school, but also in his free time, whereas another displays the opposite and can scarcely be "motivated" to learn even in class.[5]

The effects of this semantic displacement have since migrated into everyday language, insofar as it is largely perceived as more agreeable or objective to describe oneself or others as "highly motivated" or "especially capable" than as "extremely ambitious." The advantage of this new terminology is that it brackets off the ambivalent moral assessment that resonates in the word "ambition" and replaces it with a fixed scale that stretches from avoidance (motivation = 0) on one end to the extreme motivation of success at any price ("giving 100 percent")—including the destruction of the high achiever in the form of a "hero's death"—on the other. A precise reconstruction of the displacement of "ambition" by "motivation" along with its ideological consequences and implications for the history of

---

[4]Ibid., 391f.
[5]Heinz Heckhausen, *Motivation und Handeln*, 2nd ed. (Berlin/Heidelberg/New York: Springer, 1989), 2.

200 AMBITION: AN ESSAY ON THE BURNING DESIRE TO RISE

mentalities remains, as far as I can tell, a desideratum in critical discourse analysis, one that can only be mentioned in passing here. McClelland distinguished between three primary human motivations or drives, the famous "big three": the need for *achievement* (ambition), the need for *affiliation* or social *connection*, and the need for *power*.[6] His approach, highly successful in psychological practice, continues to make its influence felt in modern pedagogy and coaching, for example in the kind of political, social, and economic leadership training programs that McClelland himself conducted and studied both at Harvard[7] and later while performing field trials in India. The concept of "need" he adopted from Henry A. Murray, who defined it as follows:

> A need is a construct (a convenient fiction or hypothetical concept) which stands for a force (the physio-chemical nature of which is unknown) [...] which organizes perception, apperception, intellection, conation and action in such a way as to transform in a certain direction an existing, unsatisfying situation.[8]

The pointedly empiricist, quantitative bent of the psychology of motivation deemphasizes the fact that, in McClelland's pathbreaking works, world literature (*The Achieving Society*, 1961) and Freudian psychoanalysis (*Power: The Inner Experience*, 1975) provide the foundations for his arguments and statistical inquiries. The Thematic Apperception Test (TAT), also developed by Murray— and, despite all of the criticisms leveled against it, still used today as an instrument of clinical psychology—functions on this literary-psychoanalytical basis as an empirical method for studying and diagnosing personalities. Over the course of the test, subjects are presented with a series of ambiguous images and asked to give free rein to their imagination by inventing stories about them within a certain period of time. As McClelland notes in his book on the

---

[6]Cf. McClelland, *The Achieving Society*, 43.

[7]Cf. David McClelland, "Power Motivation and Organizational Leadership," in: McClelland, *Power: The Inner Experience* (New York: Irvington Publishers, 1975), 252–71.

[8]Henry A. Murray, *Explorations in Personality* (Oxford: Oxford University Press, 2008), 123f.

AMBITION IN MODERNITY

power motive, "In point of fact, fantasy, as reflected in such stories, has shown itself to be the most sensitive indicator of changes in motivational states of all sorts."[9]

Here I would like to recapitulate McClelland's concept of the achieving society; his study of the "need for achievement"[10] also reaches back to Hesiod's *Works and Days* as a foundational text in the history of competition and so, not least for this reason, also fits into the context of my own reflections on ambition. First, however, I must briefly sketch McClelland's psychoanalytic approach to studying the motive of power, as in the realm of economic competition, the psychological motivation of achievement is all but inevitably associated or combined with that of power, while the need for affiliation or connection by definition plays a subordinate role (at least initially). In an achieving society, the various ways in which the actors engaged in economic life deal with power, along with their respective levels of emotional maturity, naturally play a significant role and considerably influence the quality and character of both their pursuit of success and, consequently, their respective positions within economic processes. The need for achievement and the need for power are two distinct phenomena that overlap in thinking about competition, in the ambition to be "first": "Enjoying competition is the point at which *n* Achievement [the need for achievement] and *n* Power [the need for power] meet."[11]

Four Stages of Maturity

Drawing on Freud's theories about the stages of human sexual development as well as Erik H. Erikson's theory of human life-stages, McClelland differentiates between four stages of social-emotional maturity in dealing with the need for power that he sees as parallel to Freud's oral, anal, phallic, and genital phases.[12]

---

[9]McClelland, *Power: The Inner Experience*, 6.

[10]McClelland, *The Achieving Society*, 43.

[11]David McClelland, *Die Leistungsgesellschaft: Psychologische Analyse der Voraussetzungen wirtschaftlicher Entwicklungen* (Stuttgart: Kohlhammer, 1966), 284.

[12]For what follows, see McClelland, *Power: The Inner Experience*, 13–29.

202 AMBITION: AN ESSAY ON THE BURNING DESIRE TO RISE

According to McClelland, the feeling of power can be derived from *support* (by others), *autonomy* (independence from others), *self-assertion* (conflict with others), and *togetherness* (cooperation, solidarity, etc.).[13]

In *Stage I*, human beings in the *oral phase*—that is, infants—experience strength, security, and thus an early, archaic form of power through caring, motherly devotion. If infants could speak, they would say, "It strengthens me."[14] According to McClelland, people in whom this form of the feeling of power still dominates in adulthood should pursue careers in which they can serve powerful others: "Clienthood is their preferred status, because by being the client of a strong person, they themselves gain strength and feel powerful."[15]

In *Stage II*, human beings first experience the possibility of self-control; this corresponds to Freud's *anal phase*, in which the possibility of controlling one's bowel movements offers an early opportunity to say "no." In keeping with other well-known Freudian theories, McClelland also notes that obsessional or compulsive neurosis represents the pathological manifestation of the need for control. In adulthood, he argues, this anal phase lives on in the "accumulation" of prestige. At the same time, beyond such compulsions or obsessions, adults in *Stage II* also experience a sense of self-supported independence or willfulness. McClelland sharply differentiates in this context between two distinct forms of power. In *Stage II*, from a psychological perspective, "the *goal* of power *motivation* is to *feel powerful*, and [...] influencing others

---

[13]Cf. ibid., 29. Another theoretical foundation of McClelland's argument is Talcott Parsons' systems theory, particularly his major 1958 essay, "Social Structure and the Development of Personality: Freud's Contribution to the Integration of Psychology and Sociology," which elaborates the connections between personality development and collectivity structures and thus the relevance of psychology to sociology: "Psychologically, the essential point is that the process of ego development takes place through the learning of social roles in collectivity structures. Through this process, in some sense, the normative patterns of the collectivity in which a person learns to interact become part of his own personality and define *its* organization." In: Talcott Parsons, *Social Structure and Personality* (London: The Free Press, 1964), 78–111 (91f.).

[14]McClelland, *Power: The Inner Experience*, 13.

[15]Ibid., 13f.

AMBITION IN MODERNITY   203

is only one of many ways of feeling powerful."[16] A person who feels powerful because he feels steady and secure or because he has power over himself may not need the additional confirmation of fame and glory or domination over others, acclamation or continued recognition from a praising, potentially subjugated collective. Here again we can see the double-edged nature— mentioned above in the context of considering Aristotelian ethics as a form of Coriolanus' paradox—of power sought in the name of ambition. Understood as a product of the psychological vacuum of a lack of self-sufficiency, such power always brings with it new dependencies, allowing the dialectic of master and slave to play out over and over again.

In *Stage III*, corresponding to Freud's *phallic phase*, young people become conscious of various opportunities to exert influence over others, to dominate them, whether through physical assertion and aggression or through more subtle means like persuasion or even support and assistance that obliges others to express their gratitude to them or makes them dependent on them (with the double-edged consequences mentioned above). *Stage III* evinces the true *attitude of competition*, ambition in the sense that we have been discussing it to this point. And dominance, McClelland argues, is largely the aim of the ambitious pursuit of power, a genuine expression of the "will to power."

Finally, McClelland describes *Stage IV*, which corresponds to Freud's *genital phase* following the end of the latency period, as yet another form of the gratification of power consisting in the seemingly paradoxical conscious, willing subordination or integration of the powerful subject to or into a broader context, that is, in service to a higher cause (a religion, government, institution, or organization). *Stage IV* becomes less paradoxical when one recognizes—as McClelland emphasizes—its proximity to fully developed sexual love, which is aimed at generativity and consequently, in instrumentally rational terms, at securing certain corresponding social requirements (marriage, social community, etc.). From the perspective of a Machiavellian theory of power that interprets all manifestations of the power drive as "sublimations of the more primitive urge to dominate others," however, committed service to a cause necessarily

---

[16]Ibid., 17.

204 AMBITION: AN ESSAY ON THE BURNING DESIRE TO RISE

appears, as McClelland frankly admits, to be "sheer hypocrisy."[17] According to McClelland, who here cites Abraham Lincoln as an example, the principle of the need for power corresponding to *Stage IV* would be, "It moves me to do my duty."[18] Among the challenges that this poses for psychological research is not only the shadow of "messianism,"[19] the potentially pathological sense of mission of a leader at the highest stage, but also the task of offering a coherent explanation of the transition from an attitude of competition to one of cooperation, that is, from *Stage III* to *Stage IV*: "from self-assertion to selfless service to an ideal."[20]

The difference between "selfless" service to the polis, the nation, or a "cause" in the name of responsibility on the one hand and service primarily for the sake of oneself and one's own interests on the other—continually debated and discussed from Plato to Montesquieu to Max Weber's essay on politics as a vocation—thus reappears in the mid-twentieth century in the realm of clinical psychology. McClelland does not come to any firm, unambiguous conclusion here, although in his view, "it does appear that men and women who reach a Stage IV expression of *n* Power are more fully actualized."[21] In a certain sense, passing through these four stages means coming full circle, inasmuch as one's successful integration into a larger whole can ideally also mean a return, in adulthood, to the original feeling of security of one's earliest childhood, only now within a community. McClelland's concept of emotional maturity as the ability to respond appropriately in social and economic life, "to use whichever [modality or expression of the power drive] is appropriate to the situation," is also a critical component of his finely delineated theory of power:

> Immaturity involves using perhaps only one mode [of behavior] in all situations or using a mode inappropriate to a particular situation. It would be immature to compete for being the most pious Christian (Stage III behavior) or to be a Christian only

---

[17]Ibid., 20.
[18]Ibid.
[19]Ibid., 21.
[20]Ibid., 23.
[21]Ibid.

AMBITION IN MODERNITY 205

to get the immediate emotional and personal support of the minister (Stage I behavior). [...] Yet the earlier modes should remain available to provide the opportunity for a richer, more varied life.[22]

In the light of McClelland's psychoanalytically rooted theory of the four life-stages, emotional, social maturity could thus be described as the attainment of a sovereign *capacity for integration* that both supersedes the earlier stages and at the same time, when necessary, is able to call upon them without compulsively succumbing or permanently regressing to them.

As mentioned above, McClelland's clinical studies compile personality profiles of numerous men and women with the aid of the Thematic Apperception Test and additional surveys. He offers the following characterization of those men who even in adulthood have not advanced beyond the phallic attitude of competition of *Stage III*, the especially ambitious, in the colloquial understanding of that word, with a great need for power, little need for affiliation, a low threshold of inhibition, and correspondingly a high predisposition for resentment. McClelland terms this the "conquistador motive pattern," but he might just as well have called it "the profile of the average heterosexual man":

> They [...] behave in an imperious manner, but their assertiveness is neither disciplined nor channeled through organizational structures. [...] [T]hey fight more, drink more, and boast more about their sex lives. When asked to list stressful events in their lives, they do not recall many for which they could be held personally responsible. [...] They actively reject institutional responsibility. [...] Nor do they feel any obligation to share money with charities. In short, they behave like "tough guys," miniature warlords or "conquistadores."[23]

McClelland and his colleagues' studies of leading politicians (in the form of assessments of the speeches of numerous American presidents) and top managers demonstrate that one of the key factors

---

[22]Ibid., 24.
[23]Ibid., 295.

206 AMBITION: AN ESSAY ON THE BURNING DESIRE TO RISE

in the transition from *Stage III*—that of the bibulous conquistador—to *Stage IV* is a high level of restraint or fully developed capacity for self-control. In combination with a strong feeling of power, strong motivation to achieve, and little need for social connection, self-control facilitates the development of the "imperial motivational pattern"[24] that corresponds to *Stage IV*, what one might call the transition from the politician Octavian to the emperor Augustus. Men "with the conquistador motivational pattern make good feudal lords or perhaps daring tank commanders,"[25] but they do not attain the profile of a superior, responsible political leader like Franklin D. Roosevelt, "regarded by the majority of Americans during his lifetime and by historians since as one of the most successful, charismatic U.S. Presidents."[26]

In the later chapters of McClelland's book on power, which elaborate a theory of history, he supplements his study of political leaders who "have the maturity to make them wise rather than egotistic leaders" with an argument, based on Talcott Parsons' systems theory, that "explains the rise of great, well-organized empires in terms of a particular motive combination."[27] He locates the reason for this success in the "extractive capability" of a political system that understands how to effectively mobilize "material and human resources" in ways that "expand the possibilities of obtaining various goals for the system and for the society."[28] At this point, the personality profile of the ruler again comes into play, for as McClelland demonstrates via a variety of statistics from the 1970s, some countries' extractive capability is "reflected in spending more on guns and less on butter."[29] Writing in the shadow of the end of Richard Nixon's presidency under the threat of impeachment, McClelland ultimately returns to a series of now-classic reflections that go back to antiquity. It is to be hoped, he writes, that the ruler has in fact attained *Stage IV*, the highest level of maturity, and thus left his or her personal ambition behind:

---

[24]Ibid., 297.
[25]Ibid., 296.
[26]Ibid., 300.
[27]Ibid., 304.
[28]Ibid., 305.
[29]Ibid., 309.

AMBITION IN MODERNITY   207

Once he has attained this sense in Stages II and III, he should go on to an even higher level of maturity in which his participation in building better organizations out of his motivational needs will be essentially ego-less. The self is no longer in need of strengthening. If the leaders and participants in such organizations are at that stage of development, then one need not fear that the organizations will turn into ruthlessly authoritarian empires.[30]

McClelland's profile of the "imperial motivational pattern" represented by an impressive leader who combines consciousness of his own power, combat strength, self-control, resistance to regression, and effectiveness with an ethically grounded awareness that he serves a greater "cause" that transcends his individual person is effectively an elaboration of Max Weber's ideal type of the ethical, responsible politician who does not desire to get high on his own power, but rather wants to lead the cause he serves, soberly and purposefully, to success.

The Model of the Protestant Ethic of Achievement

As the author of the classic series of essays *The Protestant Ethic and the Spirit of Capitalism*, first published in 1904, Max Weber is the most important source for McClelland's work tracing the contours of the achieving society. With his writings on the Protestant ethic, McClelland argues, Weber "laid the groundwork for efforts to understand the social and psychological origins of such key economic forces as rapid technological advances, specialization of labor, population growth, and energetic entrepreneurship."[31] McClelland thus characterizes his own book *The Achieving Society* as an effort to confirm the hypothesis "that Weber's observation of the connection between Protestantism and the rise of capitalism may be a special instance of a much more general phenomenon."[32]

---

[30]Ibid., 313.
[31]McClelland, *The Achieving Society*, 11.
[32]Ibid., 70.

208 AMBITION: AN ESSAY ON THE BURNING DESIRE TO RISE

What exactly was it in Weber's theory that, as his biographer Jürgen Kaube notes, everyone could feel attacked by it, "disciples of Marxist theory, exponents of the Prussian religion of the state, Prussia's cultural elite, German historians, and friends of the money economy" alike?[33]

In light of the fact that, at the turn of the nineteenth century, successful entrepreneurs in Europe and especially the United States were statistically more likely to be Protestant than Catholic, Max Weber—whose project has been passionately and controversially debated ever since its publication—undertook to demonstrate that the Protestant denominations of Christianity, particularly Calvinism with its doctrine of predestination and Methodism with its systematization of conduct, should be acknowledged as significant factors in the development of modern capitalism. As a close reader of Karl Marx, however, Weber repeatedly pushes back against the erroneous notion that his masterpiece of modern cultural and economic sociology reduces this "tremendous confusion of reciprocal influences"[34] to a one-sided "spiritual" causal interpretation of culture and history.[35] At one point, he summarizes his brilliant theory as follows:

> [I]nnerworldly Protestant asceticism works with all its force against the uninhibited *enjoyment* of possessions; it discourages *consumption*, especially the consumption of luxuries. Conversely, it has the effect of liberating the *acquisition of wealth* from the inhibitions of traditionalist ethics; it breaks the fetters on the striving for gain by not only legalizing it, but [...] seeing it as directly willed by God.[36]

Weber's essay continues to fascinate today because it shows how originally purely religious needs and above all deep fears had tangible economic consequences, inasmuch as human work, conceived of

---

[33]Jürgen Kaube, *Max Weber: Ein Leben zwischen den Epochen* (Berlin: Rowohlt, 2014), 175.

[34]Max Weber, *The Protestant Ethic and the "Spirit" of Capitalism and Other Writings*, edited and translated by Peter Baehr and Gordon C. Wells (New York: Penguin, 2002), 36.

[35]Ibid., 122.

[36]Ibid., 115.

AMBITION IN MODERNITY

as a *vocation* to be performed as successfully as possible, in many ways rose to ultimately become "the *sole* means of making sure of one's state of grace." Ceaseless work and relentless industriousness in the place assigned to one by the Lord became duties before God.[37] What at first glance appeared to be the pursuit of purely economic success turned out upon closer inspection to be a product of the religious ambition of the "steely Puritan merchants of that heroic age of capitalism."[38] The systematic sanctification of life in the name of a vocation whose practitioner spurned consumption and consistently reinvested his profits "could almost assume the character of a business arrangement"[39] and, through the Protestant rejection of the magical practices of Catholic priests (confession, etc.),[40] effectively advanced the "disenchantment of the world" across different social classes[41]:

> Obviously, the "productivity" of work in the capitalist sense of the word was given a powerful boost by this *exclusive* striving for the kingdom of God through fulfillment of the duty of labor as a calling and through strict asceticism, since Church discipline naturally imposed this on the impoverished classes in particular.[42]

Weber's study moreover remains fascinating because it shows that the effects of this inner-worldly asceticism still define the "steel-hard shell" of capitalism today, although secularized acquisitiveness, emancipated from its religious origins, "tends to be associated with purely elemental passions, which at times virtually turn it in to a sporting contest."[43] Per Weber, the compulsive character of working life, originally founded on religious hopes and fears of eternal damnation, today continues to determine "the style of life *not only* of those directly involved in business but of every individual who is born into this mechanism." The religious foundations of the vocation-as-calling have disappeared; the idea

---

[37]Ibid., 119.
[38]Ibid., 77.
[39]Ibid., 85.
[40]On Catholic priests as "magicians," cf. ibid., 80.
[41]Ibid.
[42]Ibid., 119f.
[43]Ibid., 121.

210 AMBITION: AN ESSAY ON THE BURNING DESIRE TO RISE

of duty has remained. Another specter thus emerges alongside the "specter of communism" conjured by Marx and Engels, that of the only seemingly disempowered beliefs that, undetected, haunt and continue to define modern life:

> Even the optimistic mood of [the scientific-mechanistic worldview's] laughing heir, the Enlightenment, seems destined to fade away, and the idea of the "duty in a calling" haunts our lives like the ghost of once-held religious beliefs.[44]

Weber's scholarly, eloquent depiction of how faith is "[put] to the test [...] in secular working life"[45] and its ramifications for the economic development of Europe and North America obscures the fact that his essay also brings into play, as a factor in the evolution of capitalism, the figure of the energetic and fearless young entrepreneur, whose emergence is by no means necessarily tied to the experience of Calvinism, but more likely to a motivation to achieve, leadership skills, assertiveness, the will to rise—in short: personal ambition. In direct contradistinction to Marx's theory of the first accumulation of capital as the "original sin" that unleashed capitalism,[46] Weber offers the legend of the highly motivated young entrepreneur who, as a new subject of history, "suddenly" disturbs the "coziness" of traditional economic activity:

> What happened was often simply this. A young man from one of the putter-out families from the town moved to the country, carefully selected the weavers he needed, tightened up control over them and made them more dependent, thus turning peasants into workers. [...] At the same time, he began to carry out the principle of "low price, high turnover." There was then a repetition of what invariably follows a "rationalization" process of this kind: you either prospered or went under. Under the impact of the bitter struggle for survival that was beginning, the idyll collapsed. [...] In such cases (and this is the main point), it

---

[44]Ibid., 121.
[45]Ibid., 83.
[46]Karl Marx, *Capital: A Critique of Political Economy*, vol. 1, translated by Ben Fowkes (London: Penguin, 1990), 873.

AMBITION IN MODERNITY 211

was *not* normally an influx of new *money* that brought about this revolution—in a number of cases known to me the entire "revolutionizing process" was set in motion with a few thousand marks capital borrowed from relatives: it was the new *spirit* at work—the "spirit of capitalism." The question of the motive forces behind the development of capitalism is not primarily a question of the origin of the *money* reserves to be used, but a question of the development of the capitalist spirit.[47]

Here Weber evokes one representative of the type of the ambitious go-getter whose critical influence on economic development across various epochs and societies McClelland endeavors to establish in his book on *The Achieving Society*. McClelland wants to show, empirically and thus verifiably, that "achievement motivation is an important factor affecting the rate of economic development."[48] Weber's findings thus turn out, in McClelland's view, to represent a "special case" of a more general phenomenon. McClelland, too, positions himself explicitly against Marx. The primary motive, he argues, is not greed for profit, but the need to achieve:

> The profit motive, so long a basic analytic element among Marxist and western economists alike, turns out on closer examination to be the achievement motive, at least in the sense in which most men have used the term to explain the energetic activities of the bourgeoisie. The desire for gain, in and of itself, has done little to produce economic development. But the desire for achievement has done a great deal, and ironically it was probably this same desire that activated the low middle-class leaders of the Russian Communist Party as well as the bourgeoisie they criticized so intensely.[49]

Here again the intensity of the achievement motive is determined via the Thematic Apperception Test, on the basis of the concentration

---

[47]Weber, *The Protestant Ethic*, 21f.

[48]McClelland, *The Achieving Society*, 61.

[49]Ibid., 391. See also 234–7, where McClelland argues that, "as all our evidence indicates, [...] Western capitalists were actually motivated primarily by the achievement motive" (236).

212 AMBITION: AN ESSAY ON THE BURNING DESIRE TO RISE

of achievement-related ideas and fantasies in the stories subjects write about the ambiguous images presented to them.[50] McClelland supplements this with surveys of families with "highly motivated sons whose mothers expect self-reliance and mastery at an earlier age"[51] as well as with assessments of statistics relating to religion, "which confirmed the hypothesis [...] that Protestant boys would have higher *n* Achievement on the average than Catholic boys."[52] Surveys of American Protestants and Catholics discussed later in the book again appear to confirm Weber's thesis, showing that "Protestants [...] believe more in the worthwhileness of planning and achieving, whereas [...] Catholics [are] somewhat more fatalistic in their attitude toward life."[53]

Achievement Orientation and Economic Development

These three insights—that highly motivated subjects exhibit a high concentration of achievement-related fantasies on the TAT, that raising children to achieve is an effective parenting strategy, and the confirmation of Weber's thesis in 1950s America—form the empirical psychological basis on which McClelland is now able to pose the question of whether his findings about Protestantism can be generalized across cultures to suggest that "a high level of *n* Achievement might predispose *any* society to vigorous economic activity."[54]

McClelland begins by examining the concentration of achievement-related ideas in children's books published in modern twentieth-century societies. His study of children's books from a variety of cultures shows that "[a] concern for achievement as expressed in imaginative literature—folk tales and stories for children—is associated [...] with a more rapid rate of economic

---

[50]Cf. ibid., 39–43.
[51]Ibid., 46.
[52]Ibid., 54.
[53]Ibid., 359.
[54]Ibid., 63.

AMBITION IN MODERNITY   213

development."[55] The critical point for the psychology of motivation is the admittedly striking finding that fictional literature that promotes a commitment to achievement does not "reflect" or subsequently affirm an already existing capacity for economic achievement, but in fact *precedes* it. In stark contradiction to the classic Marxist proposition that social existence determines the consciousness of subjects, McClelland finds that, historically, a strong need for achievement comes first:

> It is difficult to argue from these data that material advance came first and created a higher need for achievement. Rather the reverse appears to be true—high *n* Achievement levels are associated with subsequently more rapid economic development. Marx appears to have been somewhat premature in dismissing psychology as a major determinant in history.[56]

In a next step, McClelland applies this procedure, only tested on modern economic nations, to societies of the past—ancient Greece, Spain in the late Middle Ages, England from the age of the Tudors through the industrial revolution, and the United States between 1800 and 1950—in order to determine whether "achievement imagery in imaginative literature increases in frequency prior to instances of marked economic growth and decreases prior to subsequent economic decline."[57]

McClelland elucidates his method in the course of discussing his first historical example, namely ancient Greece. This section is thus particularly suitable as an illustration of his procedure, which presents a challenge for both philologists and historians, starting with the fact that he works with English translations of ancient texts. The social positions of the authors (farmers, philosophers, strategists) in their respective city-states as well as the diverse literary forms and styles of the works considered are secondary to this study, which is concerned primarily with explicitly articulated ideas about achievements and objectives. The results are based not on close reading but rather on a quantitative approach of *distant*

---

[55]Ibid., 105.
[56]Ibid., 93.
[57]Ibid., 107.

214 AMBITION: AN ESSAY ON THE BURNING DESIRE TO RISE

reading. McClelland and his colleagues compile statistics on epics, dramas, poems, philosophical treatises, and political speeches by authors from Homer and Hesiod to Aristotle and Callimachus, considering them to contain achievement-related ideas

> (a) where one of the characters in the story is engaged in competitive activity in which winning or doing as well or better than others is *actually stated* as of primary concern [...]; (b) where concern for doing well in competitive activity is not explicitly stated but its importance is definitely implied by affective concern over goal attainment or references to the quality of instrumental acts (e.g., thoroughness, foresight) needed for success [...]; or (c) where some unique accomplishment is mentioned[.][58]

McClelland defines the history of ancient Greece as stretching from 900 to 100 BC, divided into three periods: growth (900–475 BC), climax (475–362 BC), and decline (362–100 BC). He counts how many instances of "achievement imagery" appear in every hundred lines of analyzed text and determines that their number continually declines over the period from ancient Greece's growth through its decline:

> [T]here were 2.01 instances of achievement imagery per hundred lines in Hesiod's *Theogony* and only.81 instances per hundred lines in the hymns to the gods by Callimachus. In every category of material scored, the highest incidence of achievement imagery occurs in the growth period, the next highest in the climax period, and the lowest in the period of decline.[59]

Figure 1 presents an overview of the results.

A comparison of the number of achievement images against the extent of ancient Greece's trade area across the Mediterranean further demonstrates that "a high level of achievement motivation precedes economic growth, [while] a lower level of achievement motivation precedes economic decline."[60] The course of ancient

---

[58]Ibid., 113f.
[59]Ibid., 119.
[60]Ibid., 120.

TABLE 4.2 NUMBER OF n ACHIEVEMENT IMAGES PER 100 LINES BY TYPE OF SAMPLE BY TIME PERIOD

Period	Man and his gods	Estate management	Funeral celebrations	Poetry	Epigrams	War speeches	Average
Growth 900-475 B.C.	2.01	3.54	7.93	2.87	4.72	7.38	4.74
Climax 475-362 B.C.	1.21	.82	5.94	.38	2.36	5.55	2.71
Decline 362-100 B.C.	.81	.00	2.54	.16	1.57	3.00	1.35

Analysis of Variance

	df	Sum of squares	Mean square	F	p
Total	17	102.15			
Time period	2	35.03	17.52	24.0	<.01
Type of sample	5	59.83	11.97	16.4	<.01
Interaction	10	7.29	.73		

FIGURE 1 David McClelland, The Achieving Society, 119.

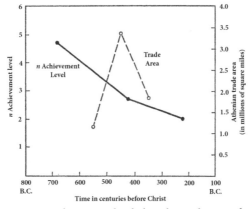

Figure 4.1 Average n Achievement level plotted at midpoints of periods of growth, climax, and decline of Athenian civilization as reflected in the extent of her trade area

FIGURE 2 David McClelland, The Achieving Society, 120.

216 AMBITION: AN ESSAY ON THE BURNING DESIRE TO RISE

Greece's economic development is established in terms of the number of vessels for wine and olive oil—the country's main exports even then—founded across the Mediterranean and displayed in Figure 2. The result, as far as McClelland is concerned, is clear: in ancient Greece, a high level of motivation brought with it real economic growth, while a decline in motivation precedes a similar decline in economic achievement. Additional statistics further show a decline over the same period in optimism or "future orientation," another important factor for a high motivation to achieve.[61] Finally, McClelland also discovers a decline in hard criteria of achievement in the education of upper-class Greek children, allowing him to identify complacency or declining ambition as a further cause of ancient Greece's decline:

> It is tempting to speculate that one reason why practically all great civilizations of the past have declined after a few generations of "climax" is because families have nearly always used their increased prosperity to turn over the rearing of their children to slaves or other dependents who "spoil" the children or keep them dependent too long. [...] [I]f prosperity becomes too general, the effect may be to diminish the number of children with high *n* Achievement below some critical point needed to maintain the civilization.[62]

Generating statistics about ancient Greece—particularly with respect to its economic development—is a murky endeavor due to the lack of available data; with greater source material, the relation between achievement imagery and economic development in England from 1400 to 1850 can be reconstructed in much greater detail. Using the same procedure—counting the number of achievement images in English literature, from *Everyman* to Marlowe's *Tamburlaine the Great* to Shelley's *Prometheus Unbound*, and comparing this to coal imports to London over the same period—McClelland is able to clearly determine "that the motivational changes *precede*

---

[61]Ibid., 124.
[62]Ibid., 128.

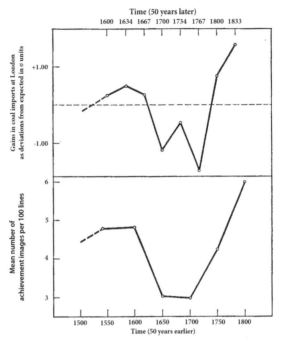

Figure 4.3 Average n Achievment levels in English literature (1550-1800 compared with rates of gain in coal imports at London 50 years later

FIGURE 3 David McClelland, The Achieving Society, 139.

the economic ones by 30-50 years."[63] The corresponding graphs are striking (see Figure 3).

Given the purely quantitative nature of this analysis, however, the question arises as to whether these numbers also correspond to *qualitative assessments* in the texts analyzed. McClelland thus performs a kind of spot check of exemplary ancient Greek literature, comparing how Hesiod, Xenophon's Socrates, and Aristotle approach the topic of farm and estate management. He finds that in Aristotle's treatment of this subject from the period of decline,

---

[63]Ibid., 138.

218 AMBITION: AN ESSAY ON THE BURNING DESIRE TO RISE

"there is practically no mention of achievement striving at all,"[64] while Socrates—in the period of climax—struggles with the idea of achievement for its own sake and, already almost a *décadent*, seems to question what use there is in "struggling to get ahead"[65] given how quickly any profits are frittered away. Hesiod, meanwhile, writing in the period of growth, "is very conscious of man's achievement strivings" and thus—as the author, if not of the *Theogony*, then certainly of the *Works and Days*, with its differentiation between the good and bad Eris—is the true progenitor of the modern achieving society under the banner of productive *agon*, the good Eris:

> He says [in the *Works and Days*], for example, "For when he that has no business looks on him that is rich, he hastens to plow and to plant and to array his house: and neighbor vies with neighbor hastening to be rich: good is this strife for man. So potter contends with potter: the hewer of wood with the hewer of wood: the beggar jealous of the beggar, the minstrel jealous of the minstrel." He takes it for granted that competition—the desire to excel—is natural to man.[66]

The spirit of competition, borne by a high need for achievement that McClelland considers so exemplarily articulated in Hesiod, finds its mythological embodiment in the god Hermes as depicted in the Homeric *Hymn to Hermes*. McClelland sees in the younger brother of Apollo "the ideal type of the capitalist entrepreneur" projected onto Olympus and declares the ambivalent traits of the god of merchants and thieves, who stole his brother's cattle on the very day he was born, to be a realistic depiction of "the conflict which was going on between the traditional propertied classes, represented by Apollo, and the *nouveaux riches* merchant classes, who adopted Hermes as their patron." The constellation of Apollo and Hermes, McClelland argues, serves as an allegory of "the relation of a growing and successful entrepreneurial class to the traditionally wealthy."[67]

It is clear that the results presented by McClelland were of great interests in economic and political circles when they were published

---

[64]Ibid., 121.
[65]Ibid.
[66]Ibid., 120.
[67]Ibid., 303.

AMBITION IN MODERNITY 219

and remain so today, as one can conclude from his investigations that economic upturns can be induced through targeted measures aimed at increasing motivation such as the widespread dissemination of highly effective achievement images, that is, through propaganda and coaching the next generation of entrepreneurs. McClelland's book thus closes with an appropriate promotional announcement:

> What each generation wanted above all, it got. What saves such a statement from banality is the new fact that the psychologist has now developed tools for finding out what a generation wants, better than it knows itself, and *before* it has had a chance of showing by its actions what it was after.[68]

Ideological Fervor

McClelland follows his historical investigations with a study of the psychology of the entrepreneur in conjunction with a series of reflections on the possible sources of the achievement motive. Here he discusses the role that discriminated-against and thus potentially highly motivated minority groups,[69] parenting practices, various religious ideas (here is where we find the abovementioned confirmation of Weber's thesis through more recent statistics), climate, and other factors play and have played in economic development. He emphasizes just one remarkable finding about pedagogy: contemporary surveys on parenting practices showed that "very high rigidity or authoritarianism, apparently particularly if it comes from the father, is likely also to lower n Achievement."[70] In his tour through the "sources of achievement," McClelland ultimately arrives at a conclusion that, in its archaic allusion to fire, recalls the world of Greek antiquity in which his study began: "There is no real substitute for ideological fervor."[71]

The ubiquity of the controversial term "neoliberalism" in contemporary academic and political debates gives occasion

---

[68]Ibid., 437.
[69]Cf. ibid., 280.
[70]Ibid., 352.
[71]Ibid., 430.

220 AMBITION: AN ESSAY ON THE BURNING DESIRE TO RISE

to exercise some restraint in using it. Nevertheless, in my view, McClelland's theory of the achieving society conclusively demonstrates that the economic productivity of the achievement motivation lends support, from the perspective of psychological expertise, to the neoliberal project of transforming the *homo politicus* into the constantly self-optimizing *homo oeconomicus*. When McClelland argues that a comprehensive change in mentality in accordance with the achievement motive will generate an economic upturn, then neoliberalism, which relies on the total responsibilization of individuals conceived of as miniature achievement-oriented businesses, can be considered a society-wide fulfillment of this postulate. What McClelland proposed primarily for entrepreneurs—heightening the need for achievement through intensive coaching—has become, under neoliberalism, a universal life maxim. Following an interlude in the 1970s in which the concept of the achieving society was critiqued and the limits of growth revealed themselves, McClelland's ideas have returned in the demands of neoliberalism, as summarized by Wendy Brown in her brilliant 2015 book *Undoing the Demos: Neoliberalism's Stealth Revolution*:

> [B]oth persons and states are expected to comport themselves in ways that maximize their capital value in the present and enhance their future value, and both persons and states do so through practices of entrepreneurialism, self-investment, and/or attracting investors.[72]

Under neoliberalism, the "ideological fervor" of the need for achievement that McClelland wrote about has become the driving force of society as a whole. The idea of "fervor" here also suggests a connection with the "burning ambition" that constitutes the primary interest of this book. If I have read closely enough, the burning, insatiable ambition that *The Achieving Society* for the most part neutralizes as "motivation" appears explicitly at at least one point, namely where McClelland discusses the work of the American sociologist and translator of Max Weber and Karl

---

[72]Wendy Brown, *Undoing the Demos: Neoliberalism's Stealth Revolution* (Brooklyn: Zone Books, 2015), 22.

AMBITION IN MODERNITY 221

Mannheim, Edward Shils. Through empirical research, Shils came to recognize a distinction between the personality profiles of efficient managers (e.g., administrative officials) and entrepreneurs willing to take risks:

> [T]he bureaucratic variant of ambition—namely, efficiency—is not conducive to economic progress. Ambition ... involves a *boundless aspiration*; its goal is not fixed in quantity at a particular point .... The more that can be achieved, the better .... Each triumph leads to another goal a little further off.[73]

Here Shils describes the tormenting, potentially infinitely one-upping logic of ambition that races from object to object, success to success, victory to victory without ever coming to a possible end. It is only here that McClelland finds himself compelled to confirm the clear connection between ambition and the motivation to achieve:

> The terminology is a little different from what we have been employing here, but it is easy to translate in terms of *n* Achievement. Ambition describes the goal of the person with high *n* Achievement precisely because what he is interested in is something that will give him achievement satisfaction. As soon as he solves one problem, he loses interest in it because he can no longer get achievement satisfaction from it [...]. If there is no challenge, he doesn't work so hard: in this sense, he would make a poor bureaucrat. He must constantly be seeking novelty or new solutions to old problems because that is the only way he can get a sense of personal achievement.[74]

At this point, where McClelland finds himself motivated by Shils to place his theory of motivation in relation to the age-old discourse of ambition, we can again see clearly the resilience of the etiology of burning ambition with its "boundless aspiration" and insatiable consumption of objects even in the clinical psychology of the 1960s. It is once again the "emulous struggle" to outdo one's past actions

---

[73]Cited in McClelland, *The Achieving Society*, 227. My emphasis.
[74]Ibid., 227f.

222 AMBITION: AN ESSAY ON THE BURNING DESIRE TO RISE

by one's future, described by Plutarch and so many others across the centuries—*ad infinitum*.

There is a marked disparity between McClelland's writings on the achievement motive and his writings on the power motive, which come together in their passionate commitment to agon. While his book on power conceives of an attainable level of "selflessness" (*Stage IV*) at which insatiable striving gives way to an ethics of responsibility in the interest of the whole that is uncontaminated by personal ambition, *The Achieving Society* is incapable of drawing any limit to ambition. The ambitious person "must constantly be seeking novelty or new solutions to old problems because that is the only way he can get a sense of personal achievement." The new terminology that replaces the concept of ambition with that of motivation seemed to promise that the two-edged nature of ambition as both a productive and a destructive force, as elaborated by Roger Caillois, had also been overcome and only the good Eris of *agon* now ruled. Our reading of this classic text on the psychology of motivation, however, creates room for the insight that the new terminology was not able to solve the old problem, it only concealed it. McClelland sees the consistently highly motivated human being, ever ready to continually improve his abilities and optimize himself, as the legacy of the productionist concept of the "human motor," the industrialized nineteenth century's "utopian image of the body without fatigue."[75] "Ambition" gives way to "motivation," the fatigue of "burnout" to the extinguishing of "fervor."

---

[75]Anson Rabinbach, *The Human Motor: Energy, Fatigue, and the Origins of Modernity* (Berkeley/Los Angeles: University of California Press, 1990), 10.

7 BURNING AMBITION
Sigmund Freud and Alfred Adler

The Masculine Protest

When we are little, our most fervent desire is to grow up, to become big and strong, so that we will finally be able to do whatever we want. As soon as we are grown, however, we wish that we were little again, so that we could once again do whatever we want: "The development of the ego consists in a departure from primary narcissism and gives rise to a vigorous attempt to recover that state."[1] Children perceive a lack that generates a desire, and it is no different with adults. The desire provides an easily flammable fuel that supplies energy to "the ambition that lies hidden in everyone,"[2] allowing it to burn or at least smolder over the course of an entire life. Human life has an inherently tragic structure: children do not know what they are doing or what they are losing when they realize their desire to grow up. They become innocently guilty. Growing up is a mistake that is as difficult as it is unavoidable, the kind of flaw known to theorists of tragedy as *hamartia*. Adults, meanwhile, understand what they have done and what they have lost, and they also know that what was lost can never be fully regained. This is the moment of recognition that theorists of tragedy call *anagnorisis*, the sudden shift from ignorance to knowledge.

The lack is stronger than any fulfillment of desire. As soon as a child stops playing, he is little once again. Likewise for adults,

---

[1] Sigmund Freud, "On Narcissism: An Introduction," in: Freud, *The Standard Edition of the Complete Psychological Works of Sigmund Freud*, vol. 14: *On the History of the Psycho-Analytic Movement, Papers on Metapsychology and Other Works (1914–1916)*, edited and translated by James Strachey (London: Hogarth Press: 1957), 67–102 (100).

[2] Sigmund Freud, "Psychical (or Mental) Treatment," in: Freud, *The Standard Edition of the Complete Psychological Works of Sigmund Freud*, vol. 7: *A Case of Hysteria, Three Essays on Sexuality and Other Works (1901–1905)*, edited and translated by James Strachey (London: Hogarth Press, 1953), 281–302 (290).

224 AMBITION: AN ESSAY ON THE BURNING DESIRE TO RISE

desires fulfilled do not last, do not remain satisfying forever, even for men as gloriously successful as Alexander the Great, whom Sigmund Freud, too, considered "undoubtedly one of the most ambitious men that ever lived." Indeed Alexander had reason to complain, a desire that remained unfulfilled: "He even complained that he would find no Homer to sing of his exploits."[3] This is the tormenting wheel of Freudian theory, the formula he found to describe the roundelay of desire, the operating mechanism of that carousel of libido that Rainer Maria Rilke also set in motion in his poem of the same name, and which he characterizes in that poem's final stanza as a blind, breathless play:

Und das geht hin und eilt sich, daß es endet	And on it goes and rushes to be done,
und kreist und dreht sich nur und hat kein Ziel.	and only circles and turns and has no goal.
Ein Rot, ein Grün, ein Grau vorbeigesendet,	A red, a green, a gray drifting past,
ein kleines kaum begonnenes Profil—.	a small, scarcely started profile—.
Und manchesmal ein Lächeln, hergewendet,	And oftentimes a smile, turned this way,
ein seliges, das blendet und verschwendet	elated and blissfully adazzle as it spends itself
an dieses atemlose blinde Spiel	on this blind, breathless play ...[4]

It is the aim of both juvenile and adult ambition to help "his majesty, the ego" to become omnipotent, even if only in one's imagination. As children are not yet grown up, there is nothing for them to do in the meantime but play at being big (as thus powerful): "A child's play is determined by wishes: in point of fact by a single wish—one that helps in his upbringing—the wish to be big and

---

[3]Sigmund Freud, *The Complete Psychological Works of Sigmund Freud*, vol. 6: *The Psychopathology of Everyday Life (1901)*, edited and translated by James Strachey (London: Hobarth Press, 1960), 108.

[4]Rainer Maria Rilke, "The Carousel," in: Rilke, *New Poems: Revised Bilingual Edition*, translated by Edward Snow (New York: North Point Press, 2001), 121–4 (123).

AMBITION IN MODERNITY

grown up. He is always playing at being 'grown up.'"[5] Among adults, who are no longer allowed to play and now have to bring the "excess of self-regard"[6] carried over from the spoiled days of their childhood under control in the name of the reality principle, fantasies and daydreams take on the function, previously served by play, of correcting "unsatisfying reality" at least *in mente*. The objects of such fantasies and daydreams "are either ambitious wishes, which serve to elevate the subject's personality; or they are erotic ones."[7]

Artists, thanks to their particular talent, enjoy the special privilege of giving such skillful form to their "erotic and ambitious wishes [...] in the life of phantasy" that they become "valued by men as precious reflections of reality."[8] For the successful artist, this public acceptance of the products of his imagination has the happy consequence of making him, in reality, the important person that previously he only was in his ambitious daydreams. In return, he creates a further source of comforting fantasies for the recipients of his art. For adults, theatrical performances (and later films and television shows) replace the play of their childhood:

> Being present as an interested spectator at a spectacle or play does for adults what play does for children, whose hesitant hopes of being able to do what grown-up people do are in that way gratified. The spectator is a person who experiences too little, who feels that he is a "poor wretch to whom nothing of importance can happen," who has long been obliged to damp down, or rather displace, his ambition to stand in his own person at the hub of world affairs; he longs to feel and to act and to arrange things according to his desires—in short, to be a hero.

---

[5]Sigmund Freud, "Creative Writers and Day-Dreaming," in: Freud, *The Complete Psychological Works of Sigmund Freud*, vol. 9: *Jensen's "Gradiva" and Other Works (1906–1908)*, edited and translated by James Strachey (London: Hobarth Press, 1959), 141–54 (146).

[6]Ibid., 147.

[7]Ibid.

[8]Sigmund Freud, "Formulations on the Two Principles of Mental Functioning," in: Freud, *The Complete Psychological Works of Sigmund Freud*, vol. 12: *The Case of Schreber, Papers on Technique and Other Works*, edited and translated by James Strachey (London: Hobarth Press, 1958), 213–26 (224).

226 AMBITION: AN ESSAY ON THE BURNING DESIRE TO RISE

And the playwright and actor enable him to do this by allowing him *to identify himself* with a hero.[9]

Freud further considers the question of how adults handle the excess of self-regard they bring with them from childhood, their "former megalomania" or "ego-libido,"[10] in his 1914 essay "On Narcissism: An Introduction." His thesis here is that not only are fantasies active in daydreams or when enjoying art, but that beyond this, they coalesce into an internally directed psychical figure that he calls the "ideal ego," of which the conscience serves as an agent or guardian:

> This ideal ego is now the target of the self-love which was enjoyed in childhood by the actual ego. The subject's narcissism makes its appearance displaced on to this new ideal ego, which, like the infantile ego, finds itself possessed of every perfection that is of value. As always where the libido is concerned, man has here again shown himself incapable of giving up a satisfaction he had once enjoyed. He is not willing to forgo the narcissistic perfection of his childhood; and when, as he grows up, he is disturbed by the admonitions of others and by the awakening of his own critical judgment, so that he can no longer retain that perfection, he seeks to recover it in the new form of an ego ideal.[11]

Freud's concept of the ideal ego has a variety of functions. He uses it, for example, to explain a mechanism of love. Where there is a discrepancy between the real ego and its ideal, love can act as an "expedient" that abolishes this discrepancy: "what possesses the excellence which the ego lacks for making it an ideal, is loved."[12] As Freud himself acknowledges and Alfred Adler later notes, however, he also introduces the concept of the ego ideal here in order to offer an alternative—one capable of rescuing his theory of the libido—to

---

[9]Sigmund Freud, "Psychopathic Characters on the Stage," in: Freud, *The Standard Edition of the Complete Psychological Works of Sigmund Freud*, vol. 7: *A Case of Hysteria, Three Essays on Sexuality and Other Works (1901–1905)*, edited and translated by James Strachey (London: Hogarth Press, 1953), 303–10 (305).

[10]Freud, "On Narcissism," 93.

[11]Ibid., 94.

[12]Ibid., 101.

AMBITION IN MODERNITY

the idea of "masculine protest"[13] that Adler had first proposed in 1910 and two years later, after his break with Freud, developed into a key concept in his 1912 magnum opus *The Neurotic Character*, where he summarizes it in a single sentence that serves as a formula for ambition: "I want to be a complete man!"[14] As Freud notes, the masculine protest is directed against "the effect of early deterrence against sexual activity" that finds its dramatic climax in the "castration complex."[15] Directly contrary to Freud, who repeatedly mentions ambition in passing but never provides any comprehensive analysis of it,[16] Adler elevates ambition born of protest, "the struggle for self-assertion,"[17] to the focal point of his own brand of individual psychology. Drawing on Nietzsche, he ascribes "absolute primacy" in mental life not to the libido and its vicissitudes, but to the pursuit of legitimacy and prestige, the will to power.[18] He sees Oedipal desire—and here his break with Freud is of course inevitable—primarily as a symptom of the "boundlessness" of ambition, which demonstrates "limitless intensity of the will to power."[19] In Adler, psychoanalysis becomes a theory of ambition, and psychotherapy finds "the best opportunity for a possible cure"

---

[13]Cf. ibid., 93f. Adler himself writes that Freud's "most recent interpretations seem to indicate that the *Freudian* theory of the libido is moving with furious speed towards our own point of view of community feeling and the striving for a personality ideal ('ego ideal'), which in the interest of increasing understanding should be welcomed very much indeed." Alfred Adler, *The Neurotic Character: Fundamentals of a Comparative Individual Psychology and Psychotherapy*, edited by Henry T. Stein, translated by Cees Koen (Bellingham: Classical Adlerian Translation Project, 2002), xvi. Adler's hope was never fulfilled. Freud considered it "quite impossible to place the genesis of neurosis upon the narrow basis of the castration complex." Freud, "On Narcissism," 92.

[14]Adler, *The Neurotic Character*, xvi.

[15]Freud, "On Narcissism," 92.

[16]In addition to the passages discussed here and in what follows, Freud also considers the substantial problem of "therapeutic ambition" in his writings on treatment techniques and elsewhere. He also repeatedly emphasizes "the ambition of the man Moses," a subject worthy of its own study. Sigmund Freud, *Moses and Monotheism: Three Essays*, in: Freud, *The Complete Psychological Works of Sigmund Freud*, vol. XXIII: *Moses and Monotheism, An Outline of Psycho-Analysis and Other Works (1937–1939)*, edited and translated by James Strachey (London: Hogarth Press, 1964), 1–138 (32).

[17]Adler, *The Neurotic Character*, 2.

[18]Ibid., 50.

[19]Ibid., 71.

228 AMBITION: AN ESSAY ON THE BURNING DESIRE TO RISE

in reconciling the warped, ossified self-image of the neurotic patient with reality.[20]

Freud concedes in his essay on narcissism that psychoanalytic research "has from the very beginning recognized the existence and importance of the 'masculine protest,'" but argues that he considers it "completely unsuited" for solving the problem of neurosis.[21] In order to be able to understand the metapsychological context of Freud's brusque repudiation of Adler, we must first ask ourselves what toehold Adler was able to find in Freud's writings for his concept of "masculine protest" in the first place: why "protest," and why "masculine"?

Above all, Adler is able to draw on Freud's highlighting of human beings' initial experiences of impotence and inferiority. As Nietzsche did before him, first in sketches drafted during the 1870s and then in more complete form in *Daybreak*, Adler derives the will to power from our primary, humiliating, and frightening experience of powerlessness. Children—all children, of all genders, not only future "neurotics"—feel "small" compared to adults and try to "compensate" for this actually existing disparity by imagining and playing at being "big" and thus powerful, "a complete man." This is the essence of the protest:

> [C]hildren [...] desire to be grown up, to be *big*, to be strong, to rule, "like the father," and are guided by this final goal. Their gestures, their physical and spiritual attitude are at every moment directed towards this final goal, to such a degree that one can easily observe an imitative facial expression, an identical mental gesture. The example becomes a signpost to the goal. Eventually, every *desire* will become an urge for compensation, a recompensation of the inferiority feeling.[22]

This early experience of inferiority does not really disappear with age. Every person whose narcissistic "ambition to stand in his own person at the hub of world affairs" feels "inferior" and thus even as an adult uses fantasies and daydreams to compensate for this

---

[20]Ibid., 45.
[21]Freud, "On Narcissism," 92.
[22]Adler, *The Neurotic Character*, 7.

AMBITION IN MODERNITY   229

feeling of inferiority. He may moreover require vanity and bravado
in order to mask the painful deficiencies of reality. Along with play
and daydreaming as efforts to alleviate the experience of being
small or frustrated, establishing an ego ideal is ultimately a third
(and potentially productive) activity for combatting the feeling of
inferiority: a fiction—Freud calls it a "projection"—that the real
ego devises from its own abilities as well as from a future in which
these abilities will unfold triumphally and without restriction. If this
projection is understood as a project that the ego actually intends
to realize, rather than allowed to languish as a sterile illusion or
empty protest, then we can reconceive the ego ideal, as Adler does,
as a "life plan"[23] for extinguishing inferiority. The "*guiding fiction
of ambition*"[24] defines a person's character, the contours of his
personality. Ambition persistently pursues the goal not just of future
triumph, but also of protecting itself from behind and from the
side, of offering "*a refuge and safeguard even against the greatest
discomfort that could possibly hit him*, against the arousal of a
distinctly experienced inferiority."[25] Burning ambition is a reaction
to the experience of burning shame.

The will to power expressed in the fiction of ambition must
repeatedly be balanced against reality if there is to be any hope
of realizing one's life plan. In Adler, too, ambition is a passion
acted out in instrumentally rational terms. And like Machiavelli,
Pettigrove, and the French moralists, he emphasizes the particular
secrecy involved in pursuing ambitious aims: "Nothing in the life
and development of man sets to work with so much secrecy as the
construction of the personality ideal."[26] The formula that Adler
finds for a successful balance between the pleasure principle and
the reality principle, which he defines as a criterion of psychological
health, is as follows:

This counter-fiction, *which invariably consists of current,
corrective examples of the community feeling*, accomplishes
the formal change of the guiding fiction by pushing forward

---

[23]Cf. ibid., 56.
[24]Ibid., 45.
[25]Ibid., 13.
[26]Ibid., 55.

230 AMBITION: AN ESSAY ON THE BURNING DESIRE TO RISE

its own considerations, by making allowances, based on their true importance, for future social and ethical demands, and in this way *it secures reasonableness, that is to say: general validity of thinking and acting.* It is a security coefficient of the guiding line to power, and the harmony of both fictions, their mutual compatibility, is a sign of mental health.[27]

Freud thus offers a precise summation of Adler's "well-known socialist world-view"[28] when he notes that his concept of the masculine protest, "which he has elevated almost to the position of the sole motive force in the formation of character and neurosis alike," is based "not on a narcissistic, and therefore still a libidinal, trend, but on a social valuation."[29] In keeping with his conception of the ego ideal as a fiction of ambition in a competitive world, Adler also modifies the interpretation of dreams. In his view, dreams are not primarily a return, in however distorted a form, of the past and repressed material provoked by recent impressions, but rather a kind of rehearsal with a view to future problems:

The dream is a sketch-like reflection of psychic attitudes and indicates, for the researcher, how the dreamer intuitively takes up a position *to a problem close at hand.*[30]

What dreams are meant to restore is a lost omnipotence (the illusionary character of which even young children are aware of, which changes nothing about the production of their desires). Against this background, the ambitious person is understood as someone who makes his ego ideal a project and plan of life, who converts his fantasy of ambition into action in order to, in Freud's words, "actually become[] the hero, the king, the creator, or the favorite he desired to be."[31] In other words, the ambitious person wants above not to be "little" again, but to be big, all grown up, "a complete man," ideally the biggest and greatest, so as to be able

---

[27]Ibid., 56.
[28]Ibid., 16, fn.
[29]Freud, "On Narcissism," 92.
[30]Adler, *The Neurotic Character*, 68.
[31]Freud, "Formulations on the Two Principles of Mental Functioning," 224.

AMBITION IN MODERNITY   231

to once again enjoy the pleasures of his original narcissism without restriction and without punishment. The fantasy of omnipotence comes into its own in the figure of the all-powerful ruler, whose physiognomy at the height of power at times again takes on certain childlike features. In Adler's view, whether ambition is "healthy" or "unhealthy"—overwrought and "neurotic"—can be seen from the relation between the ego and its ideal along with said ideal's relationship to the social world with all its demands. He thus offers a further explication of the ambivalence of ambition, which, on the one hand, is a, if not *the*, productive force in determining the shape of one's life and, on the other hand, in its excessive, illusionary form, can also lead to one's downfall: "It is impossible to overestimate the importance of the neurotic's desire *to possess everything*, and it is equally impossible to exaggerate any description of the eagerness with which *he desires to be first*."[32] If the fiction of ambition is absurd (because one's childhood experience of inferiority was absurdly cruel and harmful, as in the case of "*hated children*"[33]), it can become an abyss that swallows the ego:

> The normal child also expects the future, and more in particular his choice in love, to fulfill his ideals. But in due course of time, after letting his idea drive him as an expedient, the normal child will become able to turn away from it to confront and cope with reality. Not so the neurotic. He is unable to change his neurotic perspective by himself, to dispose of his now rigid, fixed principles; he must obey his own traits of character.[34]

The consequences of the seductive conclusiveness of this derivation of ambition from powerlessness and deficiency, from the enduring experience of the "absolute inferiority of the child,"[35] are well known. Diagnosing extremely or "pathologically" ambitious people with a secret "inferiority complex" and asserting that their ambitious striving must be an attempt to "compensate" for some painful shortcoming or deprivation—a lack of attention in childhood,

---

[32] Adler, *The Neurotic Character*, 86.
[33] Ibid., 62.
[34] Ibid., 219.
[35] Ibid., 32.

232 AMBITION: AN ESSAY ON THE BURNING DESIRE TO RISE

an early traumatizing humiliation, ingrained sexual inhibition, a physical affliction tied to bitter experiences of inclusion—has become almost a form of folk wisdom. Adler's controversial, lurid proposition that there is a "remarkable relation between organ inferiority and mental overcompensation" and that "experiences of organ inferiority will come to be an ongoing stimulus in the development of an individual's psyche"[36] is particularly salient in the collective consciousness. References to the supposed shortness of the conqueror Napoleon Bonaparte, for example, are notorious. Along with "narcissism" and the "Freudian slip," this simplified understanding of the "inferiority complex" is a textbook example of a psychological or psychoanalytic concept that has become part of the standard inventory of everyday psychological assessment in both public and private life and therefore must be taken into account as an element of the historical semantics of ambitions.

The popular reception of Adler's theory as a rule of thumb in dealing with other people, however, ignores the fact that Adler views inferiority as a fundamental experience common to all human beings, "the origins of which are deeply rooted within human nature."[37] It further ignores the fact that Adler's individual psychology is at bottom politically motivated, that "neurotics" not only suffer from "overwrought" ambition," but that their "impression that life is particularly hostile" is by no means wrong in the context of a competitive capitalist society. The fact that the neurotic feels that his "absorption into the community" has been obstructed,[38] that he "carries this feeling of inferiority with him constantly,"[39] is also an argument against existing society and its nucleus, the patriarchal family. Franz Kafka wrote his first short story, "The Judgment," in September 1912, the same year Adler's magnum opus was published. Finally, Adler's popular reception also ignores his feminism, the theoretical foundations of which he

---

[36]Ibid., 1.
[37]Ibid., 12.
[38]Ibid., 16. Adler does not differentiate between "society" and "community." His concept of "community feeling" as the antithesis of egocentrism covers a wide spectrum of meanings from empathy to social competence and maturity.
[39]Ibid., 9.

AMBITION IN MODERNITY

233

outlines in *The Neurotic Character*—which includes an analysis of "forms of the fear of women"[40] informed by literary history—and further develops in his most famous book, 1927's *Understanding Human Nature*. Adler conceives of the oppression of children, of women, and of the working class as one complex. In the section of *Understanding Human Nature* on the prejudice that women are inferior to men, he writes:

> There are so many men furthermore who not only do not show any achievements but are possessed of such a high grade of incapability that we could easily find an equal number of proofs (of course falsely) that men were the inferior sex.[41]

Ernest Jones, a student and later biographer of Sigmund Freud, illustrates how far burning male ambition—the need to always and literally everywhere be first above all others—can go in a short case study, published in 1915 and, interestingly, oriented toward Adlerian terminology, of a young man with a strong inferiority complex and thus also a "strong ambition complex." The maxim so sublimely articulated in the *Iliad* here finds its human, all too human expression in the twentieth-century confines of a public restroom:

> One day, [the young patient] reported to me the following compulsion. Whenever he entered a public restroom, he rushed to take the first empty urinal in the row [...]. If he managed to get the first urinal, he muttered to himself the words: "first before all others"; if it was the second spot he strove to take (since the first one was usually occupied), then he muttered: "second to none"; if the third: "in the top three," etc.; and if the last, the words were: "last but not least" [...]. In other words, his ambition complex flared up in the form of a compulsion whenever he urinated in the presence of other men.[42]

---

[40]Ibid., D242ff.

[41]Alfred Adler, *Understanding Human Nature*, translated by Walter Béran Wolfe (London/New York: Routledge, 2013), 132.

[42]Ernest Jones, "Urethralerotik und Ehrgeiz," in: *Internationale Zeitschrift für Psychoanalyse* III (1915), 156f. (156).

234 AMBITION: AN ESSAY ON THE BURNING DESIRE TO RISE

In this depiction of a case of compulsive ambition, Jones raises a topic that comes up just as frequently as—if not more often than—the overcompensated-for inferiority complex whenever people speak critically or mockingly of excessive ambition in or exaggerated competition among men "in the presence of other men." He alludes to archaic, primitive behaviors or rituals among boys and even grown men in awkwardly competitive situations: comparing penis size, for example, or the homosocial competition to see who can urinate best or, as Jones describes, who can secure the first spot in a row of urinals. The expulsion of urine can be "playfully" modified and the jubilant competition further refined: "This leads to the well-known contest between boys [...] regarding the distance their stream of urine can travel, the extent to which they can control its direction, and the height it can reach."[43]

These observations clarify another reason why Adler introduced the idea of the "masculine protest" specifically as a *critical* term that has only retained its relevancy in what Pierre Bourdieu calls "a society ordered through and through according to the androcentric principle."[44] Only a "complete man" who can keep with the kind of ritual Jones describes can hope to ever become the greatest. The will to power effectively proves to be a "will to masculinity"[45]:

As a boy grows older his masculinity becomes a significant duty, his ambition, his desire for power and superiority is indisputably connected and identified with the duty to be masculine.[46]

A nuanced understanding of Adler's rejection of Freud's theory of the libido in favor of a psychoanalytic theory of power intended as a critique of patriarchy stands and falls with the insight that Adler clearly describes the social construction of gender difference as a callous power relationship that produces a brutal equation based on physical violence: "'masculine' signifies worth-while, powerful, victorious, capable, whereas 'feminine' becomes identical

---

[43]Ibid., 157.
[44]Pierre Bourdieu, *Masculine Domination*, translated by Richard Nice (Stanford: Stanford University Press, 2001), 3.
[45]Adler, *The Neurotic Character*, 36.
[46]Adler, *Understanding Human Nature*, 127.

AMBITION IN MODERNITY
235

with obedient, servile, subordinate."[47] From the perspective of this equation of masculine power, there are not two genders, but only *one*—the proper man—followed by other, inferior beings who are ever less masculine, the lowest of which is called "feminine." This is the source of the "double bind" discussed in the introduction to this book.[48] A woman who is ambitious and wants to "get ahead" must renounce her femininity, "upward movement," as Bourdieu argues, "being [...] associated with the male, through erection or the upper position in the sexual act":[49]

> The feeling of inferiority and its consequences are being identified with the feeling of femininity, the compensatory compulsion in the psychic superstructure insists on safeguards in order to retain the masculine role and the meaning of the neurosis assumes the form of the antithetical fundamental idea: *I am like a woman and I want to be a man.*[50]

Thus for Adler—and, later, for Bourdieu—the dismantling of a capitalist society defined by brutal competition and the emancipation of women as the *second sex* are two aspects of a single political project:

> Adler took a position [on the question of women's rights] as early as 1908, emphasizing above all women's intellectual equality. He considered himself a socialist in this respect, seizing on Bebel's Marxist analysis and placing the struggle for the emancipation of women on a par with the class struggle [...]. In Adler's view, our society is a patriarchal one, the devaluation of women "nothing

---

[47]Ibid., 132.

[48]Pierre Bourdieu offers the following historical perspective: "Knowing thus that man and woman are perceived as two variants, superior and inferior, of the same physiology, one understands why it is that, until the Renaissance, there were no anatomical terms to describe in detail the female genitals, which were represented as comprising the same organs as those of men, but differently organized." Bourdieu, *Masculine Domination*, 14f. Adler is actually more radical than Bourdieu, inasmuch as, as noted above, he argues that nothing about this idea of *one* gender has changed with respect to actually existing power relations.

[49]Ibid., 7.

[50]Adler, *The Neurotic Character*, 15.

236 AMBITION: AN ESSAY ON THE BURNING DESIRE TO RISE

less than a driving force of our civilization," such that any change in society must begin here. The diminishment of women and overvaluation of everything masculine have obviously been reproduced in our psychic structure. [...] Wanting to be strong means "I want to be a man" and "I have to prove that I am not a woman." Adler calls this compensatory tendency "the masculine protest," which applies to both sexes. It the basis of the dynamic of neurosis.[51]

Adler's insistence on women's equality was "such a central concern that it became a constitutive part of his psychological theory and its terminology and defined his cultural critique."[52] In keeping with this, Adler energetically argued against the demonization of women as *femmes fatales* that was typical around the turn of the twentieth century:

The woman as a sphynx, as a demon, as a vampire, as a witch, as a man-murdering monster, as dispenser of mercy—the sexual impulse, excited by the masculine protest, is reflected in these images, which have their counterpart in the caricature of woman, in obscene outpourings of gall, in anecdotes and jokes, and in degrading comparisons. In the same manner the neurotic, philistine consciousness of men and the desire for superiority demands the firm convictions whose depreciation tendency directs itself towards denying women equal rights, sometimes even their right to exist.[53]

Extinguishing the Fire

Why the socialist Adler found it necessary to root the struggle for women's equality as recognition of the second sex in the structure of individual psychology can be understood from a look at Freud's

---

[51]Almuth Bruder-Bezzel, *Die Geschichte der Individualpsychologie* (Frankfurt: Fischer, 1991), 118f.
[52]Ibid., 118.
[53]Adler, *The Neurotic Character*, 221.

AMBITION IN MODERNITY 237

spectacular, speculative reflections on man's acquisition of fire, which also offer a primordial history of masculine ambition and dominance under the banner of the phallus and ultimately "forget" the second sex entirely. In a puzzling footnote to his 1930 summary of cultural philosophy, *Civilization and Its Discontents*, Freud enthrones man as the civilization-founding conqueror of fire while appointing woman the guardian of the hearth, an asymmetric division of primordial labor in the process of civilization that he justifies with reference to the anatomical differences between the sexes. There existed at the beginning of civilization a libidinous homosexual competition among men that significantly complicated everything (and still does today):

> Psycho-analytic material, incomplete as it is and not susceptible to clear interpretation, nevertheless admits of a conjecture—a fantastic-sounding one—about the origin of this human feat [the acquisition of fire]. It is as though primal man had the habit, when he came in contact with fire, of satisfying an infantile desire connected with it, by putting it out with a stream of his urine. The legends that we possess leave no doubt about the originally phallic view taken of tongues of flame as they shoot upwards. Putting out fire by micturating—a theme to which modern giants, Gulliver in Lilliput and Rabelais' Gargantua, still hark back—was therefore a kind of sexual act with a male, an enjoyment of sexual potency in a homosexual competition. The first person to renounce this desire and spare the fire was able to carry it off with him and subdue it to his own use. By damping down the fire of his own sexual excitation, he had tamed the natural force of fire. This great cultural conquest was thus the reward for his renunciation of instinct. Further, it is as though woman had been appointed guardian of the fire which was held captive on the domestic hearth, because her anatomy made it impossible for her to yield to the temptation of this desire. It is remarkable, too, how regularly analytic experience testifies to the connection between ambition, fire and urethral erotism.[54]

---

[54]Sigmund Freud, "Civilization and Its Discontents," in: Freud, *The Complete Psychological Works of Sigmund Freud*, vol. XXI: *The Future of an Illusion, Civilization and Its Discontents and Other Works (1927–1931)*, edited and translated by James Strachey (London: Hobarth Press, 1961), 57–146 (fn. 90).

238 AMBITION: AN ESSAY ON THE BURNING DESIRE TO RISE

This dreamlike speculation is puzzling at the narrative surface level, first, because it is not immediately understandable why urination is supposed to be "a kind of sexual act"—when it is actually the opposite—and, moreover, as though self-evidently, "with a male." It is further puzzling why Freud assumes a "connection between ambition, fire, and urethral erotism" and, finally, what this all has to do with the history of the acquisition of fire. Freud repeatedly asserts—in his *Three Essays on the Theory of Sexuality*, for example, as well as in his essay "The Dissolution of the Oedipus Complex"— an equivalence between childhood bedwetting and masturbation[55] or nocturnal emission.[56] In "Character and Anal Erotism," having established the nature of the "anal character," he makes reference at the very end of the essay to "the intense 'burning' ambition of people who earlier suffered from enuresis."[57] As far as I can tell, however, he never explains exactly how the nexus between enuresis and ambition should be understood. It remains unclear whether the enduring character trait in question—ambition in this case—ought to be conceived of as a stubborn continuation of childish protest (and infant sexuality), as a form of sublimation, or as a reaction formation (burning ambition as a reaction to burning shame and the threat of castration). Freud asserts the connection between urethral erotism (pleasurable sensations in the urinary tract when urinating) and ambition once again in his *New Introductory Lectures on Psychoanalysis*, again in reference to Alexander the Great:

We therefore speak of an "anal character" in which we find this remarkable combination and we draw a contrast to some extent

---

[55]Sigmund Freud, "Three Essays on the Theory of Sexuality," in: *The Complete Psychological Works of Sigmund Freud*, vol. 7: *A Case of Hysteria, Three Essays on Sexuality and Other Works (1901–1905)*, edited and translated by James Strachey (London: Hobarth Press, 1953), 123–246 (186).

[56]Sigmund Freud, "The Dissolution of the Oedipus Complex," in: Freud, *The Complete Psychological Works of Sigmund Freud*, vol. XIX: *The Ego and the Id and Other Works (1923–1925)*, edited and translated by James Strachey (London: Hobarth Press, 1961), 171–80 (175).

[57]Sigmund Freud, "Character and Anal Erotism," in: Freud, *The Complete Psychological Works of Sigmund Freud*, vol. 9: *Jensen's "Gradiva" and Other Works (1906–1908)*, edited and translated by James Strachey (London: Hobarth Press, 1959), 167–76 (175).

AMBITION IN MODERNITY   239

between the anal character and unmodified anal erotism. We also discovered a similar but perhaps still firmer link between ambition and urethral erotism. A striking allusion to this connection is to be seen in the legend that Alexander the Great was born during the same night in which a certain Herostratus set fire to the temple of Artemis at Ephesus out of a sheer desire for fame. So the ancients would seem not to have been unaware of the connection. You know, of course, how much urination has to do with fire and extinguishing fire.[58]

Such reflections, drawn from years of practical experience as a psychoanalyst, do not suggest gleefully and cruelly expanding the popular conception of the inferiority complex, namely that, according to Freud, ambitious men and women were all childhood bedwetters. A look at English and German slang is rather more illuminating: "I'm pissed off"—"Ich bin angepisst" in German— is an expression of extreme annoyance and indignation. To be "pissed" means to have been subjected to a humiliating power. Furthermore—as Freud, a passionate dog owner, well knew—the phenomenon of establishing one's territory by marking it with one's scent is well known in the animal world. Thus when the primal man imagined by Freud, just emerging from that animal world, extinguishes the flames of a fire with his urine, this is presumably a pleasure-inducing gesture of power and superiority that destroys perceived potential competitors (the phallic flames). In this sense, the "enjoyment of sexual potency in a homosexual competition" should be understood as a kind of sadistic triumph over other men. The preceding phrase, "a kind of sexual act with a male," in its typically Freudian, remarkably serene openness, nevertheless leaves homosexual enjoyment available as an option at least for free primal men, an enjoyment that is in turn also acted out in the defensively brutal initiation rites of homosocial milieus. One famous depiction of this is found in Robert Musil's early novel *The Confusions of Young Törless* (1908).

---

[58]Sigmund Freud, "New Introductory Lectures on Psycho-Analysis," in: Freud, *The Complete Psychological Works of Sigmund Freud*, vol. XXII: *New Introductory Lectures on Psycho-Analysis and Other Works (1932–1936)*, edited and translated by James Strachey (London: Hobarth Press, 1964), 1–182 (102).

240 AMBITION: AN ESSAY ON THE BURNING DESIRE TO RISE

Refraining from extinguishing the flames of the fire demonstrates the intelligence—of deferral, of delayed gratification—that plays a critical role in the establishment of civilization. A momentary triumph is sacrificed for the sake of a much farther-reaching victory and greater power. Primal man, restraining himself, masters the potentially infinite flames phallically stretching upward toward the sky and makes them his own. It is precisely here, with the sublimation of water to the flame, that ambition instates itself as a long-term project of instrumentally rational passion. Freud's primal man refrains from masturbating/urinating, thereby acquiring fire and thus also enduring power over those others who cannot control themselves and childishly extinguish the flame. The act of forcing the flame into servitude thus has a dual meaning, as Freud explains: primitive man learns to master fire and in so doing also comes to understand that the condition of the possibility of mastery is dampening the fire of his own sexual fervor. Burning ambition here appropriates the fire of mastery and domination.

Freud's designation of woman as guardian of the hearth, meanwhile, is deeply contradictory, inasmuch as it blends together the purported deficiency of women (their supposedly anatomically established inability to extinguish fire) and confidence in their reliability (they could extinguish the flames in a different way if necessary or simply let them go out by *not feeding them*). In the constellation Freud sketches, the domination of man is secured in multiple ways: through his superior ability to renounce his instincts (woman is designated guardian of the hearth because of her anatomy, *not* because she is any less capable of renouncing her instincts), his heroic acquisition of fire (mythical authority), and finally the symbolic/actual power he possesses as a result of his ability to extinguish fire at any time with the "long-range weapon" of the penis. The myth of the acquisition of fire is thus effectively a myth about the supposed, anatomically based superiority of men over women.

This reading is not unjustified, as a brief look at Freud's elaboration of his puzzling footnote in the form of a short essay titled "The Acquisition and Control of Fire," first published in 1932, will confirm. Here the story of man's refraining from extinguishing the fire is orchestrated in a mythologically striking, almost pompous way. The perfectly structured drama ends with a satyr play, introduced by a flippant quote from Heine, consisting of concrete remarks about the two functions of the male member

AMBITION IN MODERNITY   241

that concludes by triumphantly equating man with humanity: "The antithesis between the two functions might lead us to say that man [in the original German, not *der Mann*, but *der Mensch*] quenches his own fire with his own water."[59] In this phallocentric heroic tale, we find once again the "homosexually-tinged" aspect of extinguishing fire with urine,[60] which is presented—in a rather strange bit of imagery—as "a pleasurable struggle with another phallus."[61] Women, meanwhile, do not even appear at all in the homosocial world described here, not even as guardians of the hearth. Only the well-known, nasty theory that "babies are made by the man urinating into the woman's body"[62] is mentioned, and then only in passing. Freud's "The Acquisition and Control of Fire" extinguishes women.

Instead, here he tells the stories of two "great men." One is Prometheus, who stole fire from the gods and hid it in a hollow stick. In light of the theory he had already developed about the acquisition of fire in his footnote to *Civilization and Its Discontents*, Freud reads this detail via a procedure of reversal, turning it into its opposite. The hollow stick, he argues, represents the penis with its urethra: "it is the means of *quenching* fire; it is the water of his stream of urine."[63] In a brilliant turn, Freud then reads Prometheus' punishment—the chaining of the titan to a rock in the Caucasus, where every day a vulture fed on his liver—*on the one hand*, as an allegory of the painful renunciation of instinct that is always necessary in order to maintain civilization and, *on the other hand*, as a story of consolation that "gives an apt picture of the behavior of the erotic desires, which, though daily satisfied, are daily revived."[64] The daily regrowth of the liver, regarded in ancient times as "the seat of all passions and desires,"[65] thus also

---

[59]Sigmund Freud, "The Acquisition and Control of Fire," in: Freud, *The Complete Psychological Works of Sigmund Freud*, vol. XXII: *New Introductory Lectures on Psycho-Analysis and Other Works (1932–1936)*, edited and translated by James Strachey (London: Hobarth Press, 1964), 183–94 (192f).
[60]Ibid., 187.
[61]Ibid., 190.
[62]Ibid., 192.
[63]Ibid., 188.
[64]Ibid., 190.
[65]Ibid., 189.

242 AMBITION: AN ESSAY ON THE BURNING DESIRE TO RISE

signifies "a penis revivified after its collapse."[66] The second story
Freud tells, the myth of Heracles killing the hydra, again elevates
man—as in the earlier footnote—to the master of *extinguishing* fire
(in this case, the flaming severed heads of the hydra): "Prometheus
[...] had forbidden the quenching of fire; Heracles permitted it in
the case in which the brand of fire threatened disaster."[67] This is
absolute mastery, over life and death, light and shadow: the ability
to decide when the light of life will be ignited and when it will be
extinguished.

If we leave aside the hypothesis that a large majority of primitive
men preferred to indulge themselves in "pleasurable struggle with
another phallus," and instead assume that the fire of their passion
burned overwhelmingly for women, then this most strange Freudian
text suggests a different narrative. It is a text about the opposition
of "fire and water," which can be read to mean: it is about the
opposition of man and woman. With man's acquisition of fire—
understood as a renunciation of instinct—woman is extinguished
as an object of desire, even at the surface level of this second text,
which, as mentioned above, acknowledges women—specifically
"the woman's body"—*only* as victims of the men urinating into
them and otherwise entirely obliterates them. The footnote to
Civilization and Its Discontents and the essay "The Control and
Acquisition of Fire" confirm Adler's basic theory that mastery of
fire, mastery of desire—and thus mastery of women—stand at the
beginning of the development of civilization.

Freud's striking confirmation of Adler's proposition through
his brilliant decoding of the myths of Prometheus and Heracles
discourages any effort to make room for other theories about
the acquisition of fire. If we distance ourselves from the imposing
mythological framework, however, and return to the empirical
plane, we can also simply tell the story of the acquisition of fire
in reverse: Man, unable to control himself, was constantly and
childishly extinguishing fire with his proudly presented stream of
urine. Woman, meanwhile, was unfamiliar with this boyish ritual
and thus *she* was the one capable of acquiring and controlling
fire and kindling the hearth on which man then chained her as

---

[66]Ibid., 191.
[67]Ibid., 192.

AMBITION IN MODERNITY

punishment for her anxiety-inducing, civilization-founding feat. If Freud's theory about the "procedure of reversal, of turning into the opposite, of inverting relationships, which is so common in dreams,"[68] is valid, why then does he not apply it to the gender of his two masculine heroes and the gender of the monsters they fight against? As a matter of fact, the bound Prometheus then turns out to be the bound woman, Heracles, her female emancipator. And the hydra—though superficially, grammatically "feminine"—would be her opposite: her immortal head "is no doubt the phallus itself, and its destruction signifies castration."[69] Heracles' feat is thus an act of feminine protest.

[68]Ibid., 188.
[69]Ibid., 453.

The Ambition to Reject Ambition: An Afterword with a View to Montaigne

We are all hollow and empty.

MONTAIGNE[1]

As in the case of another life-determining power—namely, melancholy—working intensively with the concept "burning ambition" repeatedly reveals the intertwining of historical change on the one hand and, on the other, a relatively stable cluster of characteristics or symptoms that make it possible to trace the figure of the ambitious person through the ages. This at times striking, in many ways edifying "recognition effect" is but one reason why even old texts like the writings of Sallust or the aphorisms on ambition of the French moralists, with their "destruction psychology,"[2] should be read and reread again and again. One hesitates to claim that ambition is an anthropological constant, just as one would hesitate to claim that perceiving "family resemblances" between highly ambitious men from different epochs is pure projection. The tension between real phenomenon and discourse, between the relatively stable symptoms of a thirst for honor and glory that

---

[1]Michel De Montaigne, *The Complete Essays of Montaigne*, translated by Donald M. Frame (Stanford: Stanford University Press, 1958), 468.
[2]Hugo Friedrich, *Montaigne*, translated by Dawn Eng, edited by Philippe Desan (Berkeley: University of California Press, 1991), 161.

246 AMBITION: AN ESSAY ON THE BURNING DESIRE TO RISE

shoots dangerously beyond self-preservation and self-realization and the complex, constantly changing discussion of said thirst, is probably too difficult to ever fully resolve.

Just as the mortal sin of *acedia* is not the same thing as ancient melancholia, and just as the weltschmerz of a Lord Byron or Heinrich Heine is articulated quite differently than what we in the twenty-first century understand as depression, there is clearly a yawning abyss between Alexander the Great's drive to conquer the world and a modern-day employee's constant striving for flexibility and self-optimization under the merciless conditions of neoliberalism. And yet the similarities, down to the smallest details, in both symptoms and diagnosis continue to astound. Like Machiavelli before him, Ichheiser after him, and career-promoting public relations firms still today, Michel de Montaigne also observes that even bad publicity is more desirable than no publicity at all:

> We care more that people should speak of us than how they speak of us; and it is enough for us that our name should be current in men's mouths, no matter in what way it may be current. It seems that to be known is to have one's life and duration somehow in the keeping of others.[3]

The yearning desire to be seen, known, famous, possibly even immortal, even if only as a new Herostratus, leads Montaigne back to the notion that "we are indigent and necessitous within" and "our essence is imperfect and continually in need of betterment,"[4] an idea that Adler would revive with his theory of the inferiority complex. Like the existential philosophers of the twentieth century, Montaigne recognizes that we are all "hollow and empty," from which condition arises the enduring need for recognition that ambitious people take to its extreme with insatiable hunger. This hunger, however, cannot be satisfied by the "wind and sound"[5] of fame and glory: "There is I know not what natural sweetness in hearing oneself praised, but we make much too much of it."[6]

---

[3]Montaigne, *Essays*, 474.
[4]Ibid., 468.
[5]Ibid.
[6]Ibid., 473.

THE AMBITION TO REJECT AMBITION 247

Given the "family resemblance" of ambitious men throughout the ages, Montaigne—in a kind of supplement to the hypotheses about ambition set forth in this book—sees a distinction less in the pursuit of ambition itself and more in the varying "strength" of the souls who pursue it, and he warns against concluding that in the heart of every ambitious man lurks a potential Alexander. According to Montaigne's almost aesthetic argument, ambition is a habitus that does not suit everyone:

> Ambition is not a vice for little fellows and for undertakings such as ours. [...] This malady [of ambition] is perhaps excusable in so strong and full a soul [as Alexanders']. When these dwarfish and puny soullets behave like vain baboons and think to spread their name for having rightly judged an affair or continued the order of the guards at a city gate, the more they hope to raise their head, the more they show their tail.[7]

Montaigne supplements this refreshingly forthright assertion with a pair of anecdotes. The first tells of an ancient blowhard who, "having no other auditor of his praises or witness of his valor, boasted to his chambermaid, exclaiming: 'Oh, Perrette, what a gallant and capable man you have for a master!'"[8] The second anecdote, in an astonishing parallel to the case of the ambitious young man in the public restroom discussed by Ernest Jones, concerns a councilor who, "after disgorging a boatload of paragraphs with extreme effort and equal ineptitude, retired from the council chamber to the Palace urinal, where he was heard muttering very conscientiously between his teeth: '*Not unto us, O Lord, not unto us, but unto thy name give glory.*"[9]

As Montaigne observes elsewhere, however, even being confronted with the funhouse mirror of such blowhards or equally ambitious and naively blasphemous councilor is not enough to cure the afflicted of their ambition. Ambition, he argues, is rather the "most contrary and stubborn" of all irrational human inclinations, which even philosophers "get rid of [...] later and more reluctantly

---

[7] Ibid., 782.
[8] Ibid.
[9] Ibid.

248 AMBITION: AN ESSAY ON THE BURNING DESIRE TO RISE

than any other."[10] As with any addiction, it is almost impossible to recover from ambition by means of arguments or even chilling examples, which is why Montaigne's entertaining, brilliantly executed critique "Of Glory" is ultimately so ineffective.[11] In a short essay on our grudging reluctance to share glory with others, Montaigne thus observes:

> After you have said everything and believed everything to disown it [your thirst for glory, E.G.], it produces such an ingrained inclination against your arguments that you have little power to withstand it. For as Cicero says, even those who combat it still want the books that they write about it to bear their name on the title page, and want to become glorious for having despised glory.[12]

With respect to Cicero—whom he, too, considers the paradigmatic "most vainglorious man in the world"[13]—Montaigne concludes that "concern for reputation and glory" is so deeply rooted in human nature that "I do not know whether anyone yet has ever been able to get clean rid of it."[14] In light of the persistence of ambition, the great essay "Of Husbanding Your Will" outlines a program of ambition management, tailored to the individual, with the goal of directing ambition against itself, making it a matter of honor to face up to our ambition with the intention of rejecting it as much as possible:

> Since we will not do so out of conscience, at least out of ambition let us reject ambition. Let us disdain this base and beggarly hunger for renown and honor which makes us grovel for it before all sorts of people—*What is that praise that may be sought in the market place?*—abjectly and at no matter how vile a price. It is dishonor to be so honored. Let us learn to be no more avid of glory than we are capable of it.[15]

---

[10]Ibid., 187.
[11]Cf. Dirk Werle, *Ruhm und Moderne*, 327–36.
[12]Montaigne, *Essays*, 187.
[13]Ibid., 783.
[14]Ibid., 187.
[15]Ibid., 783.

THE AMBITION TO REJECT AMBITION 249

As opposed to seeking the glory in the market, Montaigne finds that virtuous actions "have much more grace" when they are performed not publicly, out of a craving for recognition, but "nonchalantly and noiselessly," left to be discovered accidentally by "some worthy man" who then "lifts [them] back out of obscurity to push them into the light for their own sake."[16] While Roman antiquity remains in play with the repeated references to Cicero, here a decidedly Christian idea shines through, a famous passage from the Gospel of Matthew (5:6). What Montaigne considers "graceful," what the discreet man of honor bears witness to, is actually a commandment of Jesus Christ, to be followed under the all-seeing eye of God:

> Beware of practicing your piety before others in order to be seen by them; for then you have no reward from your Father in heaven. So whenever you give alms, do not sound a trumpet before you, as the hypocrites do in the synagogues and in the streets, so that they may be praised by others. Truly I tell you, they have received their reward. But when you give alms, do not let your left hand know what your right hand is doing, so that your alms may be done in secret; and your Father who sees in secret will reward you.[17]

Montaigne's grappling with the ambition expert Cicero, his implicit, aestheticizing reference to the Gospel, and the—from a pious perspective—outrageous scene of the councilor in the palace urinal who honors God by urinating all indicate just how complex is the problem lurking behind the witty maxim that we should reject ambition out of ambition since—and this is the critical detail— we are *not* capable of doing so "out of conscience." As we can see upon closer inspection, Montaigne's emphatic reflection distances itself both from Roman tradition and from Christianity's critique of ambition, as well as from the "drive for reputation" that took the upper hand in the Renaissance,[18] in order to gain a genuinely modern perspective on ambition that leads beyond the world described by Burckhardt, which had already disappeared by the time Montaigne

---

[16]Ibid.
[17]Matthew 6:1-4 (NRSV)
[18]Friedrich, *Montaigne*, 161.

250 AMBITION: AN ESSAY ON THE BURNING DESIRE TO RISE

picked up his pen. Of his own era, the early Age of Absolutism, Montaigne writes that it is characterized by a ubiquitous, odious, "tumultuous agitation," among the ethical costs of which is that "goodness, moderation, equability, constancy, and such quiet and obscure qualities are no longer felt."[19] His notion of ambition in combat against itself is intended as an answer to these new challenges in a world in which appeals to conscience fall on deaf ears:

> See the people who have been taught to let themselves be seized and carried away: they do so everywhere, in little things as in big, in what does not touch them as in what does; they push in indiscriminately wherever there is business and involvement, and are without life when they are without tumultuous agitation. [...] Occupation is to a certain manner of people a mark of ability and dignity. Their mind seeks its repose in movement, like children in the cradle.[20]

When the busy councilor mutters between his teeth, "*Not unto us, O Lord, not unto us, but unto thy name give glory*," he is referring, probably without being aware of it (unlike Montaigne himself, of course), to a critical course shift in cultural history, as well as in the history of ambition, inaugurated by Saint Augustine in Chapters 11–19 of the fifth book of *The City of God*. The course set by Augustine, whom Montaigne quotes, was fundamental to Thomas Aquinas' critique of ambition as well as to the condemnation of ambition delivered by the apostate Augustinian monk Martin Luther. While Roman antiquity recognized the "unity of *virtus* and *gloria*" (as can be seen, for example, from Sallust's depiction of the exponents of the Roman Republic), under Christianity, virtue and glory came to form a stark opposition:

> Christianity intensifies this distinction [between *virtus* and *gloria*] into the contrast between moral inwardness for which one is answerable only before God and its reflex in the secular world, which has become meaningless.[21]

---

[19]Montaigne, *Essays*, 782.
[20]Ibid., 767f.
[21]Friedrich, *Montaigne*, 160.

THE AMBITION TO REJECT AMBITION 251

This division is both prepared and fulfilled in *The City of God*. The key point here is that Augustine, who accepts Sallust's monograph on the Catiline conspiracy as an authoritative historical account and quotes from it extensively, considers the Romans of the old Republic to be secular exemplars of devout Christian conduct, particularly Cato as Sallust depicts him. Cato and other Romans of the old school were exemplary in that they placed their ambition exclusively in the service of the virtuously established polis and found their life's fulfillment in this service. Cato gave himself up to death once the Republic was lost. Of him, Augustine writes: "For no virtue is truly such unless it is directed towards that end in which man's good—the good than which nothing better exists—is found."[22] It is on the basis of their diligent devotion to their earthly city, to which they gave all honor and even their own lives as the highest good, that Augustine presents the Romans of the old Republic to Christians as "examples for our necessary admonition":

> If, for the sake of the most glorious City of God, we do not hold fast to the same virtues that they held fast to for the sake of the glory of an earthly city, let us be pierced with shame.[23]

Ambition in the Roman Republic was virtuous as long as it served only the polis and not one's personal success, a criterion that perseveres from Sallust up through Max Weber's description of politics as, ideally, a vocation devoted to a cause that eschews the intoxication of personal power. Augustine takes this idea of the strict commitment of ambition to fostering a good earthly commonwealth and transfers it to the kingdom of God: Christian ambition is virtuous only when it is exclusively in the service of the City of God. For Christians, this means above all acting in humble awareness of the fact that not only all earthly triumph and success, but also all praiseworthy virtue ultimately comes *only* from God. Personally ascribing any glory to oneself, for example by trumpeting one's good deeds, henceforth becomes a sin, because in doing so one seizes for oneself what belongs to God. This is one reason that

---

[22]Augustine, *The City of God against the Pagans*, edited and translated by R.W. Dyson (Cambridge: Cambridge University Press, 1998), 210.
[23]Ibid., 223.

252 AMBITION: AN ESSAY ON THE BURNING DESIRE TO RISE

John Milton perceives ambition to be Lucifer's cardinal sin. Glory is due to God alone, from whom it proceeds to whom it flows back completely: *Soli Deo gloria*. In a passage that Montaigne quotes from directly at the beginning of his essay on our unwillingness to share glory with others, Augustine writes:

> It may be that, in this life, [lust for glory] cannot be completely eradicated from the heart. After all, it does not cease to tempt the minds even of those who are well advanced in virtue. But let the lust for glory be at any rate so surpassed by the love of righteousness that, if at any point "those things which are held in low esteem" should be neglected even if they are good and right, the love of human praise will blush and yield to the love of truth. If the lust for glory holds a greater place in the heart than the fear or love of God, then this vice is so inimical to godly faith that the Lord said: "How can ye believe, who look for glory from one another, and do not seek the glory which is from God alone?"[24]

Thus the devout Christian rulers whose time may yet come, "no matter how great the virtues that they are able to possess in this life, attribute them only to the grace of God, Who has given these things to them according to their good will, their belief and their prayers."[25] Christian rulers, according to Augustine, seek through their deeds solely to increase the glory of God, just as the ancient Romans before them sought solely to increase the glory of their city and empire.

With respect to the appraisal of ambition, the transition from the Middle Ages to the Renaissance can be described schematically as a return to antiquity's "idealization of glory" after Christianity's "devaluation of glory,"[26] with contemporary earthly rulers or warlords and even the public, comprised of both men and women, taking the place of Rome or God in a politically and then denominationally fragmented world. Ambition, once again

---

[24]Ibid., 214.
[25]Ibid., 225f.
[26]Friedrich, *Montaigne*, 160f. Friedrich of course makes note of the many conflicts arising from this transition, specifically referring to Petrarch, who not coincidentally has to grapple with the spirit of Saint Augustine in the *Secretum*.

THE AMBITION TO REJECT AMBITION 253

primarily secular, has been aimed at achieving success with rulers and with the public ever since. This change can clearly be seen in Baldesar Castiglione's *Book of the Courtier*, in which the courtier who ambitiously seeks success is encouraged to perform "those glorious and brave deeds" that he must perform in battle "in sight of all the noblest and most respected men in the army, and especially in the presence and (if it is possible) before the very eyes of his king or of the prince whom he serves," while at a tournament he should ensure that his attire, comportment, and conduct "attract the eyes of the bystanders as the loadstone attracts iron."[27] Montaigne deems this sort of glory to be worthless, and he ridicules the idea that great deeds should always be recorded live for both the present and posterity: "Do we think that at every harquebus shot that touches us, and at every risk that we run, there is promptly a clerk to record it?"[28]

In his essay "Of Husbanding Your Will," Montaigne distances himself from the Renaissance pursuit of ambition, but without simply returning to Augustine's position (it is in this essay that the foolish councilor appears) nor even to the ancient idea of total devotion to the polis. Instead, Montaigne, who served his king repeatedly, claims that he offered his services only "by way of loan"[29]: "I have been able to take part in public office without departing one nail's breadth from myself."[30] This *reservatio mentalis* is never relinquished: "We do like things with different degrees of effort and tension of will. The one goes very well without the other."[31] One who unreservedly dedicates himself to changing rulers or identifies entirely with the standards of the fickle public and its ever changing criteria for awarding fame and glory finds himself on the "path of ambition,"[32] a path that proves to be a perilous labyrinth of heteronomy in which one loses the one thing worthy of contemplation and reflection, oneself:

---

[27]Baldesar Castiglione, *The Book of the Courtier*, translated by Leonard Eckstein Opdycke (New York: Scribner: 1901), 84.
[28]Montaigne, *Essays*, 476.
[29]Ibid., 770.
[30]Ibid.
[31]Ibid.
[32]Cf. ibid., 783.

254 AMBITION: AN ESSAY ON THE BURNING DESIRE TO RISE

> Actions that are performed without the reflexive movement, I mean a searching and genuine reflexive movement—the actions, for example, of the avaricious, the ambitious, and so many others who run in a straight line, whose course carries them ever forward—are erroneous and diseased actions.[33]

For the aging Montaigne, whom health "happens to revisit" only "by fits and starts,"[34] Rome, God, and the public, as potential objects of identification and playing fields of ambition, give way to earnest work on the self, the consistent pursuit of "authenticity" in "being himself"[35] in the face of illness and mortality: "In short, here I am in the act of finishing up this man, not of making another out of him."[36]

Montaigne's theory of ambition turning against itself rests on this insistence on being himself regardless of the "rules and precepts of the world."[37] On the one hand, he doubts that human beings' tendency toward ambition can ever be fully eradicated; on the other, he sees the possibility of successfully managing ambition. Problematically enough, realizing this ambition against ambition means that ambition must first be aroused, but in such a way that it then turns against itself or its hypertrophy. This process gives rise to the following problems: First, the ambition to renounce ambition must itself become hypertrophic, generating a lack of drive or self-destructive apathy of the kind hideously embodied by Oblomov, who in Goncharov's novel represents anything but the ideal of a successful life. Further, if one hopes to avoid becoming alienated from working on oneself, the ambition to renounce ambition must make do without any fanfare or applause, thereby forgoing the actual object of ambitious desire. It is thus a paradox: ambition directed against itself is, in substance, no longer ambition, as it must be exercised "noiselessly" and therefore without any "sweet reward." Logically, the program of ambition management outlined by Montaigne necessarily must *precede* the in-depth work of the

---

[33]Ibid., 773.
[34]Ibid., 773.
[35]Friedrich, *Montaigne*, 160.
[36]Montaigne, *Essays*, 773.
[37]Ibid., 769.

THE AMBITION TO REJECT AMBITION   255

individual on himself in order to be able to determine what degree
of ambition the subject possesses in the first place before it can be
successfully dismantled: "Judgment must maintain its rights in all
matters; it is right that it should see, in this subject as elsewhere,
what truth sets before it. If he is Caesar, let him boldly judge himself
the greatest captain in the world."[38] Ultimately, ambition can only
be directed against itself if there is something that the subject loves
more than the laurels of fame and immortality that spectacular
success brings with it. The task that lies before the subject who
wishes to forsake ambition is thus as easy to name as it is difficult
to ever achieve. In Montaigne, the "love of righteousness" and "love
of truth" that Augustine offered against ambition in the name of the
cross give way to the challenge of filling the void in the individual
with self-love, with that

> friendship that each man owes to himself. Not a false friendship,
> that makes us embrace glory, learning, riches, and such things
> with paramount and immoderate affection, as members of our
> being; [...] but a salutary and well-regulated friendship, useful
> and pleasant alike. He who knows its duties and practices them,
> he is truly of the cabinet of the Muses; he has attained the summit
> of human wisdom and of our happiness.[39]

---

[38]Ibid., 478.
[39]Ibid., 769.

ACKNOWLEDGMENTS

This book on *Ambition* was made possible by a generous stipend from the *Volkswagen Foundation*, which financed my leave of absence in 2019/20. I would like to thank my team—Niklas Bender, Alexa Bornfleth, Aglaia Kister, Kim Luther, Max Roehl, and Julian Sieler—for smoothly and successfully running the Tübingen program for Comparative Literature while I was on leave.

I thank my dear husband Dan Poston for our conversations on this and so many other topics as well as for the happy life we are enjoying in the United States and Germany. To Gregor Gumpert, I express my gratitude for his critical reading of the entire manuscript. I am very grateful to Haaris Naqvi for accepting this book of mine for *Bloomsbury Academic*, and I would like to thank James C. Wagner for his exquisite translation from the German original.

For references, conversations, correspondence, and several other things I would like to thank Mara Delius, Libby Garland, Achim Geisenhanslüke, John T. Hamilton, Robert Kirstein, Martin von Koppenfels, Vivian Liska, Maria Moog-Grünewald, Christoph Möllers, Ernst Osterkamp, Ernst Seidl, Sebastian Schmidt-Hofner, Martin Steffen, Barbara Vinken, David Wellbery, Anja Wolkenhauer, and Guido Zurstiege. Last but not least, I would like to thank my students for their critical input and the intense discussions we had during my Tübingen seminars on ambition in drama, and beyond.

Berlin, December 2021
Eckart Goebel

INDEX

Addison, Joseph 49, 50, 103
Adler, Alfred 6, 8, 16, 17, 41, 157, 158, 226–36, 242, 246
Adorno, Theodor W. 198
Aeschylus 77
Albert, Elisa 1
Alcibiades 53, 54
Alexander the Great 3, 5, 9, 10, 28, 55–61, 84, 85, 146, 224, 238, 239, 246, 247
Arendt, Hannah 4
Aretino, Pietro 117
Aristotle 7, 14, 56, 60–7, 95 (FN 104), 203, 214, 217
Auerbach, Erich 44
Augustine 52, 88, 123, 250–5
Augustus 126, 206
Aurelius, Marcus 3

Bacon, Francis 11, 26, 36, 157
Balzac, Honoré de 11, 13, 25, 27, 38, 51, 132
Bataille, Georges 186
Benjamin, Walter 183
Bezos, Jeff 148
Bismarck, Otto von 89
Borgia, Cesare 124, 128, 131
Bourdieu, Pierre 8, 134 (FN 10), 234, 235
Braden, Gordon 107 (FN), 110 (FN 12), 113 (FN 21), 115 (FN 26), 117
Brecht, Bertolt 15, 89, 91
Brod, Max 154

Brown, Wendy 220
Bruder-Bezzel, Almuth 236 (FN 51)
Brutus, Marcus Iunius 104
Burckhardt, Jacob 12, 14–17, 37, 43 (FN 45), 51, 74–9, 82, 84, 89, 107–22, 124–31, 163, 185, 186, 194, 249
Byron, Lord 246

Caesar, Gaius Julius 3, 29, 30, 35, 55, 56, 59, 60, 84, 85, 89, 91, 95–7, 99–104, 126, 138, 141, 146, 255
Caillois, Roger 14, 17, 44, 45, 159, 185–97, 222
Callimachus 214
Cassirer, Ernst 110 (FN 12)
Castiglione, Baldesar 253
Catiline 87–91, 95–101, 103–5, 251
Cato, Marcus Porcius 60, 88, 99, 101–4, 251
Cellini, Benvenuto 12, 112, 113, 115
Cespedes, Vincent 17 (FN 48), 33, 34
Charles V 107
Cicero, Marcus Tullius 4, 15, 26, 34–6, 85, 89, 99–102, 104, 248, 249
Cioran, Emil 1
Columbus, Christoph 119
Crassus, Marcus Licinius 97, 99, 104

INDEX

Dante Alighieri 107, 110, 116 (FN 28), 117
Diogenes 56
Dostoevsky, Fyodor Mikhailovich 175

Elias, Norbert 43
Eliot, T.S. 2
Engels, Friedrich 114, 132, 133, 149, 210
Erdmann, Karl Otto 159
Erikson, Erik H. 201

Fenner, Dagmar 6 (FN 21), 176 (FN 35)
Ficino, Marsilio 109–11
Fränkel, Hermann 70–4, 77
Freud, Sigmund 17, 27, 31, 46–9, 57, 58, 78, 157, 158, 179, 187, 200–3, 223–30, 232–4, 236–43
Friedrich, Hugo 245–9, 252–4
Fuhrmann, Manfred 4 (FN 15), 34 (FN 26), 36
Fündling, Jörg 90, 94–6, 98 (FN 116)

Gamper, Michael 114 (FN 23), 116
Gay, Roxane 8–10, 46
Girard, René 42
Goethe, Johann Wolfgang 4, 10–13, 32 (FN 21), 35, 76, 77, 85–90, 113
Goncharov, Ivan Alexandrovich 18–20, 254

Hauptmann, Gerhart 159
Heckhausen, Heinz 199
Heidegger, Martin 176
Heine, Heinrich 240, 246
Henríquez, Cristina 7
Hérault de Séchelles, Marie-Jean 30, 177

Herostratus 239, 246
Hesiod 14, 66, 69–77, 79–82, 191, 193, 196, 198, 201, 214, 217, 218
Hindenburg, Paul von 159
Hitler, Adolf 159
Hobbes, Thomas 136, 194
Hölderlin, Friedrich 11
Homer 4, 66–9, 77–82, 84, 85, 214, 218, 224
Horkheimer, Max 121, 198
Huizinga, Johan 16, 112 (FN 21)
Hume, David 26, 27, 39, 40

Ibsen, Henrik 33, 139
Ichheiser, Gustav 17, 28, 150–4, 156–68, 170, 172, 174, 181, 193, 246

Jefferson, Thomas 13
Jesus Christ 15, 249
Jones, Ernest 233, 234, 247
Joubert, Joseph 4

Kafka, Franz 58, 59, 154, 183, 232
Kant, Immanuel 61, 131
Kaube, Jürgen 208
Kerrigan, William 46–9, 107 (FN), 110 (FN 12), 113 (FN 21), 115 (FN 26), 117
King, William Casey 8–10, 13, 17 (FN 48), 49 (FN 68)
Kleist, Heinrich von 11
Klibansky, Raymond 109 (FN 10)
Krause, Skadi Siiri 133–5

La Bruyère, Jean de 12, 13 (FN 39), 32, 37 (FN 31), 43, 44 (NF 46)
La Rochefoucauld, François de 31
Lacan, Jacques 158
Latte, Kurt 90 (FN 84), 94

INDEX 259

Leonardo da Vinci 117
Lincoln, Abraham 204
Louis XIV 28
Luther, Martin 123, 124, 250

Machiavelli, Niccolò 25, 31, 32,
38, 42, 70, 118, 119, 125, 126,
129–31, 163, 164, 168, 174,
177, 197, 203, 229, 246
Madonna 17 (FN 48)
Mann, Thomas 2, 3, 152, 153
Mannheim, Karl 17, 28, 64, 150
(FN 4), 152, 154, 158, 168–83,
197, 221
Marlowe, Christopher 216
Marx, Karl 114, 115, 133, 155,
164, 183, 208, 210, 211, 213,
235
McClelland, David 6, 14, 17,
198–207, 211–22
Melville, Herman 18
Michelangelo Buonarroti 112,
113, 115, 117
Milton, John 15, 48, 252
Mommsen, Theodor 15, 91 (FN
86), 97 (FN 111), 97, 99, 101
Montaigne, Michel de 17, 62, 89,
121, 245–50, 252–4
Montesquieu, Charles-Louis de 3,
29, 36, 42, 44, 51, 204
Müller, Philipp 107, 108
Münkler, Herfried 129, 130
Murray, Henry A. 200
Musil, Robert 183, 239

Napoleon Bonaparte 3, 44, 139,
146, 232
Napoleon III (Louis-Napoléon
Bonaparte) 148
Nickel, Sighard 150 (FN 4), 151
(FN 5)
Nietzsche, Friedrich 3, 14, 15, 27,
31, 37, 40–2, 51, 73, 77–85,

90, 110, 123, 177, 185, 186,
190 (FN 23), 194, 227, 228
Nieuwenburg, Paul 62 (FN 25),
64
Nixon, Richard 206

Ovid (Publius Ovidius Naso) 152,
153

Panofsky, Erwin 109 (FN 10)
Parsons, Talcott 202 (FN 13), 206
Pascal, Blaise 127
Petrarch 110, 120, 122, 123, 252
(FN 26)
Pettigrove, Glen 25–8, 31–3, 37,
39 (FN 37), 40, 43 (FN 43),
45, 46, 50, 51, 61, 74, 93, 157,
164, 175, 229
Pius II 116
Plato 25, 26, 46, 53, 54, 65, 76,
109–11, 129, 204
Plutarch 3–5, 11, 15, 34–6, 55, 56,
59, 60, 84, 137, 143, 222
Pompey 60

Rabelais, François 48, 237
Rabinbach, Anson 18, 222 (FN 75)
Reichholf, Josef H. 20–2, 76 (FN
47)
Reik, Theodor 179
Rhodes, Cecil 4, 5
Richelieu, Armand-Jean du Plessis,
1er Duc de 30, 40
Rilke, Rainer Maria 183, 224
Ritter, Henning 30, 177
Ritter, Joachim 26 (FN 3), 120
Rockefeller, John D. 148
Roeck, Bernd 32, 112, 113 (FN
21)
Romm, Robin 1, 2 (FN 4), 7
Roosevelt, Franklin D. 206
Rousseau, Jean-Jacques 25, 93
Ruehl, Martin A. 114, 115 (FN 26)

INDEX

Sallust (Gaius Sallustius Crispus) 15, 16, 51, 52, 54, 85, 87–105, 141, 150, 157, 166, 245, 250, 251
Santayana, George 25
Sartre, Jean-Paul 10
Savonarola, Girolamo 122
Saxl, Fritz 109 (FN 10)
Scheler, Max 37, 160, 180, 181 (FN 52)
Schiller, Friedrich 10, 11, 13, 139
Schöne, Wilhelm 90, 95 (FN 103), 105 (FN 134)
Schopenhauer, Arthur 70, 82, 175
Seneca, Lucius Annaeus 2, 3, 22
Shakespeare, William 5, 11, 28, 37, 42, 47, 48, 89, 95, 139, 179
Shapiro, James 95 (FN 104)
Shelley, Percy Bysshe 216
Shils, Edward 221
Socrates 17 (FN 48), 53, 54, 65, 217
Spencer, Herbert 164
Stendhal 11, 27, 44, 132, 145, 175, 177
Sulla, Lucius Cornelius 89, 90, 94–6, 98, 99, 104, 116, 138, 141, 142

Thomas Aquinas 52, 250
Thucydides 90, 94, 195
Tocqueville, Alexis de 13 (FN 40), 17, 26–33, 43, 44 (FN 47), 89, 132–50, 173

Valeriano, Pierio 128
Vauvenargues, Luc de Clapiers, Marquis de 9, 14, 15, 31
Verheyen, Nina 6, 22 (FN 65), 152 (FN 7, 9), 156 (FN 18), 171 (FN 12), 181 (FN 52)

Washington, George 13
Watson, Robert N. 5, 6
Weber, Max 29, 51–5, 83, 157, 161, 204, 207–12, 219, 220, 251
Werle, Dirk 30, 39 (FN 36), 112 (FN 21), 118 (FN 39), 248 (FN 11)
White, Hayden 112
Wilde, Oscar 12
Wrobouschek, Markus 151 (FN 5)

Xenophon 217

Young, Edward 14